Other outstanding history books by Mike Rothmiller

The Making of Adolf Hitler
The Child. The Man. The Monster

New York Times Bestselling Author
Mike Rothmiller

AMERICA — WORDS THAT SHAPED THE NATION
THE FIRST 50 YEARS
1776-1826

Volume 1 1776-1826
Mike Rothmiller
Copyright 2012. All Rights Reserved

True Stories of the OSS and CIA

by

New York Times Bestselling Author

Mike Rothmiller

True Stories of the OSS and CIA

Copyright Michael Rothmiller 2015

All Rights Reserved.

No copyrighted part of this book may be used or reproduced in any manner whatsoever without the expressed written permission except in the case of brief quotations embodied in critical articles or reviews. Original documents may be found in the public domain in the National Archives and Records Administration.

Library of Congress Card Number 1-2161000701

ISBN 13:978-1508581079

ISBN 10:150858107 xs

Dedicated To Those Who Served

Acknowledgement

I wish to thank the entire staff of the national archives for preserving these priceless documents. Since the creation of the National Archives in 1934 thousands of dedicated civil servants have been collecting, studying and cataloging literary billions of pages of government documents. The task is enormous, yet through their hard work and dedication these documents will be preserved in perpetuity. Without their wonderful work this book would not have been possible. On behalf of all Americans, thank you.

Forward

"Bring me back reliable information." Those were the orders given by Alexander The Great to his spies nearly 4,000 years ago.

"Those who know the enemy as well as they know themselves will never suffer defeat." Sun Tsu a noted Chinese warrior wrote those words 2,500 years ago.

Revelations of spying are also found in the Old and New Testament. Two spying incidents are detailed in the Old Testament; one initiated by Moses and another years later by Joshua.

During the United States war for independence General George Washington understood the value of intelligence. He organized and oversaw the first official spy ring with secret financing provided by the Second Continental Congress. The spying organization umbrella was, "The Committee of Secret Correspondence."

From the time of the earliest conflict, intelligence and psychological warfare has played a significant role, and at times, spelled the difference between victory and defeat. As the commander-in-chief or a military leader in a theater of war, knowing your enemies battle plans, strengths and weaknesses provides a remarkable strategic advantage. Likewise, if you're able to mislead your enemy into altering their plans or beliefs, you again have achieved an advantage. As in the past, today intelligence and psychological warfare play a significant role in national security and during times of war.

The United States Intelligence community as known to the public is comprised of 17 agencies that work separately, and at times, in concert to conduct intelligence activities in the field of foreign relations and national security. Members of this community include intelligence agencies, military intelligence, and civilian intelligence and analysis offices within federal executive departments. All federal intelligence agencies report to the Director of National Intelligence (DNI), who reports to the President of the United States.

However, these are not the only governmental or private organizations gathering intelligence or carrying out operations on behalf of the federal government. Various law enforcement agencies and/or their officers assist or work at the direction of various intelligence agencies, including the CIA. So, in the end, there is no way of knowing exactly how far the tentacles of federal intelligence operations reach into the American civilian population.

Additionally, it is not a secret that from time to time intelligence agencies engage in establishing and funding private corporations to provide cover for covert operations at home and overseas, or they "request" major corporations to hire CIA operatives in order to provide them legitimate cover. At times, these individuals are already in place and are later recruited by the CIA. This also includes the world of academe. Again, this is nothing new and it's done by every major country.

The vast majority of intelligence activities will never be disclosed, so the public is provided little insight into the long, distinguished, and at times, tarnished history of intelligence operations. Most intelligence operations were conceived and carried out by patriots in the interest of national security or during time of war. Without these operations, the very existence of today's United States would be in doubt and much of the free world would have faded from history. However, not all intelligence operations were successful and many were based in the theory that the end, justifies the means. This is a difficult concept for many to accept, but this is the reality of a cold, cruel and ruthless world. At times, distasteful actions and assassinations are undertaken to safeguard the masses or protect national interest. This is not to say that all governmental intelligence operations were undertaken to safeguard the country and our freedoms. At various times for purely political reasons Presidents have directed intelligence agencies to target a rival or a particular political group. In most cases this is accomplished via the Internal Revenue Service or the CIA. This is not acceptable in any free society.

In this book you will read various accounts complied from secret OSS and CIA operations. The book ranges from the establishment of the OSS to today's CIA, it's all here. These are not my interpretation of historic events; these are the accounts of the OSS and CIA. These classified stories were commissioned, expertly researched and written for internal use of the CIA. I have not edited these documents in any form. Until recently, all were classified—ranging from CONFIDENTIAL TO TOP-SECRET.

Interestingly, the CIA is notorious for their secrecy and more often than not, the agency refuses to release documents requested in a Freedom of Information Request (FOIA) or under a Mandatory Declassification Request (MDR). Yet, here's the interesting twist. These stories contain a wealth of details and scores of informative footnotes identifying the source of the information. Even if you filed a FOIA for all the documents contained in the footnotes, it would take years to obtain them—if the CIA would provide the documents. So, in an unexpected turn of events the CIA has opened Pandora's Box allowing us to review information they thought would remain secret and in some cases, would prefer remained secret. But the documents are available for review, if you know where and how to find them. As individual stories they are indeed interesting, taken as a whole, they truly enlighten and demonstrate the enormous scope of the intelligence community.

As you read these remarkable stories of covert operations, methods of operations, establishment of the OSS and CIA, spies, intelligence they gathered and intelligence rivalries within the United States, you'll gain an appreciation for the work and exploits of these men and women; and a basic understanding of how complex and daunting the world of intelligence gathering is. You may not agree with the methods employed or the outcome, but the veil of secrecy keeping intelligence Ops in the dark will be partially removed providing a rare insider's glimpse into decades of intelligence operations, the thought process of intelligence officers and the magnitude of some operations. Taken in their full context, these were truly remarkable undertakings.

These stories are just the tip of the iceberg illustrating the wide spectrum of intelligence activities carried out by the OSS and todays CIA. You'll notice that some names have been blackened out and some information redacted, this was done by the CIA.

These stories are as intriguing, informative and frightening as the best spy novels. The articles in this book were taken from the Central Intelligence Agency's (CIA) classified professional journal, "Studies in Intelligence."

In closing, you are about to enter the world of secrets, lies and deception. Your life will never been the same.

Understanding Declassification of Documents

To understand why some classified documents are released to the public, I've included the below explanation provided by the Central Intelligence Agency.

The automatic declassification provisions of Executive Order 13256 (formerly EO 12958, as amended) require the declassification of nonexempt historically valuable records 25 years or older. The EO was originally issued in April 1995 and via amendment established 31 December 2006 as the first major deadline for automatic declassification under the "25-year program". By that date, agencies were to have completed the review of all hardcopy documents determined to contain exclusively their equities. For CIA, the 2006 deadline covered the span of relevant documents originally dating from the establishment of the CIA after WWII through 1981.

The requirement to automatically declassify records 25 years or older "rolls" forward one year at a time. For example, by 31 December 2012, permanent records through 31 December 1987 were automatically declassified, unless appropriately exempted under the guidelines of the EO. In this regard, CIA maintains a program operating out of the CIA Declassification Center to review records under the purview of EO 13526 before they reach their automatic declassification deadline.

THE OFFICIAL CIA DISCLAIMER

The articles in this series are taken from the Central Intelligence Agency's (CIA) professional journal, "Studies in Intelligence." Sherman Kent created "Studies" in 1955 as a journal for intelligence professionals. In the first article published in "Studies," Kent called for the creation of literature that would support the development of intelligence as a professional discipline. Kent believed that the most important service such literature could perform would be to record and disseminate new ideas and experiences, and build toward a cumulative understanding of the profession. The series contains articles relating to intelligence organizations and activities in a number of countries, methods relating to intelligence gathering and analysis, and intelligence activities throughout history. The articles also contain a number of reviews of relevant books. The CIA puts the following disclaimer on all "Studies in Intelligence" articles: All statements of fact, opinion or analysis expressed in "Studies in Intelligence" are those of the authors. They do not necessarily reflect official positions or views of the Central Intelligence Agency or any other U.S. Government entity, past or present. Nothing in the contents should be construed as asserting or implying U.S. Government endorsement of an article's factual statements and interpretations.

Table of Contents

PRESIDENT FRANKLIN D. ROOSEVELT ESTABLISHES THE OFFICE OF STRAGTIC SERVICES (OSS)..15

PRESIDENT HARRY S. TRUMAN ESTABLISHES THE CIA.......................................18

A BIBLE LESSON ON SPYING...22

A SHORT TOUR THROUGH THE HISTORY OF INTELLIGENCE..............................28

A CABLE FROM NAPOLEON..42

PROJECT TERMINATION AND A CHANGE OF ADMINISTRATION........................64

GENERAL WILLIAM DONOVAN'S MARCHING ORDERS......................................70

INTELLIGENCE RIVALRIES IN WARTIME..102

THE OSS ASSESSMENT PROGRAM..111

VIRGINA HALL, AN AMERICAN SPY...126

THE LIFE AND WORK OF STEPHAN HALLER..131

INTELLIGENCE OPERATIONS OF OSS DETACHMENT 101..................................146

PRESIDENT HARRY S. TRUMAN ON CIA COVERT OPERATIONS..........................160

COVER IN UNCONVENTIONAL OPERATIONS...172

REMINISCENCES OF A COMMUNICATIONS AGENT……………………………...178

PHOTO INTELLIGENCE AND PUBLIC PERSUASION…………………………….185

THE CIA AND ACADEME…………………………………………………………...189

CRANKS, NUTS AND SCREWBALLS……………………………………………….200

TRUTH DRUGS IN INTERROGATION…………………………………………...212

THE COVERT COLLECTION OF SCIENTIFIC INFORMATION…………………….232

SOME FAR-OUT THOUGHTS ON COMPUTERS……………………………………..242

THE INTELLIGENCE COMMUNITY POST-MORTEM PROGRAM. 1973-1975…………255

BASIC NATIONAL SECURITY STRATEGY NSDD 238……………………………...270

CIA PUBLIC AFFAIRS AND THE DRUG CONSPIRACY……………………………….290

President Franklin D. Roosevelt

President Franklin D. Roosevelt's order establishing the Office of Strategic Services (OSS) the forerunner of today's Central Intelligence Agency (CIA) is below;

BY virtue of the authority vested in me as President of the United States and as Commander in Chief of the Army and Navy of the United States, it is ordered as follows:

1. The office of Coordinator of Information established by Order of July 11, 1941, exclusive of the foreign information activities transferred to the Office of War Information by Executive Order of June 13, 1942, shall hereafter be known as the Office of Strategic Services, and is hereby transferred to the jurisdiction of the United States Joint Chiefs of Staff.

2. The Office of Strategic Services shall perform the following duties:

(a) Collect and analyze such strategic information as may be required by the United States Joint Chiefs of Staff.

(b) Plan and operate such special services as may be directed by the United States Joint Chiefs of Staff.

3. At the head of the Office of Strategic Services shall be a Director of Strategic Services who shall be appointed by the President and who shall perform his duties under the direction and supervision of the United States Joint Chiefs of Staff.

4. William J. Donovan is hereby appointed as Director of Strategic Services.

5. The Order of July 11, 1941, is hereby revoked.

General William J. Donovan, first director of the OSS

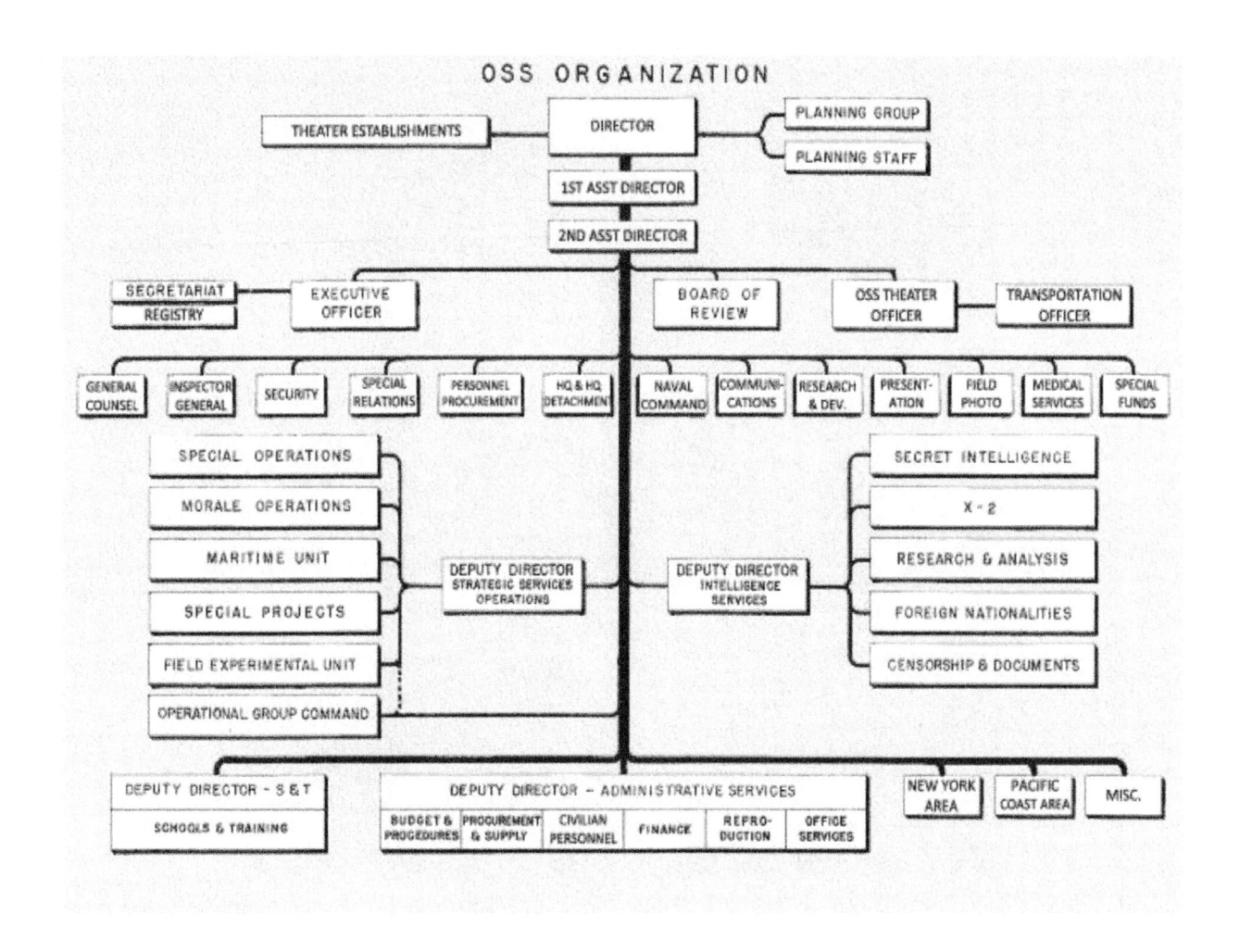

ORGANIZATIONAL CHART OF THE OSS

OSS Insignia

President Harry S. Truman

The National Security Act of 1947 (Synopsis provided by the CIA)

President Harry S. Truman signed the National Security Act of 1947 (P.L. 80-235, 61 Stat 496) on July 26, 1947. The act – an intricate series of compromises – took well over a year to craft. It remained the charter of the U.S. national security establishment until significantly altered with the passage of the National Security Intelligence Reform and Terrorism Prevention Act of December 2004, which created the Office of the Director of National Intelligence.

This landmark legislation reorganized and modernized the US armed forces, foreign policy, and the Intelligence Community apparatus. It directed a major reorganization of the foreign policy and military establishments of the US government. And it created many of the institutions that US presidents would find useful when formulating and implementing foreign policy.

A Brief Overview of the Act

The act:

- Established the National Security Council (NSC)
- Merged the War and Navy departments into the National Military Establishment (NME) headed by the secretary of defense, and
- Recognized the US Air Force as an independent service from the Army.

Initially each of the three service secretaries maintained quasi-cabinet status, but the act was amended on August 10, 1949 to formalize their subordination to the secretary of defense. At the same time the NME was renamed the Department of Defense.

In the intelligence field, the act ratified President Truman's creation (in 1946) of the post of Director of Central Intelligence (DCI), and transformed the Central Intelligence Group into the statutory Central Intelligence Agency (CIA), the nation's first peacetime intelligence agency.

Most of these provisions prompted sharp debates in the Executive Branch and Congress. Several compromises were struck in order for the act to win passage. These compromises would have far-reaching implications for the Intelligence Community.

President Truman's Goals:

Unify the Armed Services & Reform Intelligence

President Truman's main goal in guiding this legislation through Congress was to modernize the nation's "antiquated defense setup" by unifying the armed services under a civilian chief. Intelligence reform was a secondary goal, and the White House kept the bill's passages on intelligence as brief as possible to ensure that its details did not hamper prospects for military unification. This tactic almost backfired.

When the president sent his bill forward in February 1947, the brevity of its intelligence provisions caused Congressional scrutiny. More than a few members of Congress read the bill with concerns about its proposed concentration of military power.

They also eventually debated almost every word of its bill's intelligence section. Some members argued that the DCI and the new CIA could become a menace to civil liberties--an "American Gestapo." Administration witnesses alleviated this concern by reminding Congress that the Agency's authorized mission would be foreign intelligence.

The Act Establishes the Role for CIA

When lawmakers finished editing the section on intelligence, however, the language managed to summarize and ratify most of the crucial arrangements already made by the Truman administration. The National Security Act would:

- authorize a Central Intelligence Agency (but leave the powers and duties of the Agency's head for a separate bill to enumerate);
- that CIA would be an independent agency under the supervision of the NSC;
- that CIA would conduct both analysis and clandestine activities, but would have no policymaking role and no law enforcement powers;
- and, finally, that the DCI would be confirmed by the Senate and could be either a civilian or an officer on detail from his home service.

The legislation gave America something new; no other nation had structured its foreign intelligence establishment in quite the same way.

The CIA would be an independent, central agency, overseeing strategic analysis and coordinating clandestine activities abroad. It would not be a controlling agency. The CIA would both rival and complement the efforts of the departmental intelligence organizations. This prescription of coordination without control guaranteed competition as the CIA and the departmental agencies pursued common targets, but it also fostered a healthy exchange of views and abilities.

What the act did not do, however, was almost as important as what it did. It helped ensure that American intelligence remained a loose confederation of agencies lacking strong direction from either civilian or military decision makers. President Truman had endorsed the Army and Navy view that "every department required its own intelligence." The National Security Act left this concession intact. Only later would the Defense Intelligence Agency be created to coordinate military intelligence.

Separation Between Foreign & Domestic Intelligence

The act also made a crucial concession to members concerned about threats to civil liberties. It drew a bright line between foreign and domestic intelligence and assigning these realms, in effect, to the CIA and the Federal Bureau of Investigation, respectively. The CIA, furthermore, would have no "police, subpoena, or law enforcement powers," according to the act.

The importance of the National Security Act cannot be overstated. It was a central document in U.S. Cold War policy and reflected the nation's acceptance of its position as a world leader.

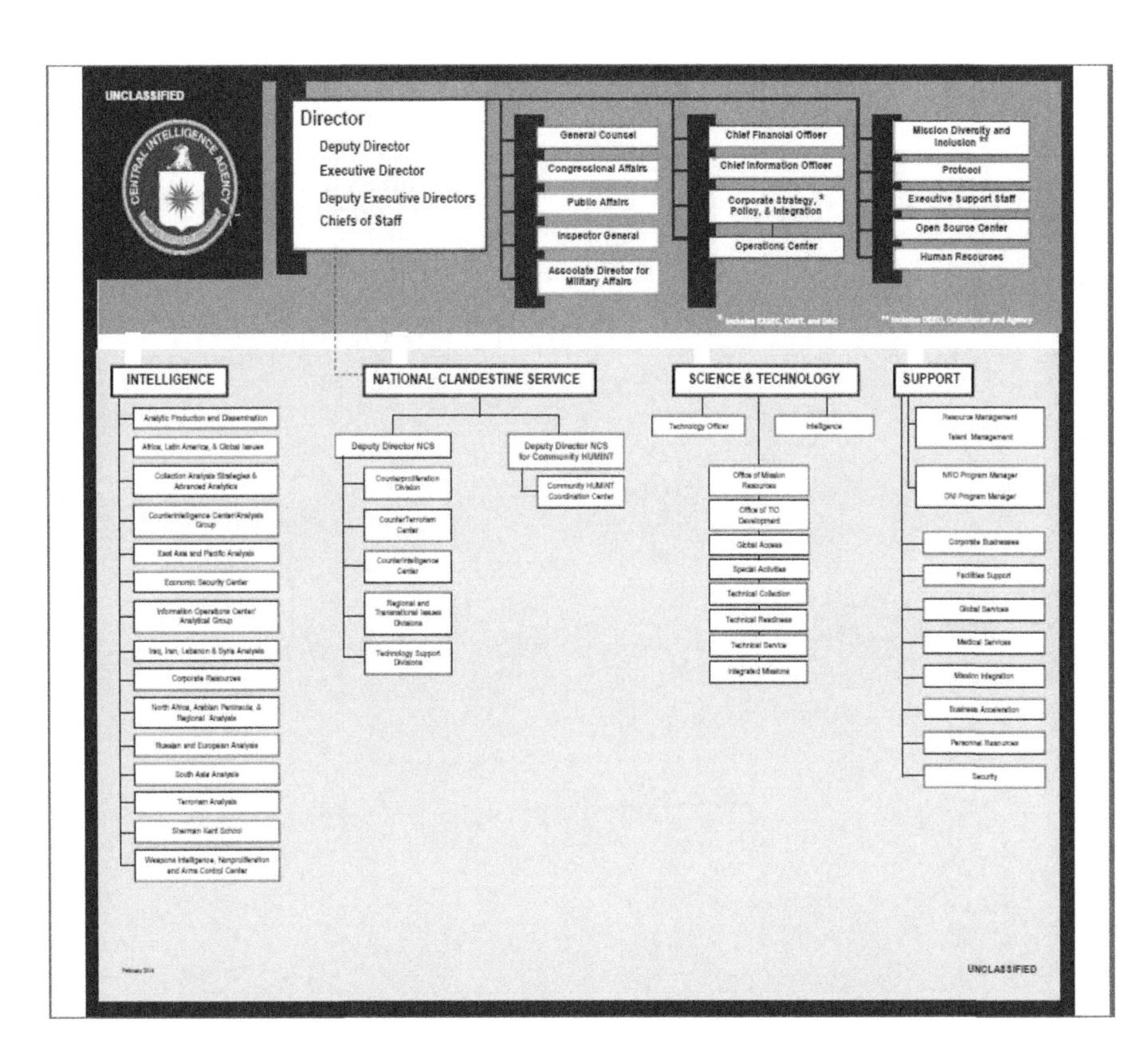

ORGANIZATIONAL CHART OF THE CIA

A BIBLE LESSON ON SPYING

*One more round with espionage
by Moses and Joshua*

A BIBLE LESSON ON SPYING

JOHN M. CARDWELL

For the past few years the Central Intelligence Agency has come under considerable scrutiny. Major issues have been raised regarding oversight and control, the intent being to insure accountability and legality. With the advent of the Carter administration, the issue of morality has also been made a major concern. Today the CIA and the nation are confronted with a perplexing situation: how can we engage in secret operations with oversight of these operations lying essentially in the public domain (Congress) and conduct inherently insidious spying activities that must also conform to traditional non-spying standards of ethical conduct and morality.

In an effort to seek some solutions to these problems, it is natural that we should explore historical precedents to determine what lessons and insights the past might offer. One rich source of information that should not be overlooked is the Holy Bible. The purpose therefore of this discussion is to explore the issue of spying as it occurs in the Bible and examine the lessons it might offer. Perhaps new perspectives can be found that will offer guidance regarding how "... one Nation, under God..." should go about the business of spying.

The subject of spying appears in numerous places throughout the Old and New Testament.[1] Spies were used by the Israelites against their adversaries, and on occasion various factions within the tribes of Israel used spies against each other. In the New Testament, spies were used by the political forces opposed to the emerging Christian movement and by members of the early Christian church to protect itself. There are many additional incidents in which individuals clearly engaged in espionage activities but are not normally referenced using those terms. For example, Judas could be described as having been a secret agent for the Sanhedrin because of his role in the betrayal of Jesus.

Spying as an activity is not treated as an issue in either the Old or the New Testaments and is discussed or mentioned only as an event worth reporting. As a consequence, the lessons to be learned from examining the Scriptures must be inferred in the context of narrative experiences. Guidance to be derived from the study of biblical spying events is therefore subjective and dependent upon the approach and depth from which inferences are drawn. In this discussion, however, the objective has been to emphasize the facts and keep interpretations to a minimum.

The earliest mention of spying in the Old Testament occurs in the story of Joseph.[2] After Joseph had been sold by his brothers into bondage and had later maneuvered himself into a position of influence in the Egyptian government, his

---

[1] All references cited in this article can be found in the *Holy Bible*, Revised Standard Version, Thomas Nelson and Sons, New York, 1959.

[2] Genesis 42:6-17

brothers came to Egypt to buy food during a famine. They were brought before Joseph but did not recognize him. Joseph, however, did recognize them, and in an effort to hide his recognition, accused them of coming to Egypt not to buy food but to spy. Evidently spying was an established fact of life, well familiar to Joseph.

There are only two spying incidents in the Bible in which methods and sources are discussed in any detail, and both occur in the Old Testament. The first incident occurred under the direction of Moses shortly after he led the Israelites out of Egypt.[3] They had camped in the wilderness of Paran near the boundary of the Promised Land, and Moses used spies to determine what the Promised Land was like. The second occurred approximately 40 years later under the direction of Joshua.[4] At that time, the Israelites had completed their sojourn in the desert and were again about to enter the Promised Land. There is a remarkable contrast not only in terms of methods and sources used by these two outstanding biblical leaders, but also in the different administrative procedures governing these two operations and the kinds of people involved. From an analysis of these two operations, biblical experience and perspectives with respect to spying are revealed.[5]

The children of Israel were divided into 12 tribes, or family groups, each tribe having its own leaders and hierarchy. The society was predominantly patriarchal in nature with the leader of each tribe acting as a kind of benevolent dictator or governor over his group. In him was vested the responsibility for providing administrative, legal, military, social, economic, and religious guidance and leadership. Moses was the overall leader and spokesman of the tribes but he exercised final authority only upon the consensus of the people and the leaders of the 12 tribes. Forty years later Joshua occupied roughly the same position as Moses. Both men, therefore, were not absolute rulers of the tribes of Israel. The people could, and occasionally did, reject their leadership.

Moses conducted the earliest spying operation recorded in the Bible. As previously mentioned, the purpose of this operation was to "spy out" Canaan.[6] He chose 12 prominent individuals, one from each of the 12 tribes, to be his spies and instructed them to go into the Promised Land and learn what the land was like. To provide proof that indeed it was a "land flowing with milk and honey," he instructed his spies to return with samples of fruit. These spies spent 40 days in the Promised Land, returned as instructed with information regarding the cities and the population, and delivered samples of fruit. Upon their return, they reported their findings publicly to Moses and the 12 tribes. They brought back a uniform opinion regarding the cities, number of people, lay of the land, and the fact that the countryside was indeed "flowing with milk and honey." Ten of the spies, however, reported that the people were so physically large and well organized that if an invasion was attempted, the Israelites would be destroyed. Only two of the spies reported that they were confident that they could succeed and argued strenuously to go forward with the invasion. In the ensuing public debate, the Israelites became frightened by the negative report of the 10 spies and lost confidence that they could succeed in an invasion. They advocated stoning the two spies who said that an invasion should be attempted.

---

[3] Numbers 13-14

[4] Joshua 2

[5] Intelligence operations by Moses and Joshua have previously figured in "Decision Trees" by Dr. Edwin G. Sapp, *Studies* XVIII/4, and "Scientific and Technical Intelligence" by Robert M. Clark, *Studies* XIX/1, pp. 46-47.

[6] The complete story of the espionage mission can be found in Numbers 13 and Numbers 14:1-10. The consequences are described in Numbers 14:10-34.

Biblical Spying

Moses was distraught at the loss of confidence by the Israelites, especially after they had been safely delivered out of Egypt and had successfully crossed the Red Sea. Their attitude brought them dangerously close to losing their status as God's chosen people, but Moses argued successfully on their behalf. They were nevertheless severely punished for their failure. They were told that they would be required to remain in the wilderness one year for every day the spies spent in the Promised Land, that is, 40 years for the 40 days spent spying. They were furthermore told that everyone over the age of 20 would be denied entry into the Promised Land, and that the only exceptions would be the two spies who maintained their faith. Even Moses was told he would not enter the Promised Land, and he did not.[7] Thus the first spying operation discussed in the Bible ended in failure and had disastrous consequences for the population.

Forty years later the Israelites found themselves again preparing to enter the Promised Land, this time under the leadership of Joshua.[8] Joshua was, by the way, one of the two surviving spies who had participated in the operation conducted under Moses.[9] As before, there was a need to send spies into the Promised Land to get intelligence to support the invasion. Joshua, however, went about things quite differently. He chose two young men whose names are not recorded and instructed them to go into Canaan and to reconnoiter the city of Jericho.[10] The spies went to Jericho and visited a harlot named Rahab. Although the presence of the spies was reported to the local authorities, Rahab hid the spies and kept them from being captured. She told the two spies that the people had been expecting an Israelite invasion for some time. She reported that—despite the fact that the city was well fortified and the army well trained—the people were frightened of the Israelites and had lost the courage to stand up to them. The escape of the Israelites from the Egyptians, their successful crossing of the Red Sea, the subsequent destruction of Pharaoh and his armies, and their exploits during their 40 years of wandering in the desert were well known to the people and had convinced them of the Israelites' superiority. Rahab likewise was convinced the city would fall and made an agreement with the spies that she would help them leave the city and not reveal what she had told them if in return they would spare her and her family during the attack. The spies agreed and with Rahab's help they successfully escaped capture and eventually made their way back to their own people. The spies reported to Joshua everything that had happened, especially the information given to them by the harlot regarding the fear of the people.

Using this information, Joshua made plans for the invasion and reported his plan to the 12 tribes. The plan was approved, the invasion proceeded, and the attack, capture, and subsequent destruction of the city of Jericho was successful.[11] Rahab and her family were, as agreed, spared by Joshua during the battle of Jericho.[12]

The contrast between these two incidents is significant. Moses used 12 people, all amateurs, each with both political and military responsibilities in his own tribe. Each was a prominent individual who is named in the Bible. On the other hand, Joshua apparently used two professional (throughout they were referred to only as "spies") anonymous (their names are not given) people to conduct his mission. Moses' spies brought back reports only of the physical characteristics of the land, whereas Joshua's also reported the attitude of the people. The spies Moses sent made their report

---
[7] Deuteronomy 1:37
[8] Joshua 1:1-2
[9] Deuteronomy 1:38
[10] The mission into Jericho is described in Joshua 2.
[11] Joshua 3, 4, 5, and 6:1-21
[12] Joshua 6:22-25

openly, and the discussion that followed was conducted in public. Joshua's spies, by contrast, reported only to Joshua, who then made the necessary decisions. Moses' spies, who also would have been principals in any military actions to be taken, participated in the decision-making process. Joshua's spies neither had leadership responsibilities nor did they participate in the policy-making decision process. The consequences of these two operations are significantly different. Moses' operation, conducted by amateurs more or less in the public domain, resulted in a weakening of Moses' position of authority, led to a loss of the people's confidence in themselves, and precipitated an extended period of severe national punishment. Joshua's operation, conducted in private by professionals, led to an achievement of national destiny.

An implicit point is made regarding the procedures used during these two spying operations. It is not specifically stated, but one is left with the impression that the 12 spies sent by Moses more or less went about their business as tourists, and the report they brought back is typical of the kind of thing that a tourist would report. The information reported to Moses consisted both of facts and conclusions drawn by the spies. The negative report given by the majority of the spies, for example, reflected their perception regarding the consequences of military actions, which, if taken, they would be called upon to lead. The people agreed with the negative position, not because of facts reported, but because of the negative interpretation given these facts by individuals of prominence.

Joshua's spies, on the other hand, went in secret (although they were discovered) and visited a harlot who gave them valuable information regarding the attitude of her people. The spies did not interpret this information but simply reported to Joshua what they had been told. No moral judgment was made regarding the fact that Joshua's spies visited a harlot, nor is the information provided by her judged to be of questionable validity.

The relationship between Rahab and the spies was evidently amoral. No conditions of "conversion" were imposed in the recruitment, but merely an agreement for conspiratorial silence in exchange for a harlot's life. Joshua made no recorded comment or judgment regarding his spies' recruitment of or the agreement with the harlot. He did, however, honor the agreement, despite the fact that he had not given his prior approval and took no part in making it. After the Battle of Jericho, Rahab joined the Israelites and lived with them. No mention is made of whether or not she continued to practice her old profession. All references to her, in both the Old and the New Testament, refer to her only as "Rahab the harlot."

If there is a lesson to be learned, it would appear that a strong case is made for the conduct of spying activities in secret by professionals, unencumbered by other political or military responsibilities, and that these professionals should report in secret to higher authority who would make policy decisions without debate. Spies should definitely not participate in the policy-decision-making process, nor should they take their cases to the public. When that occurs, although stoning is passé, the people are likely to throw figurative rocks at the wrong people for the wrong reasons.

It can be argued that the Moses operation suffered from complications that arose because of oversight and political issues. The selection of twelve spies, one from each of the twelve tribes, was probably motivated by political considerations, and the very specific instructions given by Moses to the spies were probably necessary in order to define the specific objectives and procedures in order to obtain approval from the twelve tribes. All the Israelites knew that the operation was to occur, who was going, and what they were to accomplish on the mission. When they returned, their report

Biblical Spying

was likewise made in public, the results of which have been noted earlier. It is noteworthy that the spies successfully accomplished all mission objectives. The point at which the Moses operation actually failed can be traced to the negative comments made during the public "mission debriefing." Taken overall, it can be argued that the negative report of the spies and the loss of control over the situation was actually stimulated because of too much oversight and the tightly controlled administrative procedures used. In summary, this episode is a classic example of an operation that was successful, but in which the "patient" died.

The contrasts offered by the Joshua operation are startling. Joshua certainly did not have an oversight problem, nor did he worry about defining a politically acceptable mission scenario. His spies were sent in secret, were given absolutely minimal instructions, "Go, view the land, especially Jericho," and reported back only to Joshua. The operational scenario could hardly have been predicted, and if it could, it is questionable that it would have been met with approval. Joshua handled all administrative matters alone, provided flexible and responsive support to his spies by keeping their bargain, and made the necessary judgments required to successfully lead his people to victory. From a purely administrative point of view, the Joshua mission was a nightmare; nevertheless, the operation can only be judged as an unqualified success.

A SHORT TOUR THROUGH THE HISTORY OF INTELLIGENCE

We will be moving rather quickly—to understate the case

A SHORT TOUR THROUGH THE HISTORY OF INTELLIGENCE

Edward F. Sayle

Tonight, we have an almost impossible task—to review for you the history of intelligence as reflected in the literature and to do so in an hour. To understate the case, we will be moving quickly.

The Ancients

The oldest known military treatise, *The Art of War*, written in China about 500 B.C., addresses the need for intelligence. In it, Sun Tsu wrote:

> "Those who know the enemy as well as they know themselves will never suffer defeat. . . . What enables the wise sovereign and the good general . . . to achieve things beyond the reach of ordinary men is foreknowledge."

Two centuries later, about 300 B.C., the Brahmin Kautilya tells us in his *Arthasastra* that by the collection of intelligence,

> ". . . the wise king shall guard . . . against the intrigue of foreign kings."

The *Holy Bible*, recounts no less than eleven episodes of espionage, including the familiar instruction by the Lord to Moses to send spies into the land of Canaan—with collection requirements as detailed as one might find today. Elsewhere, we might tend to agree that Rahab's sheltering of Joshua's spies in Jericho probably is the first documented use of a "safe house."

Among the ancients we encounter the use of ciphers, agent networks, courier systems and even mail intercepts, the latter attributed to Alexander the Great. The earliest extant intelligence report is a clay tablet written about 2000 B.C., but it is another dating back to 1370 B.C. that provides the ageless injunction:

> "Bring me back reliable information."

The literature of Hannibal and Julius Caesar abounds with the tales of informants and intrigue, intelligence networks, the use of cover legend and the like. Of Hannibal, for example, Polybius records,

> "For years before he undertook his campaign against Rome, he had sent his agents into Italy and they were observing everyone and everything. He charged them with transmitting to him exact and positive information regarding the fertility of the trans-Alpine plains and the Valley of the Po, their populations, their military spirit and preparations and, above all, their disposition towards the government at Rome."

These early civilizations recognized the necessity of intelligence collection. They were also most aware of deception—or what we would call disinformation. But, it is not until later, in reviewing the victory of William the Conqueror at the Battle of Hastings, we learn in detail how extensive early deception operations were.

Adapted from a talk delivered to the Senior Officers Development Course, Center for the Study of Intelligence, 7 January 1981.

A Short Tour

The Origins of Modern Services

In Britain, we find the first formal employment of *espials* about 1434, during the reign of Henry the Sixth—but it was not until fifty years later that the intelligence service took on any organized form. During the reign of Henry the Eighth the chief of military intelligence was designated the "Scoutmaster"—a term used by another intelligence officer, Robert Baden-Powell, centuries later in establishing the scouting movement.

British intelligence includes such figures as Walsingham, Christopher Marlowe, Daniel Defoe, William Earl of Cadogan, and a host of other better known for other accomplishments.

My favorite of these is the first Duke of Marlborough—"The First Churchill"—whose intelligence service was credited with being the best in Europe, yet was tactfully ignored in the B.B.C. dramatization of his life. I believe you will agree with me that Marlborough showed himself to be an intelligence professional when he wrote:

> "I cannot suppose that I need say how essential a part of the Service this (intelligence) is, that no war can be conducted successfully without very early and good intelligence, and that such advices cannot be had but at a very great expense. Nobody can be ignorant of this that knows anything of secret correspondence, or considers the numbers of persons that must be employed in it, the great hazard they undergo, the variety of places in which such correspondence must be kept, and the constant necessity of supporting and feeding this service, not to mention some extraordinary expenses of a higher nature, which ought only to be hinted at."

Much has been written of the early British service, with a heavy focus on the period of Elizabeth I and Walsingham's thoroughly repressive, but effective, intelligence and counterintelligence establishment. Unfortunately, the most revealing episodes of British intelligence history are more or less buried in the histories and biographies of the many monarchs and prime ministers and such departments as the Post Office, the Treasury and the Foreign Office.

For example, one discovers that the Royal Post Office was created with the express design of centralizing the mails for intercept purposes, and learns how one family had the responsibility for over 100 years of deciphering codes found in the mail. Now, that's job tenure! Or, one may wish to read more of George Downing, the American from Salem, Massachusetts, who headed British intelligence under both Cromwell and the restored Stuarts, and whose home at No. 10 Downing Street is now known for another reason.

Some historians credit Frederick the Great as being the real founder of organized spying in modern times. He once boasted that his spies outnumbered his cooks by a ratio of one hundred to one. Aside from its vulnerability to epicurean puns, I doubt that his service is a particularly good model of an intelligence organization in a democracy, to say the least.

With France, as another example, there are Napoleon's spymasters Fouche, Savary and Schulmeister; Louis the Fifteenth's military intelligence under the Count deSaxe and the unilateral political intelligence nets of the Count deBroglie; the colorful security risk Chevalier dÉon; and, of course, Beaumarchias, duPont, and others involved in France's extensive covert action operation which insured the success of the American Revolution.

A Short Tour

The American Service

Our own roots are not shallow; many derive from the Revolution. The founding fathers in the Continental Congress formalized intelligence with the creation, in November 1775, of the Committee of Secret Correspondence, our first intelligence directorate, and in making legislative provision for the protection of sources and methods while providing some measure of legislative oversight.

The intelligence committee recognized something then of which our present-day intelligence oversight committees also are most aware and on guard. On October 1, 1776, a courier arrived in Philadelphia conveying the oral report of Doctor Arthur Lee, the American intelligence resident in London, that the French—through Beaumarchais—had agreed to provide covert support to the American cause. Benjamin Franklin and Robert Morris, the only members of the committee in Philadelphia at the time, wrote:

> "We agree in opinion that it is our indispensable duty to keep it a secret, even from Congress. . . . We find, by fatal experience, the Congress consists of too many members to keep secrets. . . ."

Noble as this decision was, when Richard Henry Lee returned to Philadelphia he was briefed, as was his right, on the exciting news from his younger brother. He subscribed in writing to Franklin and Morris' decision on secrecy—then leaked the information to a friend. Within the month, the leak came to the attention of future Chief Justice John Jay, who was then engaged in counterintelligence activities. He was quick to admonish Morris:

> ". . . Communicate no other intelligence to Congress at large than what may be necessary to promote the common weal, not gratify the curiosity of individuals."

The Continental Congress established Secret Journals governing sensitive intelligence and foreign relations matters and imposed restrictions on access to and the copying of them. It enforced secrecy of intelligence data to the point of passing a patently false resolution of the Congress to protect intelligence relationships with France, and by firing the talented writer Tom Paine for leaking classified information. (The French hired him almost immediately.)

The Continental Congress authorized covert action operations, propaganda activity, deception operations, positive collection, and even adopted strict rules governing mail intercept after noting abuses.*

The Congress also found a way to fund intelligence operations with gold and silver at a time its own salaries were paid with paper money "not worth a Continental." And, in accepting accountings for funds thus expended, the Congress permitted the deletion of the names of intelligence sources who were paid.

Intelligence even contributed to the text of our Declaration of Independence. One of the charges leveled by Thomas Jefferson in that document, you may recall, accuses George the Third

> ". . . is at this time, Transporting Armies of Foreign Mercenaries to compleat the works of death, desolation and tyranny. . . ."

This indications and warning intelligence—in the form of copies of the agreements reached by George the Third with the German princes for provision of merce-

---
* See: Intelligence Vignette—The First Challenge to Secret Agencies, P #75.

naries (we lump them together in history as the "Hessians")—had been smuggled from London to Philadelphia via Canada by George Merchant. It arrived in Philadelphia on May 18, 1776, providing a timely input to our basic document.

The Congress also learned the hard way about excessive compartmentation. Working with American sympathizers on Bermuda, Morris engineered a highly successful "smash and grab" raid on the Royal gunpowder magazine in the colony. But, he neglected to tell General Washington of the mission. Washington, learning independently of the powder supply, launched his own raid. By the time his men arrived in Bermuda, the gunpowder was long gone and the Americans ran into a hornet's nest of British ships. This says something about the need for a *central* intelligence agency.

My favorite achievement of the Continental Congress grew from the ill-fated military and covert action effort led by Benjamin Franklin, Samuel Chase, Charles Carroll and Father John Carroll to acquire Quebec as the fourteenth colony. On February 26, 1776, in one of its secret resolutions, the Congress dispatched Fluery Mesplat, his printing equipment and family, to Canada

> ". . . to establish a free press . . . for the frequent publication of such pieces as may be of service to the cause of the United Colonies."

Our political operatives and their military forces were forced to withdraw, but Mesplat—undetected—remained behind, establishing the first French-language press in Canada, and founding Quebec's first newspapers, one of which, the *Montreal Gazette*, is still published today. I guess we might call this U.S. intelligence's longest-running proprietary and covert action operation, although one might suspect that somewhere along the line we lost control of it.

The Continental Congress also established many precedents for our service. It dictated the first requirements for an oath of secrecy for those employed in sensitive positions, and adopted a more stringent oath for its own members. It authorized gratuities for foreign figures to be influenced and it granted funds for what we would now call "operational entertainment." It dedicated ships exclusively for intelligence work under the control of the secret committees—not the Navy. It established an effective system of covert procurement, a counterintelligence system complete with penetration agents, adopted codes and ciphers and used chemical secret writing for intelligence communications, established our first foreign publications procurement program, and legislated our nation's first espionage act. (That act, it might be mentioned, was cited by the U.S. Supreme Court in its ruling against the German saboteurs during World War II.)

The Continental Congress requested and received the first intelligence estimate, strangely enough formatted as answers to certain key intelligence questions.

The Congress was concerned, even then, about the Russian menace. Since we hoped to pay for our foreign military procurement with tobacco, William Carmichael, an agent of the Committee of Secret Correspondence, was tasked with determining if Russian tobacco exports posed a threat to our plans. He reported the following from Amsterdam in November 1776:

> "You have been threatened that the Ukraine would supply Europe with tobacco. It must be long before that time will arrive. I have seen some of its tobacco here, and the best of it is worse than the worst of our ground leaf. Four hundred thousand pounds have been sent here this year."

There is also one other intelligence precedent from that conflict, one which has effected all of us at one time or another—travel vouchers. Yes, even for his famous

A Short Tour

"early warning" operation. Paul Revere had a travel order from the Committee of Safety and was required to fill out a travel voucher. After he filed his voucher, his per diem was reduced!

With victory over Britain, the new nation set about writing its Constitution. The Constitutional Convention provided in Article One for continuation of the Secret Journals, and tackled the future of intelligence. A citation from the *Federalist Papers* might best illustrate this. Jay wrote:

> "There are cases where the most useful intelligence may be obtained, if the persons possessing it can be relieved from apprehensions of discovery. Those apprehensions will operate on those persons whether they are actuated by mercenary or friendly motives; and there doubtless are many of both descriptions who would rely on the secrecy of the President, and who would not confide in that of the Senate, and still less in that of a large popular assembly. The Convention have done well, therefore, in so disposing of the power of making treaties that although the President must, in forming them, act by the advice and consent of the Senate, yet he will be able to manage the business of intelligence in such a manner as prudence may suggest."

One other important decision made by the Constitutional Convention was placing foreign intelligence activities in the hands of a civilian entity—rather than the military. The Secretary of the United States of America for Foreign Affairs—the forerunner of the present-day Department of State, received the task.

After George Washington took office, the founding fathers were true to their word. When Washington asked for a "competent fund," the Congress understood. And, on 1 July 1790, it gave the President the "Contingent Fund of Foreign Intercourse"—the so-called secret service fund—which required accounting only by certificate when necessary, the same procedure delegated to the DCI by the Central Intelligence Act of 1949.

You might find interesting a later description of the activities Gouverneur Morris, the first intelligence agent dispatched abroad under the Constitution by President Washington. Of him, William McClay said:

> "He has acted in a strange kind of capacity, half pimp, half envoy, or perhaps more properly a kind of political evesdropper."

Washington's secret service fund the first year was only $40,000. By the third year it had risen to one million dollars, or 12% of the national budget. Much of the money was for ransoming American hostages held in Algiers, for paying off foreign officials and, in effect, "buying peace."

During his term, President Jefferson received intelligence from France suggesting that Napoleon would be willing to coerce Spain into yielding the Floridas to the United States for seven million dollars—with Napoleon pocketing most of the money. Jefferson sought, and in secret session the Congress appropriated, an even greater secret discretionary fund—two million dollars—to start negotiations from which Napoleon later backed out.

Earlier, Jefferson had convinced the Congress to appropriate a sum of money

> "For the purpose of extending the external commerce of the United States."

The legislation was public, but its cryptic language masked the funding of the Lewis and Clark expedition which, despite what the schoolbooks tell us, was planned as an intelligence mission, most secret in nature, to enter the territories of foreign states with whom we were at peace, for the purpose of locating and mapping fortifications.

During Madison's administration, document security procedures were formalized with the markings: Secret, Confidential and Private. (We had to wait until this century to add Top Secret to the list to contend with British Most Secret information.)

Madison, like his predecessors, recognized the need for intelligence, dispatching secret agents to South America, Nova Scotia, Bermuda and Turkey.

But, like Jefferson, his eyes were on the Floridas, and in 1810 he sent agents to West Florida to convince American settlers there that in the event they separated from Spain, they would be welcome to join the United States. The settlers responded, adopted a "lone star" flag, captured Baton Rouge, and declared West Florida to be "free and independent." Within two days of receipt of reports of the "lone star" declaration, Madison proclaimed American control over the territory and sent troops.

Madison then took on the rest of the Floridas, dispatching General George Matthews on the secret mission. Matthews opted once again for the "lone star" revolution tactic, and in March 1812 a group of "patriots," which included Georgia militia in mufti and other volunteers, supported by American gunboats, occupied their first town and moved on to San Marcos near St. Augustine. They failed in this second conquest attempt but, undaunted, organized a government, chose a governor and ceded East Florida to the United States.

But, back in Washington, the situation had changed. President Madison had just paid $50,000 for the letters of John Henry, a British spy, which laid bare British efforts to woo the Federalists. The documents had been well-publicized, and the British thoroughly denounced for intervention in our domestic affairs. It was a bit of embarrassment, to say the least. The British had been doing only a little bit of spying and buying; General Matthews had successfully incited a revolution, seized Spanish territory, and had employed U.S. naval forces to boot.

Although there had been secret Congressional support for launching Matthews' mission, the President had no choice but to reprimand him and to promise to return the land to Spain—but he didn't; and it was left to Andrew Jackson to administer the coup de grace during the War of 1812.

It was also during Madison's regime that a successful—if unholy—alliance was made with gangsters for intelligence purposes. The pirate Jean Laffite and his men were used to scout, spy and sometimes fight with General Andrew Jackson in Louisiana.

Earlier, I mentioned the Secret Journals of Congress. In 1818, the question of declassifying those journals first arose. Recognizing the role of the Executive Branch, the Congress permitted the President to withhold those matters related to foreign affairs that he deemed to require continued protection. Thus, the published Secret Journals of the Revolution, declassified in 1818, and the Confederation period, declassified in 1820—much like information released these days under the Freedom of Information Act—are incomplete and fragmentary. Even then, there was embarrassment to some; for example, disclosure of the unanimous secret resolution authorizing the Secretary of State to open any letter—except those to and from members of Congress—in any post office for reasons of national interest.

From time to time, there had been rumblings in the Congress about secret agents and the sums to support them, but it was not until March 1818, nearly 29 years after Washington had sent his first secret agent abroad, that the issue erupted in the Senate as a purely political one. By then, framers of the Constitution and the founders of the government had all retired or had died. The issue was raised by young men, examining the system they had inherited.

A Short Tour

One, Henry Clay, objected to including in the appropriations bill monies for three individuals, saying that he felt the Contingent Fund was primarily, if not exclusively, to be used for secret agencies. The issue was resolved quickly—the money was struck from the appropriations bill—and added to the Contingent Fund!

It arose again, in 1825, with Adams as President and Clay Secretary of State, with the opposition condemning the sending of official observers to the Panama Congress—and several suggesting from the floor that secret agents, paid from the Contingent Fund, should have been sent, instead.

Six years later, in 1831, the appropriations bill was again at issue—this time over treaty commissioners. To put an end to queries, the Administration moved to transfer money from the appropriations bill to the secret service fund. The opposition indicated that it did not mind using the Contingent Fund for paying secret agents but that treaty commissioners were another thing. They lost, and the issue was buried in the secrecy of the Contingent Fund.

It was during these debates that the first full public statement of the purpose of the secret fund surfaced. Senator John Forsyth, later to be Secretary of State to Presidents Jackson and Van Buren, declared:

> "The experience of the Confederation having shown the necessity of secret confidential agencies in foreign countries, very early in the progress of the Federal Government a fund was set apart, to be expended at the discretion of the President of the United States on his responsibility only, called the Contingent Fund of Foreign Intercourse. . . . It was given for all purposes to which a secret service fund should or could be applied to the public benefit. For Spies, if the gentleman pleases. . . ."

Later challenges were defeated in 1838 and 1842, with one buried and the second settled by removing payment of Department of State dispatch agents from the secret fund.

This early period of our Republic contains a number of fascinating intelligence episodes.

In 1823, President Monroe, concerned at the possibility of European intervention in South America, dispatched Alexander McRae to Europe to follow the events on the scene. McRae's letter of instruction contained this admonition, one with which we would not be unfamiliar:

> "You will assume no public character, but take passports of a private citizen of the United States. . . . And you will take proper precautions for avoiding any appearance or suspicion of your being employed by a public agency. . . ."

That same year, Monroe sent George Bethune English to the capital of Islam, both representing himself as, and garbed in the costume of, an American Musselman. English managed to obtain a copy of the Turkish treaty with France "quietly and without observation," he said, but refrained from attempting to get certain others for fear it would "rouse suspicion." I would guess that George English comes the closest to the popular storybook spy—disguise and all.

After Joel Poinsett failed to purchase Texas from Mexico for five million dollars even after some realigning of the border, President John Quincy Adams, dispatched Anthony Butler as Poinsett's replacement. Butler attempted to bribe Mexican officials into selling, came up with the idea of an unpayable loan to them with Texas as collateral and was charged by the Mexicans with being behind attempts to recruit so-called "colonists" to revolutionize Texas.

A Short Tour

A "lone star" uprising eventually succeeded—and as we all know, there was no sign of U.S. intervention. In fact, when General Santa Anna was defeated in 1836, President Jackson removed all suspicion that the "lone star" tactic had been used once more. He felt it necessary to send a secret agent to inquire into the political, social and economic conditions in the Republic, the military strength of the Texans, their financial resources, and the ability of Sam Houston's government to meet its international obligations. The agent, Henry M. Morfit, came back with the word, in effect, "They're not ready yet," leading Jackson to advise the Congress that the U.S. stand aloof. That's one bad mark any Texan can hold against our service. All I can say is that by March of the following year the situation had changed and the United States finally recognized the Republic of Texas.

Another of President Jackson's agents is worth noting, if only because the case reflects how little our fledgling nation knew about the world. Edmund Roberts was assigned to investigate the operations of the British East India Company and sailed in 1832 for the Far East rated as the "captain's clerk" on the sloop *Peacock*. Only the captain knew his true status. Unfortunately, information at the Department of State regarding the countries he would visit was not very extensive or exact. In fact, titles and identities of some of the national leaders he was to approach were unknown in Washington. Simple—he was given a quantity of passports with blank spaces so that he might enter the necessary information on the spot. And, since he might be able to negotiate a treaty here and there, he was furnished with a supply of letters of credence with similar blank spaces. By the time Roberts died in Macao four years later, he had concluded treaties with Siam and the Sultan of Muscat!

President Tyler also had a bit of controversy over the natural combination already mentioned: Texas, secret agents and the Contingent Fund. Duff Green, a newspaper publisher, was sent to England to collect intelligence and engage in a bit of covert action related to the possible annexation of Texas. One of his letters about Texas was published in the British press, naturally not over his true name—creating such a stir that the Congress asked Secretary of State Calhoun to identify the writer and summon him before Congress. Calhoun replied that he couldn't ascertain the identity of the writer.

Congress tried again, closer to target, asking if Duff Green had been employed in Europe. Calhoun obviously winced before responding that there was

> ". . . no communication whatever either to or from Mr. Green, in relation to the annexation of Texas, to be found in the files of the Department."

The Senate went into executive session and tried again. By resolution it asked President Tyler if Duff Green had received any monies out of the Contingent Fund.

By then, the Senate had already rejected the treaty for annexation, and the secret no longer needed to be held. President Tyler answered that although he was not *required* to tell the Senate whom he paid from the Contingent Fund, he would oblige—this once. Yes, Duff Green had been employed to collect information about a negotiation being contemplated, but later abandoned. You will note that he didn't answer the original question—who wrote the controversial letter?

But Tyler, after leaving office, was not to hear the last of his Contingent Fund. It was charged in the Congress that a Secretary of State, Daniel Webster, had used some $17,000 from the Fund for propaganda in the U.S. religious press to win popular support for an unpopular treaty with Canada.

By deposition, Tyler told the investigating committee that this was a secret matter and that Webster had been deputized to carry it out. The committee back-tracked. It

A Short Tour

said it had no intention of investigating the acts of secret agents or of judging the propriety of using them within the United States.

The full House wasn't mollified. It called upon President Polk to surrender the accounts of all payments from the fund during Tyler's administration. Polk refused disclosure, noting:

> "The experience of every nation on earth has demonstrated that emergencies may arise in which it becomes absolutely necessary for the public safety or the public good to make expenditures, the very object of which would be defeated by publicity. . . . In no nation is the application of such funds made public. In time of war or impending danger the situation of the country will make it necessary to employ individuals for the purpose of obtaining information or rendering other important services who could never be prevailed upon to act if they entertained the least apprehension that their names or their agency would in any contingency be revealed."

I have cited a lengthy excerpt from President Polk's statement because it recognizes a clear linkage between "obtaining information," i.e. collection, and "rendering other important services," undefined. Rather like the phrase "to perform such other functions and duties related to intelligence affecting the national security . . . " in the National Security Act of 1947.

Polk had good reason to defend the integrity of the Contingent Fund and to include "rendering other important services" in addition to collection—he was then using the fund for agents to Mexico and to California for what we would now call covert action to assure that California and Texas would drop into the U.S. basket.

As war clouds thickened, Polk received an intelligence report that Mexico might cede California to Britain, effectively and permanently blocking American dreams of stretching to the Pacific. He authorized Thomas Larkin to assure the Californians that

> "Should California assert and maintain her independence, we shall render her all the kind offices in our power, as a sister Republic."

Should the question of annexation arise, Larkin was empowered to say that the United States had no such aspirations

> ". . . unless by the free and spontaneous wish of the independent people of adjoining territories."

Larkin was instructed to propound these ideas secretly, but back in Washington, the opposition in Congress got it all wrong—they claimed that Larkin had been instructed to produce a revolution in California and that Col. John Fremont had been given authority to sustain it.

The war with Mexico broke out in 1846, and once more President Polk turned to a secret agent, this time Moses Yale Beach, a journalist and a founder of the New York Associated Press. Beach travelled to Mexico, using a British passport, and under instruction

> ". . . Never to give the slightest intimation, directly or indirectly, that you are an agent of this Government."

Beach is said to have done well. He met with prominent Mexicans and became actively involved in the political and social life of Mexico City, all with the objective of seeking a way toward peace, a task some historians say he almost accomplished. Interestingly, the suspicious American press never unmasked his mission.

Another precedent under President Polk was the establishment of the Army's first "spy company," commanded, appropriately enough, by Ethan Allen Hitchcock, grandson and namesake of the leader of the Green Mountain Boys during the War of Independence.

President Taylor also had his spy flap, and handled it with a flourish. It surfaced in the Congress that he had dispatched an agent to take soundings of the Hungarian revolt—and perhaps do a bit more if it looked as though the Magyars would win. They didn't, and the Congressional leak resulted in a strong note from the Austrians saying that had the agent been apprehended, he could have been treated in a manner traditional for spies. President Taylor, in angry response, defined a spy as one sent by one *belligerent* against another to gain secret information for *hostile* purposes. The United States was a neutral in the conflict, ergo the man was an observer, not a spy. Furthermore, the President of the United States took great offense at the suggestion that this country would employ spies.

President Pierce, as Polk, made extensive use of agents and covert action. He acquiesced to the formation of an exile army in New Orleans for the "liberation of Cuba," sent an agent to Cuba, approved a plan to encourage European money-lenders to call in their notes from the Spanish Crown to force Madrid to sell Cuba to the United States to pay the debts; dabbled in covert action in Canada, and even came up with intelligence from intercepted mail of British plans to sell guns to Costa Rica for use in war with Nicaragua and to drive out the North Americans. When political realities forced him to end his support to the exile army's invasion of Cuba, he used positive intelligence on Cuban fortifications to convince an old friend, who was the leader of the "army," to call it off.

President Buchanan had his spies, too. Francis J. Grund, the newsman credited with being the father of the sensational style of journalism, served in Europe as a roving spy-at-large, investigating a number of issues of concern to the President. He was authorized to reveal his true status only to U.S. Ministers in whatever countries he visited, but to all others he was to be only an interested and inquisitive private citizen.

Hours could be spent on the Civil War: the exploits of the civilian Pinkertons and the military men of Lafayette Baker's Secret Service Bureau; overhead reconnaissance by Professor Lowe's "Aeronaut Corps" of balloonists; President Lincoln's fascination with communications intelligence; and uncounted espionage cases. I will leave these to your private reading, and tantalize you with mention of a few of our intelligence activities abroad during the conflict:

    a. Agents with some ten million dollars to engage in preclusive purchasing in Great Britain.

    b. Some two dozen agents in Britain and on the continent to identify secret sales and ship construction as part of British and French covert support of the Confederacy. (They had little difficulty in recruiting clerks in business houses and shipyards to obtain the information.)

    c. Seizure on the high seas of a Scots-registry ship with a British crew sailing with false destination papers because we knew it was being delivered to the South.

    d. Attempts to recruit General Garibaldi to accept senior rank in the Union Army.

    e. Operations into Canada to thwart Confederate operations being launched from there and to build a case proving Canadian and British covert assistance to the Confederates.

A Short Tour

A landmark court decision regarding our intelligence service stems from the Civil War. William A. Lloyd, under personal contract to President Lincoln, was sent south to collect tactical and political information. He was to be paid $200 a month, but when the war ended and he returned north, he was only reimbursed for his expenses. He took the matter to the Court of Claims seeking additional compensation.

The U.S. Supreme Court, in deciding the case, acknowledged that the President had the authority to employ secret agents, that all such agent contracts are binding on the government, and that the sums should be paid from the Contingent Fund. Yet, because Lloyd had taken the matter to the courts, it ruled against him stating:

> "The service stipulated by the contract was a secret service; the information sought was to be obtained clandestinely and was to be communicated privately; the employment and the service were to be equally concealed. Both employer and agent must have understood that the lips of the other were to be forever sealed respecting the relation of either to the matter. This condition of the engagement was implied by the nature of the employment, and is implied in all secret employments of the Government. . . . If upon contracts of such matters an action against the Government could be maintained in the Court of Claims . . . the whole service in any case and the manner of its discharge with the details of its dealings with individuals and officers, might be exposed to the serious detriment of the public. A secret service, with liability to publicity in this way, would be impossible. . . . The publicity produced by an action would itself be a breach of a contract of that kind, and thus defeat recovery. . . ."

It is in this decision one finds roots for the so-called "Glomar defense," that is, we are not saying that such information exists, but *if* it does indeed exist, it would be properly classified. The Supreme Court said in its decision:

> "It may be stated, as a general principle, that public policy forbids the maintenance of any suit in a court of justice, the trial of which would inevitably lead to the disclosure of matters which the law itself regards as confidential, and respecting which it will not allow the confidence to be violated. . . . Much greater reason exists for the application of the principle to cases of contract for secret services with the Government, as the existence of a contract of that kind is itself a fact not to be disclosed."

After the Civil War, Presidents continued to dispatch agents, with Canada a favorite destination. In 1869, for example, President Grant dispatched John Wickes Taylor to the area of the Red River Rebellion in Canada, to determine if sentiment existed for annexation of the Selkirk area—or even more—by the United States. It didn't. We had called it wrong. The dissidents did not want to leave Canada—they just wanted to be a second Quebec.

In 1881, the Army devised the idea of "Hunting and Fishing Leave," a means by which officers could be dispatched to conduct terrain reconnaissance, yet providing some degree of official deniability.

Captain Daniel Taylor performed such a reconnaissance along the St. Lawrence River to obtain military information in 1881; in 1890, Lt. Andrew Rowan (of later "message to Garcia" fame) did a detailed reconnaissance of the entire line of the Canadian Pacific Railway; and in 1897, Lt. Henry M. Whitney infiltrated Puerto Rico as a crew member on a British tramp steamer. The need for information was great and in 1902, the Military Information Division of the Army instructed commanding officers of a number of frontier posts to send secret tactical reconnaissance missions into Canada for mapping purposes. (Should you be curious, "Hunting and Fishing Leave" existed in Army regulations, in one form or another, until 1928.)

A Short Tour

The period saw heightened interest in military intelligence. The Office of Naval Intelligence was formed in 1882, followed by the Bureau of Military Intelligence in the Army in 1885. It was in that year also, that President Cleveland authorized the posting of military and naval attaches at our foreign legations.

But perhaps the best evaluation of this period is that of Thomas Miller Beach, a British intelligence agent who served under cover in the United States from 1867 to 1888, as part of a network the British and Canadians maintained along the border and in such cities as Chicago, Detroit and Buffalo. In his memoirs, Beach provides this critique of the American service:

> "America is called the Land of the Free, but she could give England points in the working of the Secret Service, for there, there is no stinting of money or men."

In 1909, there was a joint intelligence operation involving a two year reconnaissance of Taiwan, the Ryukyus, the Japanese home islands, Korea and Manchuria by Commander Joseph Thompson of the U.S. Navy Medical Service, and 1st Lt. Consuelo A. Seoane, 3rd Cavalry. Traveling under assumed names and South African nationality and posing as naturalists, the two officers mapped Japanese fortifications and coastal facilities. To enhance their cover, they collected specimens and maintained bogus diaries of botanical finds—for the benefit of Japanese surreptitious entry teams—and checked in regularly with British consular authorities to affirm Crown protection due South African nationals.

We've leap-frogged rather quickly from the Civil War, and now find ourselves with World War I, and the familiar story of the Zimmerman Telegram—involving foreign liaison, communications intelligence and cryptography—which led President Wilson to ask the Congress for a declaration of war against Germany.

I bring focus on the Zimmerman Telegram, and President Wilson's major policy decision based on that intelligence data, for a reason.

Perhaps, as we have made our quick tour through what can be learned from the literature of intelligence, I am certain there have been a few things mentioned which prompted you to say quietly, "Gee, I didn't know that."

Obviously, there is much to be learned from the literature of any profession, and intelligence is no exception. Those who engage in our profession, and those in the national and foreign policy spheres who must employ us, have an obligation to learn from the literature, or they might someday find themselves in the quandry faced by President Wilson in acting on the intelligence we know as the Zimmerman Telegraph. As he said later:

> "You have got to think of the President of the United States as the chief counsellor of the Nation, elected for a little while but as a man meant constantly and every day to be the Commander-in-Chief of the Army and Navy of the United States, ready to order them to any part of the world where the threat of war is a menace to his own people."

> "And you cannot do that under free debate. You cannot do that under public counsel. Plans must be kept secret."

> "Knowledge must be accumulated by a system which we have condemned, because it is a spying system. The more polite call it a system of intelligence."

> "You cannot watch other nations with your unassisted eye. You have to watch them with secret agencies planted everywhere."

A Short Tour

"Let me testify to this, my fellow citizens, I not only did not know it until we got into this war, but I did not believe it when I was told that it was true, that Germany was not the only country that maintained a secret service. Every country in Europe maintained it, because they had to be ready for Germany's spring upon them, and the only difference between the German secret service and the other secret services was that the German secret service found out more than the others did, and therefore Germany sprang upon other nations unaware, and they were not ready for it."

Thus, we end our review—with President Wilson's candor, and what I believe is the best endorsement to come to mind for the proper study of the literature of intelligence.

A CABLE FROM NAPOLEON

The story of a critical intelligence finding almost unrecorded in the history of French intervention in Mexico during and after the Civil War is reconstructed here from official records in the National Archives.

A CABLE FROM NAPOLEON
Edwin C. Fishel

The years 1864–67 saw the United States facing one of the severest international problems in its history: an Austrian prince ruled Mexico and a French army occupied the south bank of the Rio Grande. It was toward the end of this period that the Atlantic cable went into permanent operation. Thus the United States had both the motive and the means for what was almost certainly its first essay in peacetime communications intelligence.[1]

The nation had emerged from the Civil War possessing a respectable intelligence capability. Union espionage activities were generally successful, especially in the later stages of the war; Northern communications men read Confederate messages with considerable regularity (and received reciprocal treatment of their own traffic from the rebel signalmen); and there were intelligence staffs that developed a high degree of competence in digesting and reporting these findings.[2]

---

[1] No earlier use of communications intelligence by the United States in peacetime is known to the writer. Any reader who knows of one is urged to present it.

[2] At the beginning of the war the government's conception of military intelligence work was so limited that it employed Allan Pinkerton, by that time well known as the head of a successful detective agency, as the chief intelligence operative in Washington. Pinkerton proved effective in counterintelligence work, but his intelligence estimates so greatly exaggerated Confederate strength that he is commonly given a large share of the blame for the supercaution that caused his sponsor, General McClellan, to stay close to Washington with far superior forces. Pinkerton left the service with McClellan in 1862, however, and long before the end of the war competent intelligence staffs, entirely military in character though composed of men drawn from civil life, served the principal headquarters.

A Cable From Napoleon

With the war over in 1865, this new capability was turned against Napoleon III and his puppet, Emperor Maximilian of Mexico. In the struggle to get the French army out of North America and Maximilian off his throne, this government had the use of an intelligence enterprise which, though conducted on a small scale, turned out to be very effective. Up to the last weeks this intelligence operation consisted of competent reporting on the part of espionage agents and diplomatic representatives; but when a crisis developed at that point, these sources were silent, and it was a cablegram from Napoleon to his commanders in Mexico that yielded the information needed by the nation's leaders.

As an intelligence coup the interception and reading of this message were hardly spectacular, for it passed over fifteen hundred miles of telegraph wire accessible to United States forces and, contrary to later assertions that it had to be deciphered, it appears to have been sent in the clear. Nevertheless, the event was an outstanding one in the history of United States intelligence operations, not simply because it represented a beginning in a new field but also because the message in question was of crucial importance.

State of the Union, 1861–65

The crisis in which America's intelligence capability asserted itself did not come until after the nation had spent five anxious years watching the European threat develop.

Napoleon had sent an army to Mexico late in 1861, assertedly to compel the payment of huge debts owed by the government of Mexico. His object, however, was not simply a financial one: a new commander whom he sent to Mexico in 1863 received instructions (which leaked into the press) to the effect that the Emperor's purpose was to establish a Mexican government strong enough to limit "the growth and prestige of the United States."[3] At a time when the American Union appeared to be breaking up under pressure from its southern half, such a statement meant to American readers that Napoleon had no intention of stopping at the Rio Grande.

---

[3] J. Fred Rippy, *The United States and Mexico* (New York, 1926), p. 261, citing Genaro y Carlos Pereya Garcia, *Documentos inéditos o muy raros para la historia de Méjico* (20 vols., Mexico City, 1903), XIV, pp. 8–20.

A Cable From Napoleon

CONFIDENTIAL

In June 1863 French arms swept the Liberal government of President Benito Juárez from Mexico City, and in the summer of 1864 Napoleon installed the Archduke Ferdinand Maximilian, thirty-two-year-old brother of Emperor Franz Joseph of Austria, on the new throne of Mexico. During this period the Northern people, their belligerence aroused by the Southern rebellion, were clamoring for action against France — action that might well bring disaster upon them. Aggressive behavior by the United States might give Napoleon the popular support he needed to join hands with the Confederacy in a declaration of war, a development that could provide Secession with enough extra strength to prevail.

While the Civil War lasted, Congress and the public were held in check largely through the prestige and political skill of the Federal Secretary of State, William H. Seward. But when the War was over — by which time the government had reason to believe that Napoleon had become disenchanted with his puppets in Mexico — Seward was ready to turn his people's aggressive demeanor to advantage, and he warned Napoleon that their will would sooner or later prevail. Before this statement reached Paris, however, the United States Minister there, John Bigelow, who had been mirroring Seward's new firmness for some months, had in September 1865 obtained a tentative statement from the French that they intended to withdraw from Mexico.[4]

While Bigelow was shaking an admonitory finger at the French Ministry of Foreign Affairs, an American military fist was being displayed before the French along the Rio Grande. Promptly upon the silencing of Confederate guns, General Grant sent Philip Sheridan, second only to William T. Sherman in the esteem of the General-in-Chief, to the command of the Department of the Gulf, with headquarters at New Orleans. A considerable force was posted along the Mexican frontier and designated an "army of observation."

---

[4] Rippy, *op. cit.*, pp. 264-65 and 269-72; Seward to Bigelow, September 21, 1865. All diplomatic correspondence sent or received by United States officials that is cited herein will be found in the *Papers Relating to Foreign Affairs Accompanying the Annual Message of the President* to the First Session, Thirty-Ninth Congress (covering the year 1865), Second Session, Thirty-Ninth Congress (1866), and Second Session, Fortieth Congress (1867-68).

Sheridan and Intelligence

Sheridan, thirty-four years old and the possessor of a reputation as a gamecock, adhered strongly to an opinion prevalent in the Army that a little forceful military action now would save a full-scale war later. The audacious statesman who was directing foreign policy at Washington was, to Sheridan, "slow and poky," and the general found ways of giving considerable covert aid to the Juárez government, then leading a nomadic existence in the north of Mexico.[5] Sheridan and Seward, though the policy of each was anathema to the other, made an effective combination.

One of the ways in which Sheridan could exercise his relentless energy against the Imperialists without flouting Seward's policy was in collecting intelligence on what was going on below the border. There was an interregnum at the United States Legation in Mexico City, and all the official news reaching Washington from below the Rio Grande was that supplied by the Juarist Minister to the United States, Matias Romero, a scarcely unbiased source if a prolific one.[6] Sheridan quickly undertook to fill the gap.

This task must have been decidedly to the general's taste, for he had been one of the most intelligence-conscious commanders in the Civil War.[7] He had achieved something of an innovation in organizing intelligence activities when, during his 1864 campaign in the Shenandoah Valley, he established a group of intelligence operatives under military control. His previous sources of information, local citizens and Confederate deserters, had both proved unreliable. "Sheridan's Scouts" were a military organization in a day when it was customary to have civilians perform most of the intelligence-gathering tasks other

---

[5] John M. Schofield, *Forty-Six Years in the Army* (New York, 1897), p. 381; Philip H. Sheridan, *Personal Memoirs* (2 vols., New York, 1888), II, pp. 215–19; Percy F. Martin, *Maximilian in Mexico* (London, 1914), p. 432.

[6] Dozens of examples of this intelligence will be found in the Romero-to-Seward correspondence in the *Papers Relating to Foreign Affairs* described in footnote 4.

[7] When a division commander in 1862–63, Sheridan had exercised an initiative in intelligence collection that was more likely to be found in an army commander. His *Memoirs* reveal a constantly high interest in intelligence activities.

than battle-zone reconnaissance. After the war, Major Henry Harrison Young, the Scouts' commander, and four of his best men went to the Gulf Department with Sheridan.

Sheridan also, in common with numerous other commanders North and South, had an acquaintance with communications intelligence as it was produced in the field command of that day. By the time the Civil War was well advanced, Signal Corpsmen in every theater had learned how to solve the enemy's visual-signaling alphabets, and they derived much information for the commanders by keeping their field glasses trained on enemy signal stations.[8] There was not likely to be any opportunity for such methods along the Rio Grande, however, and no more likely was the possibility of tapping telegraph lines carrying useful information.

Young and his four men were dispatched to important points in northern Mexico to report on movements of the Imperial forces and the various projects of ex-Confederates who were joining Maximilian's forces and attempting to establish colonies under his flag.[9] Judged by the accuracy of the reports reaching Sheridan and the strong tendency of the Southerners' projects to abort after coming under his notice, the work of these five men was most effective.[10]

1866, Year of Telegrams and Tension

The critical question — whether the French would tire of their venture and withdraw — was, however, one to which no intelligence service could divine an answer, for the French for a long time did not know the answer themselves. In 1865 Marshal François Achille Bazaine, now Napoleon's commander in Mexico, was informed by the Minister of War that he must bring the army home, and at about the same time he received

---

[8] *War of the Rebellion: Official Records of the Union and Confederate Armies* (Washington, 1884–1901) contains hundreds of decipherments resulting from such interceptions, chiefly in the operations of 1863–65 in Tennessee and Georgia, the operations along the South Carolina coast beginning in 1863, and the Richmond-Petersburg siege of 1864–65.

[9] Sheridan, op. cit., II, p. 214.

[10] See, for example, intelligence reports sent by Sheridan to Grant, March 27, May 7, June 24, July 3 and 13, 1866. All Army correspondence cited hereafter in this article will be found in the United States National Archives, except where otherwise indicated.

word to the opposite effect from the Emperor himself.[11] Napoleon's treaty with Maximilian by which the latter accepted the throne of Mexico contained a secret clause providing that French military forces to the number of 20,000 were to remain in Mexico until November 1867.[12] As events were to prove, however, this compact was less likely to determine Napoleon's course of action than were the pressures on him represented by the United States' vigorous diplomacy and the rising military power of Prussia.

In April 1866 Minister Bigelow succeeded in pinning Napoleon down to a definite understanding, to the effect that the 28,000 French soldiers in Mexico would be brought home in three detachments, leaving in November 1866 and March and November 1867. Seward's reply to this promise was characteristic of his tone at this time: dwelling only briefly on the diplomatic niceties, he suggested that the remaining period of occupation be shortened if possible. The Secretary was in high feather; in the same month a protest by him induced the Austrian government to abandon an effort to send substantial reinforcements to the small Austrian force in Maximilian's army.[13]

In June Maximilian received a studiously insolent letter from Napoleon containing the stunning announcement that the French would withdraw. Attention now focused on whether he would attempt to hold his throne without French arms. The unhappy sovereign reacted first by dispatching his Empress, twenty-six-year-old Carlota, to Paris in a vain attempt to change Napoleon's mind. He soon decided to abdicate, then determined to remain on his throne, then wavered for many weeks between abdicating and remaining.[14]

Napoleon meanwhile had to contend not only with his protégé's indecision but with some apparent recalcitrance on the

---

[11] Philip Guedalla, *The Two Marshals* (London, 1943) p. 130.

[12] *Ibid.*, p. 112.

[13] Seward to de Montholon, April 25, 1866; Seward to J. Lothrop Motley (United States Minister to Austria), April 6, 16, 30, May 3, 30, 1866; Motley to Seward, April 6, May 1, 6, 15, 21, 1866; James M. Callahan, *American Foreign Policy in Mexican Relations* (New York, 1932), p. 235.

[14] Martin, *op. cit.*, pp. 266–267 and 272–273.

A Cable From Napoleon

part of Bazaine, who was variously suspected of having a secret agreement with Maximilian to remain in the latter's support, of being secretly in league with the Mexican Liberals, of profiting financially from his official position, and of having hopes of succeeding Maximilian. (There is evidence to support all these suspicions.) [15] Soon Napoleon realized he had made a bad bargain with the United States; to attempt to bring the army home in three parts would risk the annihilation of the last third. Early in the autumn of 1866 the Emperor sent his military aide, General Castelnau, to Mexico with instructions to have the army ready to leave in one shipment in March, and to supersede Bazaine if necessary. Thus the evacuation was to begin four months later than Napoleon had promised, but to end eight months earlier.[16]

No word of this important about-face was, however, promptly passed to the United States government. At the beginning of November — supposedly the month for the first shipment — the best information this country's leaders possessed was a strong indication that Napoleon intended to rid himself of Maximilian. This was contained in a letter written to Maximilian by a confidential agent whom he had sent to Europe; it showed the failure of Carlota's visit to Napoleon. Somewhere between its point of origin, Brussels, and its destination, the office of Maximilian's consul in New York, it had fallen into the hands of a Juarist agent.[17] Soon after Minister Romero placed it in Seward's hands, Napoleon's new Foreign Minister, the Marquis de Moustier, wrote his Minister in Washington, de Montholon, that the evacuation timetable was raising serious difficulties but that in no case would the November 1867 deadline for its

---

[15] Castelnau to Napoleon, December 8, 1866, quoted in Georges A. M. Girard, *La Vie et les souvenirs du General Castelnau* (Paris, 1930), pp. 112–124; Marcus Otterbourg (United States charge d'affaires in Mexico) to Seward, December 29, 1866; Martin, *op. cit.*, pp. 298–99; Lewis D. Campbell (United States Minister to Mexico) to Seward, November 21, 1866.

[16] De Moustier (Foreign Minister) to de Montholon (Minister to the United States), October 16, 1866, in *Foreign Affairs*; Bigelow to Seward, November 8, 1866; Martin, *op. cit.*, pp. 56–57; Guedalla, *op. cit.*, p. 133; Girard, *op. cit.*, p. 122.

[17] Romero to Seward, October 10, 1866; *New York Tribune*, January 4, 1867.

completion be exceeded.[18] This note should have reached Seward in early November (1866), but if it did, its strong hint that there would be no partial evacuation in that month was apparently lost on him.

When the French felt able to promise complete withdrawal in March, de Moustier revealed to Bigelow the abandonment of the three-stage plan. So alarmed was Bigelow by the prospect of a major outbreak of anti-French feeling in America that he refrained from sending the news to Seward until he had heard it from the Emperor himself, whom he saw on November 7. The November shipment had been cancelled for reasons purely military, the Emperor said, showing surprise that the United States had not known of the change. The order had been telegraphed to Bazaine and had been sent in the clear in order that "no secret might be made of its tenor in the United States."[19] Undoubtedly the Emperor was perfectly sincere in implying that he expected the United States government to make itself a tacit "information addressee" on telegrams of foreign governments reaching its territory.

Receiving Bigelow's report of this interview, Seward struck off a peremptory cablegram to Paris: the United States "can not acquiesce," he declared. The 774 words of this message unfolded before Bigelow on November 26 and 27, their transmission having cost the State Department some $13,000. On December 3 Bigelow telegraphed the Foreign Minister's assurance that military considerations alone were responsible for the change of plans and his promise, somewhat more definite than the previous one, that the French "corps of occupation is to embark in the month of March next."[20]

So strongly had this government relied on Napoleon's original promise that President Johnson had dispatched an important diplomatic mission to Mexico (republican Mexico, that is) — a mission that was already at sea, expecting, on arrival at Vera

---

[18] De Moustier to de Montholon, October 16, *loc. cit.*

[19] Bigelow to Seward, November 8, 1866.

[20] Seward to Bigelow, November 23, 1866; Dexter Perkins, *The Monroe Doctrine, 1826–1867* (Baltimore, 1933), p. 534; Bigelow to Seward, December 3, 1866.

A Cable From Napoleon

Cruz, to find the French leaving and Juárez resuming the reins of government. The mission consisted of ex-Senator Lewis D. Campbell, newly appointed Minister to Mexico, and General William T. Sherman, sent with Campbell to give the mission prestige, to advise Juárez in regard to the many military problems that would be plaguing him,[21] and possibly to arrange for the use of small numbers of United States troops to assist the Liberal regime by temporarily occupying certain island forts.[22]

Evidence was accumulating that Maximilian and his European troops would soon be gone from Mexico,[23] but it stood no chance of general acceptance in Washington. Such was the degree of trust now accorded Louis Napoleon that his promise to evacuate Mexico would be believed on the day when the last French soldier took ship at Vera Cruz.

At this juncture Sheridan's headquarters came into possession of a copy of a coded telegram to Napoleon from Bazaine and Castelnau. The message had left Mexico City by courier on December 3 and had been delivered to the French Consulate at New Orleans, from where it was telegraphed to Paris on the 9th. As will be explained below, there is every reason to believe that this message went unread by United States cryptographers. The possession of its contents would have been of great value, for the message (as translated from the version given by Castelnau's biographer) said:

---

[21] Seward's instructions to Campbell, dated October 25, 1866, are perhaps the most impressive of the numerous masterful documents produced by the Secretary in the Mexican affair. Grant was the President's first selection as the military member of the mission and was excused only after a number of urgent requests. Correspondence relating to the inception of the Sherman-Campbell mission includes: Andrew Johnson to E. M. Stanton, October 26 and 30; Grant to Sherman (at St. Louis), October 20 and 22; Grant to Johnson, October 20 and 21, and Grant to Stanton, October 27.

[22] Sherman to Grant, November 3, 1866 (Sherman MSS, Library of Congress); Grant to Sheridan, November 4, 1866. Sheridan was directed to "comply with any request as to location of troops in your department that Lt. Gen. Sherman . . . may make."

[23] Campbell to Seward, November 21, 1866; unaddressed, unsigned military intelligence report dated at Washington, November 18.

CONFIDENTIAL

A Cable From Napoleon

New Orleans, 9 Dec 1866

To His Majesty the Emperor Napoleon at Paris.
Mexico, 3rd December.

Emperor Maximilian appears to wish to remain in Mexico, but we must not count on it. Since the evacuation is to be completed in March, it is urgent that the transports arrive. We think that the foreign regiment must also be embarked. As for the French officers and soldiers attached to the Mexican Corps, can they be allowed the option of returning?

The country is restless. The Campbell and Sherman mission, which arrived off Vera Cruz on November 29 and left December 3, seems disposed to a peaceful solution. Nevertheless it gives moral support to the Juarists through the statement of the Federal government.

Marshal Bazaine and General Castelnau [24]

As December wore on, rumblings from Capitol Hill indicated that Congress — the same Congress that was even then moving to impeach President Johnson — might attempt to take the management of the entire affair out of the Administration's hands. Word arrived from Bigelow that transports to bring the army home were ready to sail from French ports, but that information would by no means be convincing enough to reassure Washington. And that word was the last to be heard from Bigelow, as competent a reporter as he was a diplomatist. He was relieved as Minister by John Adams Dix, ex-senator, ex-general, who did not manage to turn his hand to report-writing until mid-February, after the crisis was past.[25]

Similarly, nothing that would clarify the situation was coming out of Mexico. General Grant received a report from Sherman, at Vera Cruz, containing two items of intelligence, highly significant and completely contradictory: two ships, waiting at Vera Cruz to take Maximilian home, had been loaded with tremendous quantities of royal baggage; and the Emperor had just issued a proclamation to the Mexican people announcing

[24] Girard, op. cit., pp. 117-18.
[25] New York Herald, December 7, 1866, p. 4, col. 3; Bigelow to Seward, November 30, 1866; Morgan Dix, Memoirs of John Adams Dix (2 vols., New York, 1883), II, 150; Dix to Seward, December 24, 1866.

A Cable From Napoleon   CONFIDENTIAL

First and last pages of the five-page message to Napoleon III from his commanders in Mexico, reporting on the situation there and asking instructions concerning the evacuation of the European forces. The French clear-text version, as repeated by General Castelnau in a letter to Napoleon on December 8, 1866 (and quoted by Castelnau's biographer), reads:

> L'empereur Maximilien paraît vouloir rester au Mexique, mais on ne peut y compter. L'évacuation devant être terminée en mars, il est urgent que les transports arrivent. Nous pensons que le régiment étranger doit être aussi embarqué. Quant aux officiers et soldats français détachés aux corps mexicains, peut-on leur laisser la faculté de revenir? Le pays est inquiet. La mission Campbell et Sherman arrivée devant Vera Cruz le 29 novembre et partie le 3 décembre semble disposée à une solution pacifique. Elle n'en donne pas moins un appui moral aux Juaristes par la déclaration du gouvernement fédéral.

his intention to remain. Sherman and Campbell were facng a dilemma, in that they could not reach Juárez without crossing territory held by the Imperialists, with whom they were supposed to have nothing to do. Sherman invited Grant to instruct him to go to Mexico City to see Bazaine, who, he was sure, would tell him the truth about French intentions, but nothing came of this suggestion. Wrote the general of the colorful pen and the fervid dislike of politics: "I am as anxious to find Juarez as Japhet was to find his father, that I may dispose of this mission." [26]

Tension mounted in Washington early in January as the Senate prepared for a debate on the Mexican question, and a wide variety of reports circulated, the most ominous being that half of the French forces were to remain in Mexico through the summer, and that Assistant Secretary of State Frederick W. Seward, who had sailed mysteriously from Annapolis on Christmas day, was on his way to see Napoleon. (He was en route to the West Indies on one of his father's projects for the purchase of territory.) [27] But on January 12, before the Senate got around to the Mexican question, the War Department received a message from Sheridan at New Orleans transmitting the following telegram:

Paris Jany 10th

French Consul New Orleans
for General Cast[elnau] at Mexico.

Received your dispatch of the ninth December. Do not compel the Emperor to abdicate, but do not delay the departure of the troops; bring back all those who will not remain there. Most of the fleet has left.

NAPOLEON.

---

[26] Sherman to Grant, December 1 and 7, 1866. Sherman, despite his reputation for hard-headedness, was not one of those who favored military action by the United States in Mexico. He wrote Grant, "I feel as bitter as you do about this meddling of Napoleon, but we can bide our time and not punish ourselves by picking up a burden [the French] can't afford to carry."

[27] *New York Herald*, January 3, 1867; New York *Evening Post*, January 8, 1867; Frederick W. Seward, *Reminiscences of a War-time Statesman and Diplomat* (New York and London, 1916), pp. 348–55. Seward's project, a very closely kept secret, was the acquisition of a harbor in San Domingo. A treaty was later concluded but buried by the Senate.

A Cable From Napoleon

Napoleon III's "Bring the army home" message, and the one by which General Sheridan transmitted it in translation to General Grant. The notation on the Sheridan-to-Grant message "Recd 230 PM In cipher" refers to its receipt and decipherment in the War Department, and so does not bear on Sheridan's later assertion that Napoleon's message was sent in cipher.

The phrase "will not remain there" was a translation error. It was corrected to "are not willing to remain" when Sheridan forwarded a confirmation copy of his telegram by mail later on January 12. "Most of the fleet has left" (referring to the departure of transports for Mexico) would have been better translated "Most of the ships have left."

CONFIDENTIAL   A Cable From Napoleon

Here now was a conclusive answer to both of the pressing questions, the French evacuation and Maximilian's future. The entire French force must be leaving; else there would scarcely be a question of compelling Maximilian to abdicate. And with the French gone, Maximilian, even if he remained firm in his decision to keep the throne, could hardly stand against the rising Liberals very long. The European threat to American soil could be considered virtually at an end.

How It Happened

Because of the historical importance attaching to the interception of this message and the Mexico-to-Paris message of a month earlier, the circumstances surrounding the interception are worth examining.

The two telegrams owed their existence to the successful installation of the Atlantic cable a few months before. The cable's own history went back to August 1857, when the first attempt to lay it ended in failure. A year later a connection was completed and the cable was operated for eleven weeks before it went dead, apparently because the use of a very high voltage had broken down the insulation. Renewal of the attempt awaited the development of better electrical techniques and the end of the Civil War. In 1865 a new cable was laid from Valentia, Ireland, but was lost six hundred miles short of Newfoundland. Another was started July 13, 1866, and brought ashore at Heart's Content, Newfoundland, on July 27. The ill-starred steamer *Great Eastern*, which laid it, then picked up the buried end of the 1865 cable and ran a second line to Newfoundland. Service to the public opened August 26.[28]

Thus Napoleon's September message to Bazaine passed after the permanent operation of a telegraph line across the Atlantic had been a reality for only a few weeks, and it must be conceded that the United States was reasonably prompt in availing itself of this source of intelligence — despite Napoleon's opinion to the contrary.

---

[28] Robert Luther Thompson, *Wiring a Continent* (Princeton, 1947), pp. 299-301, 319-20, 323, 433-34; S. A. Garnham and Robert L. Hadfield, *The Submarine Cable* (London, 1934), pp. 19-40. The cable laying was the only success in the long career of the leviathan *Great Eastern*, which bankrupted a succession of owners as a passenger and cargo ship, as an exhibition ship, and finally as a gigantic dismantling and salvage operation. Its history is told by James Dugan in *The Great Iron Ship* (New York, 1953).

A Cable From Napoleon

Although the first interception took place only a month after the French Emperor had virtually invited this government to read his mail, it appears that Napoleon's suggestion had nothing to do with it. The author of the intercept scheme, in all probability, was General Sheridan, and it is highly unlikely that Napoleon's remarks would have been communicated to him. In any case, no instructions for surveillance of the telegraph lines to obtain French messages appear in the correspondence to the Gulf Department from Army Headquarters.[29]

Years later Sheridan explained how the job was done: his telegraph operator and cipher clerk, Charles A. Keefer, one of the numerous Canadians who entered the Union and Confederate telegraph services, had succeeded in "getting possession of the telegraph and managing [a] secret line,"[30] which presumably connected his office with the Western Union wires in New Orleans.

Keefer's "secret line" may not have been so remarkable a thing as Sheridan's cryptic account makes it seem, for there was a high degree of integration between the Military Telegraph system to which Keefer belonged and the commercial system over which the messages passed. Throughout the occupied areas of the South during and after the Civil War, the Military Telegraph service took over commercial and railroad telegraph facilities wherever they existed. These Military Telegraph offices accepted commercial as well as government business, and commercial offices of course sent and received thousands of military telegrams; many a telegraph circuit had a military office at one terminus and a commercial office at the other.

As the Reconstruction period advanced, this integration became even closer; when the wires were returned to the use of the companies that owned them, Military Telegraph officers remained on duty to take care of government business and exercise a loose kind of supervision over the commercial opera-

---

[29] Correspondence from August 1 to December 10, 1866, has been examined for evidence of such instructions. Sheridan's papers in the Library of Congress appear to be incomplete for this period.

[30] Unaddressed official statement signed by Sheridan December 8, 1877 (sic); William R. Plum, *The Military Telegraph During the Civil War in the United States* (2 vols., Chicago, 1882), II, pp. 343 and 357, is authority for the information on Keefer's nationality.

tions. At some places military and commercial operators worked side by side. The fact that Keefer's copies of the French telegrams were written on Western Union message blanks makes it appear that New Orleans was one of the cities where this arrangement was in effect. If it was not, and the Military Telegraph and Western Union offices there were located separately, they were nevertheless using the same wires for communication with distant points, which would have made it comparatively easy for Keefer to connect a "secret line."

This integration of operations went all the way to the top of the two telegraph systems. General Thomas T. Eckert, who had been the second-ranking member and active head of the Military Telegraph service, continued to be closely connected with it after becoming Assistant Secretary of War in 1866. In the period now under study Eckert was apparently occupying his War Department position and at the same time resuming his activities in the industry as Eastern Division superintendent for Western Union at New York.[31]

Sheridan also credited Keefer with having solved the French "cipher,"[32] but there is strong evidence to the contrary:

(1) The amount of material Keefer could have had to work with was very small. The cable in its early years was used sparingly because of the very high tolls (note the $1,979.25 charge, in gold, that the French Consulate paid for the December 3/9 message). Thus Paris was still awaiting word from Castelnau at the end of November,[33] although he had been in Mexico nearly two months. The only French messages referred to in any of the documents examined in the present study are the clear-text message that Napoleon said he sent Bazaine in September,[34] the message of December 3/9, and the message of January 10. Accordingly, as the January message (to be discussed in detail below) was almost certainly sent in the clear,

---

[31] Plum, op. cit., II, pp. 345–48. The War Department records for 1866 and 1867 contain frequent cipher telegrams to Secretary Stanton from Eckert in New York; some of these messages bear dates subsequent to Eckert's resignation from the Deparment.

[32] From Sheridan's statement of December 8, 1877, and his *Memoirs*, vol. II, p. 226.

[33] Bigelow to Seward, November 30, 1866.

[34] This message has not been found by the writer in either French or United States records available in Washington.

A Cable From Napoleon

it is highly probable that the December 3/9 message from Bazaine and Castelnau to Napoleon was the only encrypted French telegram that passed between Mexico and France during the entire period of the French intervention.[35] It is extremely unlikely that the code — for the message was in code and not cipher — could have been solved from this one message of eighty-eight groups.

(2) An examination of all available United States records that could reasonably be expected to contain such an item (if it existed) fails to uncover a decrypted version of the December 3/9 message or any other evidence that the government during the ensuing weeks had come into possession of the information it contained.[36]

Somewhat surprising is the apparent fact that Sheridan did not send the message to the War Department cryptographers for study. On several occasions during the Civil War, these men had been able to read enemy messages referred to them. This experience (so far as it is recorded) was, however, limited to the solution of certain ciphers (some of which were relatively complex for that day),[37] and the French code would have presented them with a strange and much more difficult problem. Union cryptographers at New Orleans had also once solved a captured message,[38] a fact which may have induced Sheridan to rely on his own headquarters' capability and not turn to Washington.

---

[35] This message and the French version of the January 10 message are filed in the National Archives with telegrams sent from the military headquarters at New Orleans during the years 1864–69. This filing is clearly in error, for the messages are foreign to the rest of the material in this file and they bear none of the marks that an operator would have placed on them had he transmitted them. War Department and Army Headquarters records do not show their receipt.

[36] Besides the government records cited elsewhere, the following collections have been searched for such evidence: the Andrew Johnson MSS, Sheridan MSS, Grant MSS, Edwin M. Stanton MSS, all in the Manuscripts Division, Library of Congress, and the contemporary correspondence between the War Department and State Department in the National Archives. Despite the extreme improbability that the message contents were obtained by solving the French code, this search took account of the possibility that the developments reported in the message were learned by other means.

CONFIDENTIAL   A Cable From Napoleon

It was the January 10 message from Napoleon, the only message mentioned in Sheridan's account of this episode, that the general said Keefer had solved. But there is every reason to believe that the French clear-text of this message is the message as received in New Orleans, and not a decoded version of that message. Note:

(1) The message heading. It is filled out in precisely the way that was standard procedure in telegraphic reception at that period. A considerably different format was used for the delivery of plain-text versions of friendly messages received in cipher, and since Keefer was also a Military Telegraph cipher clerk, he would probably have used that format or a similar one in writing up the plain text of a foreign cipher or code message. (This format is illustrated by the photostat of the deciphered version of Sheridan's January 12 message, of which Napoleon's message of the 10th was a part.)

(2) The difficulties that the copyist had with French spellings (Castelnau, *décembre, forcez, abdiquer, navires*). These are the difficulties of a telegraph operator receiving in a strange language. A cryptographer in writing up a decoded message would scarcely have made so many false strokes and misspellings; and with such a poor knowledge of the French language, he could scarcely have solved a coded message in French.

In addition to the above evidence, there is the extreme unlikelihood that this message added to the earlier one would have given Keefer enough material to have solved the code. There is also reason to believe, from Napoleon's statement to Bigelow regarding the message he sent Bazaine in September,

---

[*] The Confederates used two kinds of cipher, both involving the substitution of one character for another. What appears to be a representative if not a complete account of the cryptanalytic experiences of the Washington cryptographers is given by David Homer Bates, *Lincoln in the Telegraph Office* (New York, 1907), pp. 66–85. Bates was in the War Department telegraph and cipher office throughout the Civil War. The infrequency of such activity was plainly the result of the difficulty in obtaining intercepts (except at the front, where the traffic intercepted was almost always visual). All the cryptanalytic episodes reported by Bates involved intercepted courier and mail dispatches rather than messages obtained by wiretapping.

[*] Plum, *op. cit.*, I, pp. 36–39.

A Cable From Napoleon

that political considerations might well have induced the Emperor to send this message through the United States in the clear.

Impact and Epilogue

Rare indeed is the single intelligence item that is at once so important and so unmistakable in meaning as the intercept of January 10. Its effect on events, however, can only be estimated, for no reference to it appears in the records of the developments that followed.

On the 17th the French Minister came to Seward proposing that France and the United States enter into an agreement for the governing of Mexico during the period that would follow the departure of the French troops. France's only stipulation was that the interim government exclude Juárez. The United States, having consistently pursued a policy of recognition of Juárez and nonrecognition of Maximilian, could never have voluntarily accepted such a proposal. And since southern Texas was well garrisoned with troops remaining from the magnificent army that had subdued the Confederacy, involuntary acceptance was likewise out of the question. But Seward might reasonably have entertained the proposal and then engaged in time-consuming negotiations, awaiting news from Mexico that the French were gone. Instead, he dismissed Napoleon's Minister with little ceremony;[29] his firmness probably stemmed largely from knowledge that the French withdrawal was already well advanced and the Emperor's proposal could be only an effort to save face.

The effect that Sheridan's communications intelligence enterprise had on international affairs, then, was probably this: it did not induce a change in policy or any other positive action, but it materially helped the government ride out a dangerous situation simply by sitting tight.

The Administration's domestic position, however, was as weak as its international position was strong. When the Senate on the 15th got around to its foreign policy debate, an earnest effort was made to embarrass the Administration (although the threatened attempt to take foreign policy out of

---

[29] Seward to Minister Berthemy, January 21, 1865 (memorandum of conversation of January 17).

its hands did not materialize). The debate continued into the 16th, when Senator Charles Sumner, chairman of the Foreign Relations Committee, saw fit to announce that he had reliable information (including a copy of a dispatch to the State Department from the United States Consul at Vera Cruz) that the French were withdrawing. That ended the matter.[40] Neither Seward nor the President seems to have said anything to counter the unfriendly speechmaking, having in Sumner a more direct means of silencing the opposition. Although the senator was no friend of the Administration, at least some of its intelligence information had been given to him for that purpose. From the conviction with which Sumner addressed his colleagues, one is tempted to believe that intelligence much more sensitive — and more convincing — than the consular dispatch had been confided to him.

Seward's ability to close out the Mexican affair with firmness and surehandedness must have substantially bolstered the Presidential prestige, which in that year was at the lowest ebb it has reached in the nation's history. Had the government's resistance to the French intervention been anything but a resounding success, Andrew Johnson might well have failed to muster the one-vote margin by which the impeachment proceedings against him were defeated.

Before January ended, the intelligence conveyed by Napoleon's cablegram was supported by details of the French withdrawal received from other sources, one of them an unnamed spy who was sent by Sheridan to the Vera Cruz area and returned with convincing evidence of preparations for the embarkation of the Army.[41] Bazaine led the last remnants of the French force out of Mexico City on February 5. Two weeks later embarkation had begun at Vera Cruz, and by March 11 it was complete.

Maximilian's regime quickly collapsed. He foolishly bottled up his small army of Mexicans, Austrians, and Belgians in Querétaro, a hundred miles northwest of the capital. An agent

---

[40] *Congressional Globe*, January 16, 1867.

[41] Sheridan to J. A. Rawlins (Chief of Staff to Grant), January 4, 1867. The ordinary period for transmittal of mail would have caused this dispatch to arrive in Washington perhaps a week later than the January 10 telegram from Paris via New Orleans.

of Sheridan, with this army by permission, late in February reported the Imperialists marching out of Querétaro and driving the enemy before them, but the offensive was shortlived. Soon Maximilian was back in Querétaro under siege, and on May 19, as a result of treachery by a Mexican Imperialist officer related by marriage to Bazaine, the garrison was captured.[42]

Seward had literally "scolded Napoleon out of Mexico," but if the final issue of *l'affaire Maximilien* was a triumph for American diplomacy, the fate of the unhappy sovereign himself was a sorry story of nonperformance of duty by an American diplomat. After Sherman had been excused from further participation in the mission, Minister Campbell stationed himself at New Orleans and determinedly resisted repeated efforts by Seward to get him into Mexico. In April, when it had become plain that the siege of Querétaro would end in the capture of Maximilian, Seward sent an urgent plea for Maximilian's life, instructing Campbell to find Juárez and deliver the message in person. It was delivered to the head of the Mexican government not by Campbell, ex-colonel, ex-senator, but by James White, sergeant. Such pleas delivered later on by a diplomatic Chief of Mission were heeded, but this one was of no avail, and Maximilian lost his life before a firing squad at Querétaro on June 19, 1867. Four days earlier, too late to affect the fate of the misguided prince, Seward had given Campbell a new title: ex-Minister.[43]

---

[42] Martin, *op. cit.*, 295-97; unsigned letter to Sheridan from his agent in Querétaro, February 26.

[43] *New York Herald*, December 7, 1866; Seward to Campbell, December 25, 1866, January 2, 8, 23, April 6, June 1, 5, 8, 11, 15, 1867; Campbell to Seward, December 24, 1866, January 2, 7, February 9, March 12, and June 3, 6, 10, 15, and 16, 1867; Martin, *op. cit.*, pp. 408, 411; Sheridan, *op. cit.*, II, p. 227.

PROJECT TERMINATION AND A CHANGE OF ADMINISTRATION

*Wrapping Up a Track II
Operation in Poland*

PROJECT TERMINATION WITH A CHANGE OF ADMINISTRATION

Edward F. Sayle

It had been twenty-two years since Charles was indoctrinated into the secret project.

He was only thirty-two at the time, and after an unusually rapid advancement in the military, found himself honored with appointment as ambassador to Poland. It was known, of course, that his political backers had strong links to that country. The appointment signaled to them that there apparently has been no foundation to rumors that the chief of state planned to take a more aggressive stance against the Russian influence in that land.

Eight days after announcement of the ambassadorial appointment Charles was approached by a confidant of the chief of state, bearing a letter. The letter, signed by the chief of state personally, told Charles to put his faith in matters about which the confidant would brief him, and thereafter he "will not speak of it to a living soul."

His written, diplomatic instructions required he exert himself to sustain the existing government in Poland, and told him to be vague and reserved when asked his government's attitude toward those who would seek to change Poland's leadership. His secret instructions from the chief of state's confidant clearly were for a Track II operation. He was ordered to cultivate, most secretly, Polish nationalists who would be expected to be favorably inclined toward his government. He was to oppose the pro-Russian elements in power and to counter increased Russian intervention through the secret funding and other support of the Polish nationalist movement.

Charles thus was ordered not only to implement a policy contrary to the instructions of his diplomatic superiors, but one which was in direct conflict with the views of his political backers. These overt connections would serve as cover for what he was actually to do, and would help relieve suspicion if any mis-step resulted in unwanted attention. The secret instructions had gone one step further. Not only were his diplomatic superiors to be kept unwitting of the Track II effort, but Charles was to attempt through his dispatches and other reporting, to sway their judgment into accepting as their own the goals of the secret policy.

Over time, the operation grew to include other agents and to encompass secret operations in other countries, but the operation in Poland, despite successes and failures, remained the crucial link-pin for Charles. The conflicts between his overt instructions and his secret charge were relieved somewhat in the fifth year, when the chief of state approved the briefing of the principal desk officer responsible for communicating with the ambassador.

The desk officer, a careerist, then could receive Charles' enciphered reports through the safety of the diplomatic pouch and deliver them to the chief of state without the diplomatic hierarchy being aware. Responses from the chief of state could be handled in the same way; they could be inserted in the pouch just before it was sealed by the desk officer. There was another advantage, as well. Should the ambassador's superiors dictate instructions in conflict with Charles' secret mission, the desk officer could modify them slightly and blunt their effect. For a while, Charles was shielded from the confrontation certain to come.

The Russians augmented their garrisons and Charles' major effort had to be curtailed. He was ordered home, but not before he could arrange for secret subsidies to the Polish nationalists through an agent—who was to remain behind in Poland. Above all, those forces had to survive.

Relieved of his ambassadorial post, Charles returned to his military career, assuming even greater responsibilities for maintenance of the secret operations. He continued to receive the reporting of the other agents in the network; to this was added all the diplomatic correspondence between his government and its ambassadors in Poland and Russia. He assumed the role of analyst, providing the chief of state with assessments through yet other secret channels without the knowledge of either his military superiors or senior diplomats.

The senior diplomatic desk officer was the first to fall when his superiors became suspicious and lacking any proof arranged to dismiss him for other causes. Operating in retirement, the desk officer continued his role in the operation, providing the all-important link between the net and the chief of state. The overt diplomatic correspondence which he had obtained previously through his official position continued to pass through the man's hands to Charles'. Others in the network, utilizing their continued access in the nation's embassies abroad would copy it and send it back to him in cipher. It was slow—but it worked.

In Charles' tenth year of involvement, it came his turn to fall from grace. He, too, was dismissed for causes unrelated to the operation, and retired to his home some distance away in disgrace. The chief of state, however, desired the secret operation to be continued, even if it was necessary to brief additional people ensure that the secret correspondence to and from Charles could continue unimpaired. Even the death of the former desk officer had little effect on the operation. Secret reporting flowed directly to Charles, in his exile, and his analyses went unopened to the chief of state, through alternate secret channels, with none of the cabinet or department heads any the wiser.

Thus it had been for twenty-two years, when the chief of state died. What was to become of the extensive hip-pocket intelligence and covert action operation? That was the situation in 1774 for Charles Francois, Count de Broglie, upon the death of Louis XV and the ascent of Louis XVI, the dead monarch's grandson.

Charles had to confront the problem quickly. Publicly he was perceived as disgraced and dismissed from public service; yet, he was also an important confidant of the late King and the sole channel for the secret network. Three days after Louis XVI's accession, Charles sent him a resume of the operation from its inception, expecting the new King to summon him to explain the curious communication. No such summons was forthcoming.

Instead, by return post he received an unsigned letter indicating that the writer, Louis XVI, had no intention of compromising himself. It read, in part:

"... M. d'Ogny [the Postmaster General] had asked to speak to me on Saturday, when he handed me the letters in cypher. I opened them to see what the cypher was like, never having seen one. He was greatly astonished to learn that I knew already of this correspondence, and he assured me that he did not know whence the letters came, or wither they went ... I return the letters by the

Project Termination

same way, with your pay for the month of May. You may keep your bureau till the month of July, when I will have more definite commands conveyed to you. But, send me back the cypher, and be assured of the most impenetrable secrecy..."

It was not the reception Charles had anticipated. He made another attempt through the secret channel for permission to brief the new King and to secure the safe custody of any incriminating papers that might be in royal quarters. Fearing particularly that extensive intelligence collection which had been conducted in Britain for a contingency invasion plan would fall into the hands of Britain's spies or friends in court, Charles wrote his sovereign:

"... As for the papers, I do not know whether his late Majesty kept in his desk the whole of the papers, memoranda, maps, and plans, which I sent to him. Certain of them, of the year 1765 or 1766, relating to England, have maps in long tin boxes. All these should be carefully concealed. If M. d'Aiguillon could get possession of them, he would probably communicate their contents to Lord Stormont [the British Ambassador to France], in order to stand well with the Courts of all the foreign Powers, which he is trying his utmost to do."

The King's response six days later provided good news for Charles and his restoration to public life, but bad news for the operation:

"... Having maturely examined these correspondences, I have come to the conclusion that they serve no purpose, and indeed may be injurious to my service. This is not on account of M. d'Aiguillon (for he is no longer anything), but in general; they hamper the Minister of Foreign Affairs if he is not acquainted with them, and they give rise to vexations if he is ... I will send you your pay for the month of June, as the last payment; after that you will dissolve your cabinet, and I require from you not only secrecy on the subject of this former correspondence, but also that you will burn all the documents in any way concerning it. This precaution cannot fail to be useful to you, and by acquitting yourself sincerely of it and not mixing yourself up with any affair in future, you will merit to be permitted to return to Court."

It was clear that Charles could win the monarch's favor by destroying the compromising correspondence, but it was also clear to him that both he and the other members of the net could equally be discarded and forgotten. He advised the King through the secret channel that burning the secret correspondence could be a disadvantage. The papers, stored in a number of places, he said, should be gathered together and a final accounting made. There is also the matter:

"... of all those who had pensions and emoluments fixed by the late King, and from whom it is evident that the King, whose benevolence, goodness and justice are well known, would not wish to withdraw them. It must also be observed, that persons employed in affairs of such importance and secrecy, should not be deprived of the recompenses that have been accorded to them, which they have merited by their fidelity, and which most of them would be unable to do without. The late King set aside ten thousand francs a month for this purpose."

It was a bold move—and an exceedingly dangerous one. Charles was challenging the Crown in its desire to distance itself from an activity with serious potential for embarrassment, both internally and with a number of foreign governments. Fortunately, it was successful. In the interim, there had been a shake-up in the bureaucracy. M. de Vergennes, the French Ambassador to Sweden, had been elevated to Minister of Foreign Affairs.

Project Termination

The secret correspondence was now at the helm of foreign affairs. Vergennes had been one of the earliest members of the network and, no doubt, its most distinguished member. The changed attitude at Court was reflected in Louis XVI's response to Charles' resettlement appeal:

"I have found in the King's apartments, as you told me I should, several maps and papers, which I have locked up; since then I have inquired about you, and all that I have heard shows me that you have done nothing except by orders of the King. Therefore I permit you to return to Paris, and to the Court at Compiegne. I approve of your writing to the Ministers to tell them to discontinue the correspondence. I send you the formula of the letters, which you must send back to me for signature. As for you, on your arrival in Paris, you will collect all your papers, leave them with M. de Vergennes, and afterwards you can take your repose."

The King was true to his word. After a review of the papers by Vergennes and two other confidants, Louis XVI granted annuities to all the members of the network. He was particularly generous to one who had gone to the Bastille rather than compromising the operation by explaining his conduct. There were even twenty thousand francs for the fading Polish nationalists. Recognition was granted Charles, Duke de Broglie, in a letter from his sovereign which said, in part:

". . . it has been proved to me that you have behaved with all the zeal and fidelity which you owed to him [Louis XVI], and which were never slackened by the sometimes embarrassing circumstances in which you found yourself; and, in every respect, you acquitted yourself of this commission in the most prudent manner, and in that most conformable to the wishes of the late King. It has been proved to me, moreover, that during the last few years you have found yourself compromised in a matter in which you had no share, and on suspicions which could only have taken rise in the ignorance that prevailed respecting your relations with the late King and the studies which you undertook by his command, and yet this has never induced you to betray his secret . . ."

The secret correspondence, or the King's Secret as it has since been known, had drawn to a close. But, there was still one matter that remained undone.

One agent remained to be resettled. He was a threat to the Crown and a security risk, as well. He was the Chevalier d'Eon who had been dismissed from the French Embassy in London after a confrontation with an unwitting Ambassador who had been offended by his behavior, including a penchant for wearing women's clothing. Banished from polite society, d'Eon's "beat" became the offbeat, particularly the London taverns frequented by the press. His colorful reports had detailed the gossip of Parliament and the unpublished scandals of the ruling party. His frequent demands for salary increases and his half-threatening letters would have made him an excellent candidate for separation from the net except for one thing—he held documents spelling out the nature of the intelligence operation. Particularly incriminating was a set of the contingency plans for the invasion of England to which Louis XV had carelessly affixed his initials.

Earlier efforts to encourage d'Eon to part with the papers and to return home had failed. He had even told the press of one of the approaches, concealing only the existence of the net and his secret bargaining points. This time the task fell to the Caron de Beaumarchais, a secret agent of Vergennes. Beaumarchais, the poet and playwright, was in London attempting the preclusive purchase of a pamphlet scandalizing Marie Antoinette, a task similar to one he had undertaken to Britain in behalf of Louis XV to prevent publication of a work dealing with Madame du Barry.

Project Termination

The playwright and d'Eon struck it off immediately. Said d'Eon, "We were drawn together by the natural curiosity of two extraordinary beings to meet each other."

A deal was struck. d'Eon would surrender the incriminating papers to Beaumarchais and return to France in exchange for permission to declare as and dress as a woman there, to receive a pension, and to wear the order of a Knight of the Royal and Military Order of St. Louis for service in the King's Dragoons. In return for d'Eon's agreement not to take male clothing back to France, Beaumarchais provided two thousand crowns to purchase an expensive feminine wardrobe.

The business of the secret correspondence was at long last finished, but the London affair had not ended. d'Eon had gravitated toward the coterie of John Wilkes, Lord Mayor of London, and Beaumarchais had followed. Wilkes, a political intriguer, had gained notoriety for his membership in the orgiastic Hell Fire Club and for his clandestine printing of erotica. He was also a friend of American independence. With little difficulty, Beaumarchais penetrated the circle. At Wilkes' home, Beaumarchais met Dr. Arthur Lee of Virginia, an agent of the Committee of Secret Correspondence of the Continental Congress. Beaumarchais, whose command of the English language was reportedly limited to "Goddam," was pleased to be cultivated by Lee, an American speaking fluent French. Lee quickly persuaded Beaumarchais of the American will, claiming for example that some 80,000 Americans were beseiging the British garrison at Boston, and pointing out that the wealth of North America then being siphoned off by Britain could, in victory, be the object of major trade with France. Beaumarchais was equal to the task—assuring Lee that Foreign Minister Vergennes would support the American rebels through covert means.

But, that's another story.

General William Donovan's Marching Orders

How it all began:

DONOVAN'S ORIGINAL MARCHING ORDERS

Thomas F. Troy

Two quotations will set the stage for this inquiry into the orders under which Colonel William J. Donovan was set up in business by President Franklin D. Roosevelt as this nation's first chief of intelligence and special operations.

The first quotation comes from Breckinridge Long, Assistant Secretary of State, 1939-1944, a man who figures no more in this paper but who was a close observer of much to be narrated here and who, moreover, kept an interesting diary. As one of three assistant secretaries working under Secretary of State Cordell Hull and Under Secretary Sumner Wells, "Breck" Long administered both the Department of State and the Foreign Service and, as he perhaps understandably complained in his diary, was responsible for 23 of the 42 divisions of the Department. This wide-spread coverage several times brought him in contact with the work of the new Coordinator of Information (COI)—the job FDR officially gave to Donovan on 11 July 1941; and Long was quick to arrive at the following characterization of this New York Irishman, military hero, and Wall Street lawyer:

> "Bill Donovan—'Wild Bill' is head of the C.I.O. [sic]—Coordinator of Information. He has been a thorn in the side of a number of the regular agencies of the Government for some time—including the side of the Department of State—and more particularly recently in Welles'. He is into everybody's business—knows no bounds of jurisdiction—tries to fill the shoes of each agency charged with responsibility for a war activity. He has had almost unlimited money and has a regular army at work and agents all over the world. He does many things under the *nom de guerre* of 'Information'." [1]

The second quotation gives the other side of the coin, and quite appropriately comes from Donovan himself. With reference to a different matter than the specific one which provoked Long's outburst, and writing not in a diary but to the President, the Colonel, "angry and indignant," denounced the circulation of "the well-worn lie" that he had 90 representatives working in Latin America. He attributed the repetition of this story to an effort to prove that he had "gone into a field which you had not allocated to me." Then Donovan laid it on the line: "You should know me well enough to know that I do adhere strictly to *my orders* and make no attempt to encroach upon the jurisdiction of anyone else." [Italics mine.] [2]

"My orders" . . . ah, there was the rub! Just what were those orders? That was, in effect, the question that many in Washington, throughout the summer

---

[1] Breckinridge Long, *The War Diary of Breckinridge Long: Selections from the Years 1939-1944*, ed. Fred L. Israel (Univ. of Nebraska Press, Lincoln, Neb., 1966) p. 257. This passage was written on 10 April 1942; on 20 December 1941 Long had noted (pp. 233-34) that Donovan was hard to "control," and that his organization was "composed largely of inexperienced people" who were also "inexperienced . . . in dealing . . . with . . . confidential information."

[2] Memorandum from William J. Donovan to President Roosevelt, No. 452, 27 April 1942, Donovan Papers, "Exhibits Illustrating the History of OSS," Vol. II, "The Office of the Coordinator of Information," Tab YY. Hereafter the short title is Donovan Papers, "Exhibits," and this will cover both Vols. I and II.

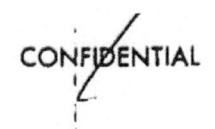

and fall of 1941, wanted answered definitely. That was, in effect, the question—as will be seen—that prompted the Director of the Bureau of the Budget twice in the first seven months of Donovan's official existence to recommend to the President that COI's area of activity be newly defined. That question, indeed, also caused Donovan himself, three months after taking office, to tell the President that their original decision to put nothing in writing was wrong. That question, in fact, has never really been answered; and it is the purpose of this inquiry to make an attempt to do so.

The answer will be sought in reconstructing three episodes in roughly the first six months of COI's history: (1) Donovan's meeting with the President on 18 June 1941 when FDR gave the go-ahead sign on COI; (2) the drafting of the order which made COI official on 11 July; and (3) the next few months when that order was implemented.

The Roosevelt-Donovan Meeting, 18 June 1941

Contrary to a common misconception, Bill Donovan was not a close friend of the President. They had been at Columbia Law School at the same time but had not known one another. They were from opposite sides of the State of New York: Donovan from Buffalo, and FDR from the Hudson River Valley. They were also from opposite sides of the socio-economic tracks; Donovan was an Irish Catholic, the grandson of immigrants, the son of a railroad yards superintendent, while FDR, the squire of Hyde Park, was a WASP before the acronym was common coin. Also, and more importantly perhaps, they were from opposite sides of the political fence; Donovan was as much a life-long Republican as FDR was Mr. Democrat. Their paths had only occasionally crossed as when, for example, Donovan unsuccessfully ran for the governorship of New York when Roosevelt was elected President in 1932. It was not, then, until 1940 that Donovan, in his fifty-seventh year, and FDR, one year older, were brought together on the same side of the tracks.

What accomplished this was Adolf Hitler and the European War he launched in September 1939. There is no need here to do more than state the common revulsion and alarm felt by both men at the prospect of Nazi hegemony in Europe and abroad. Donovan, probably because he was a private citizen, was way out ahead of the President, however, in urging all-out aid to Britain as an essential element in the defense of the Western Hemisphere. Because of this attitude, because of his prominence in Republican and national affairs, because of his recent travels in Germany, Ethiopia, and Spain, and probably on the recommendation of his good friend, the new Secretary of the Navy, Frank Knox, Colonel Donovan was sent by President Roosevelt to England in the summer of 1940 to report on Britain's chances against the expected Nazi assault. Six months later the President again sent him abroad, this time on a three-months tour of Britain, the Balkans, the Middle East, Spain, and Ireland.[3]

After both trips, Donovan, the President's representative who talked day after day with heads of state and their chief advisors, reported to the President—at least on 9 August 1940 and 19 March 1941. There are no good records of these conversations, but it is safe to say that Donovan, whose mind ranged over

---

[*] See this writer's "COI and British Intelligence: An Essay on Origins," (CIA, 1970), esp. Chs. II and III. Hereafter referred to as "COI."

every aspect of the war in Europe, particularly singled out for the President's attention the whole range of unconventional warfare activities that had been brought to the fore by the Fifth Column and British counter-measures. He must have given Roosevelt some idea, however brief, of his thinking on a new agency to handle "white" and "black" propaganda, sabotage and guerrilla warfare, special intelligence, and strategic planning.[4]

Donovan Proposes "Service of Strategic Information"

Eventually, probably late in May of 1941, Donovan was asked by the President to put his proposal in writing, and this he did in a "Memorandum of Establishment of Service of Strategic Information," dated 10 June 1941. The document, which of course is fundamental in the long line of papers outlining the COI-OSS-CIA objectives and tasks, is as interesting for what it does not say as for what it does say. Since it was soon, on 18 June, to receive the Presidential stamp of approval, it is well here to take a close look at it.[5] (Appendix A)

In a few words—934—Donovan laid out his argument, proceeding from general to particular, for a "Service of Strategic Information." The basic proposition was the interrelationship of strategy and information: without the latter, strategy was helpless; and unless directed to strategy, information was useless. The second proposition measured the information required in terms of total war—"the commitment of all resources of a nation, moral as well as material"—and Donovan particularly stressed the dependence of modern war on "the economic base." The third proposition was the flat assertion that despite the activity of the Army and Navy intelligence units, the country did not have an "effective service" for developing that "accurate, comprehensive, long-range information without which no strategic board can plan for the future." The conclusion was the essentiality of "a central enemy intelligence organization which would itself collect either directly or through existing departments of government, at home and abroad, pertinent information" on the total resources and intentions of the enemy.

As an example, he cited the economic field where there were many weapons that could be used against the enemy. These weapons were so scattered throughout the bureaucracy, however, that they could not be effectively utilized in the waging of economic warfare unless all departments of the government had the same information. This brief passage will appear more important, in this inquiry into Donovan's marching orders, when we touch upon the difficulty that Donovan was soon to have with the Economic Defense Board, which considered economic warfare its bailiwick.

Another brief—and apparently deliberately vague—passage is the one dealing with radio as "the most powerful weapon" in "the psychological attack against the moral and spiritual defenses of a nation." Certainly Donovan was one of the first fully to appreciate the significance of the Nazi use of the radio as an element of "modern warfare." In this memorandum, however, he contented himself with boldly stating that the perfection of radio as a weapon required planning, and planning required information, which could then lead to

---

[4] *Ibid.*, Chs. IV and VIII.
[5] Donovan Papers, "Exhibits," Vol. I, Tab B.

action by appropriate agencies. There was no felt need to spell out the role of radio in psychological warfare and clandestine communications.

In terms of secret activities, the most revealing part of this Memorandum is not the text but the organizational chart accompanying it. Where one would expect frankness, he gets obscurity, and vice versa. Hence, the coordination of information—the main subject of the paper—is entrusted to directors of "Collection and Distribution" and of "Classification and Interpretation"; and the radio weapon is the province of the "Director of Supplementary Activities"; whereas the chart shows what the text nowhere mentions, namely, the two directors of "Mail, Radio, Cable Interception (Censorship)" and of "Codes and Cyphers." Only the "Director of Economic Warfare Material" accurately reflects its textual counterpart.

Presumably Donovan sent this Memorandum to the President on or shortly after 10 June. At least on the next day FDR told Grace Tully that he wanted to see Ben Cohen, old friend, adviser, and legal draftsman, before he returned to his London post and "also Bill Donovan."[6] Presumably again, at least in the light of subsequent events, the President wanted to see both men on the same matter. On 13 June, Donovan told Secretary of the Treasury Henry Morgenthau, Jr., who wanted Donovan to take the full-time job of running the Treasury's Bond Drive in New York State, that he first wanted to tell the Secretary "something about the President."[7] Again, on the 17th Donovan told the importunate Secretary that he was in Washington "today because I'm supposed to have a date this morning . . ." to which the Secretary interjected the knowing "uh uh" and Donovan replied with "That's the reason you haven't heard from me."[8] Actually, it was not until 12:30 the next day that Donovan and Cohen, accompanied by Secretary of the Navy Knox, met with the President.[9]

What went on in that meeting? Unfortunately, there is no nice transcript of the proceedings; nor is there any indication as to how long or detailed and orderly the proceedings were. Indeed, given the reputation of meetings with the President, there could have been a good deal of what Robert Sherwood called "wildly irrelevant" talk.[10] Still, there are four accounts within the first two days of the meeting, and these show that all went well for the Colonel's plan and provide us with basic information on just what the President and Donovan agreed the latter was to do.

President Roosevelt Agrees

Surely the most important is the note which the President dashed off on the cover sheet of the Memorandum and addressed to "J. B. Jr.," who was John Blandford, Jr., the Acting Director of the Bureau of the Budget: "Please set this up *confidentially* with Ben Cohen—military—not O.E.M." It was initialed

---

[6] Memorandum from Roberta Barrows to Gen. Watson, 11 June 1941, Franklin D. Roosevelt Papers (Franklin D. Roosevelt Library, Hyde Park, N.Y.) PPF 6558 (William J. Donovan).

[7] Transcribed telephone conversation between Morgenthau and Graves, 13 June 1941, Henry J. Morgenthau, Jr., Diary (Roosevelt Library), Book 408, p. 4 (CLOSED).

[8] Telcon between Morgenthau and Donovan, *ibid.*, Book 408, pp. 151-52.

[9] *Composite Presidential Diary*, Roosevelt Papers.

[10] Robert E. Sherwood, *Roosevelt and Hopkins: An Intimate History* (Harper, New York, 1950, p. 265).

"FDR." [11] (Fig. 1.) Thus, the President underwrote Donovan's 934 words and the chart; and then he added that the new Service was to have a military flavor and was not to be part of the Office of Emergency Management, which had been set up a year earlier as a framework for running the numerous new war agencies.

The next two accounts come from Donovan, the first directly, and the second indirectly. On the 20th, Donovan called Secretary Morgenthau in order to establish liaison with the Treasury's intelligence department and prefaced his request with this awkwardly worded explanation: "I just wanted to tell you myself that along the lines that you and I talked, the President accepted in totem (sic) . . ." [12] We shall see as we go along that Donovan was firmly convinced that he and FDR had agreed on many things that were not explicitly put forth in the original Memorandum.

Even before this conversation with Morgenthau, indeed, some time on the 18th itself, Donovan had given a more substantive briefing on the day's proceedings to a very interested observer. This was William S. Stephenson, a Canadian who was serving in the United States as His Majesty's Director of British Security Coordination (BSC); actually he was the head of British intelligence in this country. Moreover, he had played a major role in persuading Donovan to recommend and take on the job of running America's first foreign intelligence establishment. Donovan, with a Presidential mandate in his pocket, so preoccupied as to forget to call the impatient Morgenthau, and hustling off to New York on a 3:30 flight, nevertheless found time to talk with Stephenson, who that night cabled London: "Donovan saw President today and after long discussion wherein all points were agreed, he accepted appointment. He will be coordinator of all forms [of] intelligence including offensive operations equivalent SO-2 [sabotage]. He will hold rank of Major General and will be responsible only to the President." Here at last is a direct statement of Donovan's function as an intelligence chief; what is meant by "all forms [of] intelligence" must be gathered from Stephenson's own organization, which he had in mind in his dealings with Donovan, and BSC was responsible for "secret" intelligence, counterintelligence, propaganda, and "special operations." Here also is the first reference to Donovan as Major General, a promotion which, as we shall see, the military managed to forestall.[13]

The last fresh account comes indirectly and largely from Ben Cohen, but it also reflects John Blandford's understanding of what the President wanted done. Cohen had been directed, on the 18th, to work with the acting director of the Bureau of the Budget, who, in turn, was personally directed on the morning of the 19th to work with Cohen. Consequently, later that morning Cohen met with Blandford and two of the latter's subordinates, Donald C. Stone and Bernard L. Gladieux. It was Gladieux who summarized the conference.[14]

Three paragraphs are particularly worth quoting, because they shed additional light on what the President had discussed with Donovan. The first raises

---

[11] Records of OSS, Bureau of the Budget, Box 23, Folder 211. These records referred to hereafter as BOB Records.

[12] Telcon between Morgenthau and Donovan, Morgenthau Diary, Book 411, pp. 67-71.

[13] "COI," Ch. VIII.

[14] Memorandum of "Conference with Ben Cohen on Strategic Information." BOB Records, Folder 210.

6/10/41

> J.B. Jr.
> Please get this
> up confidentially
> with Ben Cohen —
> Military — not
> C. Sorol.
>
> FDR

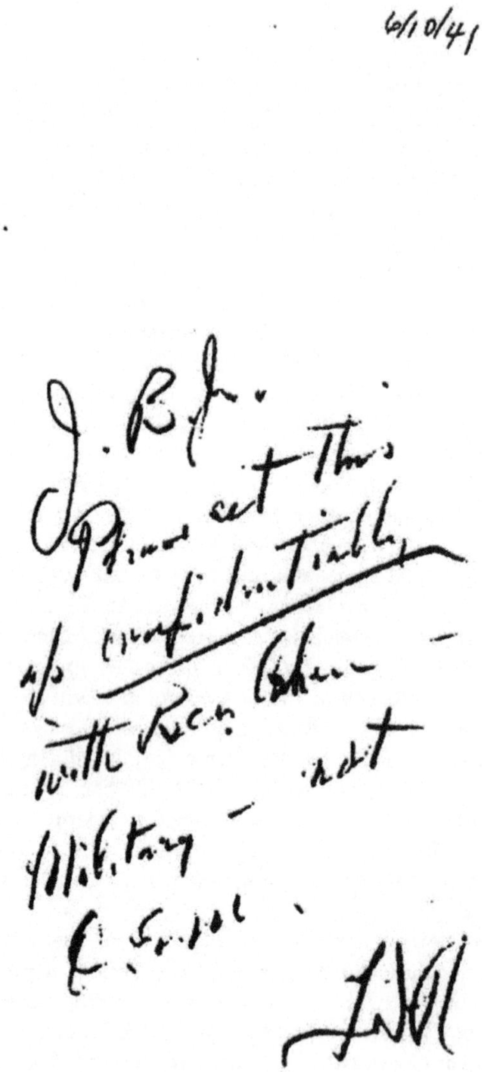

Fig. 1 Roosevelt's Covering Note.

a subject which may surprise the modern reader, who is accustomed to CIA's absorption in *foreign* activities:

> "Cohen has tried to keep the [domestic] morale function separate from strategic information. However, the President has apparently been struck by the thought that Donovan might take the morale job on temporarily or at least for exploratory purposes. He will cooperate with La Guardia on the morale and propaganda aspects. At least we do not need to take La Guardia and his activities into account in setting up this service."

This, of course, is not the place to tell the story of the establishment of the Office of Civil Defense, and of the appointment and activity of New York's Mayor Fiorello La Guardia as that Office's first Director. Suffice it to say that "the morale function" and civilian defense had long been bruited about in the upper echelons of the government as needs that the President had been slow in satisfying. Donovan, along with others, had been considered for the job, although he may or may not have known it. Even so, Donovan apparently took quite readily to the idea of responsibility for domestic morale, inasmuch as his concept of what needed to be done was not, at least at this time, divided into the foreign and domestic fields. This was total war, and there had to be unity in the response. Hence, his memorandum of 10 June had spoken of his proposed "central enemy intelligence organization" collecting information directly or indirectly through other government departments "at home and abroad"; and, as will be seen, he had the same unified approach to the subject of economic defense information.

Conflict with New Economic Agency

This can be seen, albeit dimly, in the next two paragraphs from Gladieux; these raise the question of the relationship between COI and a new agency to handle economic defense, which, like civilian defense, had long been agitating some of the President's advisors. Wrote Gladieux:

> We were particularly concerned about the relationship of this new agency to the Office of Economic Defense, since so much of the strategic information required will relate to economic defense problems . . . Cohen believes that there is nothing here to interfere with the setting up of the economic defense agency. He believes, however, that the Office of Economic Defense would get much of its information from this service.

Even so, Cohen was worried; in the next paragraph: "Cohen agrees that it would be unfortunate if this proposal were to preclude the establishment of the Office of Economic Defense, and thinks that the present Economic Defense Order should be approved." It was; six weeks later, on 30 July, the President signed the order establishing the Economic Defense Board (EDB); and what kind of functions were given this organization whose future was at one time put in doubt by the appearance of Donovan's COI? The list is impressive, if one thinks of them as somehow subsumed under the umbrella of the Coordinator of Information: advise the President on economic defense measures; coordinate the government's activities in this field; develop integrated plans and programs for coordinated action by the agencies of government; advise the President on the relationship of economic defense measures to *postwar economic reconstruction*; and review and recommend economic defense legislation! As late as the day FDR signed the EDB order, Gladieux was reporting that Vice President

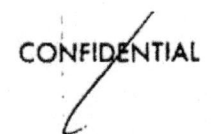

Wallace, who was to head the Board, wanted to know how Donovan's plans for "extensive economic defense activities" squared with EDB's charter.[15]

In conclusion, then, our earliest accounts of FDR's meeting with Donovan on 18 June show the President endorsing the appointment of a "Coordinator of Strategic Information" with a vaguely-worded mandate to coordinate information, do something with radio, carry on all forms of intelligence including sabotage, have something to do with domestic propaganda, and to be somehow involved in economic defense matters. This vagueness of function did not bedevil the drafters of the COI charter, simply because the President and Donovan had apparently agreed to put precious little in writing. How little was put in writing we will see when we review the drafting of the order.

The Drafting Stage: 19 June – 3 July 1941

The business was in the hands of Cohen and the men from the Budget Bureau—Blandford, Stone, and Gladieux—and was coordinated chiefly, if not solely, with the military, especially the Army, and of course with Donovan himself. The process of drafting lasted from 19 June to 3 July when the drafters' handiwork was forwarded to the President for approval and signature. It would be most useful if the surviving documents showed clearly all the changes that were made and by whom they were made; as it is, the record, while instructive, is incomplete.

The process began with a "Brief Outline of a Service of Strategic Information Based on Memorandum Submitted by Colonel Donovan."[16] There is no need to recapitulate this, except for one point, because it is basically a re-organization of Donovan's paper in terms of an order to be signed by the President and also because all the items will show up more clearly as the drafting process is reviewed. The one exceptional point is the relatively lengthy gloss on the six units which, according to Donovan's chart, were to be set up in COI. This gloss adds a few words which must have emanated from the Roosevelt-Donovan meeting. Mail, radio, and cable interception required a special unit "because of the need of especially close and immediate cooperation with the radio and postal authorities"; and the "specialized character" of codes and cyphers also required a special unit. So also with "A Unit of Economic Warfare Materials" which was being set up to provide all agencies concerned with such warfare "the widest and most comprehensive range of informational materials"; it was pointed out that the Coordinator would not coordinate such activities, "but his work should greatly facilitate such coordination." The supplementary activities unit would handle activities "not now being covered by any service or department"; and these activities "would probably involve principally activities in foreign countries calculated to assist friendly elements and to retard and undermine hostile elements. Such activities necessarily would have to be conducted along unorthodox lines, but with the greatest possible circumspection."

Perhaps the most interesting aspect of this review of the six units is that no mention of the business of intercepting communications, of codes and cyphers, of economic warfare, or of the delicate nature of special operations will appear

---

[15] "Memorandum for the President," 30 July 1941. See Note 38, *infra*.

[16] BOB Records, Folder 210. While undated and unsigned, the document clearly originated at the time mentioned.

in the writing and re-writing of the Presidential order. We cannot go on to that work without first calling attention to the pious hope wih which it ended: "The work of the Service should not require an unusually large staff..."

Actual drafting began with two drafts, testing whether the final order should be an Executive Order establishing the agency in the Executive Office of the President, or a Military Order designating Col. Donovan to perform certain functions. The former established a "Strategic Information Service" in the President's Office, based the order on the President's authority as derived from the Constitution and the statutes of the United States, and did not specifically mention Donovan. According to the Military Order, "Colonel William J. Donovan" was "hereby designated as Coordinator of Strategic Information," and this was done by virtue of FDR's position as President and Commander-in-Chief. Under both orders, Donovan had the same three functions: (1) to collect, review, and analyze information bearing on "national defense strategy"; (2) to interpret and correlate such "strategic" data and to make it available to the President and other agencies of the government; and (3) to carry out, when requested by the President, "such supplementary activities as may facilitate the securing of strategic information not now available to the Government." Incidentally, these "supplementary activities," about which there was no argument, referred to the open collection or purchase through agents of information to be used in conducting a psychological counteroffensive, and to subversion and sabotage to be carried out in wartime against the Axis military, political, and industrial machine; the term did *not* refer to a worldwide secret intelligence service, which, as a matter of fact, Donovan did not undertake to establish until so requested by the Army and Navy in September 1941. Finally, both orders provided that other agencies would make available the data required by the Coordinator, and that the Coordinator could appoint such advisory committees as he thought necessary.

In following these preliminary drafts through to the final paper, it may help the reader to single out beforehand the recurring problems as well as the "nonproblems." In this last category, the provisions for ensuring access to data and the appointment of advisory committees caused no problems; this is also largely true of the three functions except as their description was tailored to ease a concern of the Army's. What did bother people were: the type of order, the name of the new service, the kind of reference to Donovan—his name, title, his status as civilian or military—and the relationship to the military services.

While it now is anybody's guess, it appears that Blandford and his associates made a choice as between the two orders and then submitted that choice, a Military Order, to Ben Cohen on the 23rd. (Fig. 2) On that day Blandford and Cohen revised the document, and on the 24th Blandford sent his co-worker several clean copies of the revision.[17] The chief, and perhaps only substantive, revision may have appeared to them as half style and half the necessity of establishing the military character of Donovan's position. Instead of starting out with "Colonel William J. Donovan is hereby designated as Coordinator of Strategic Information," the revision began, after the preamble, with "There is hereby established the position of Coordinator...," and was then ended with this brand new line: "William J. Donovan, United States Army, is hereby designated as Coordinator of Strategic Information." The military, however, were soon to

---

[17] Memorandum from Blandford to Cohen, 24 June 1941, *ibid.*

CONFIDENTIAL   Donovan

MILITARY ORDER
- - - - -

DESIGNATING A COORDINATOR OF STRATEGIC INFORMATION

By virtue of the authority vested in me as President of the United States and as Commander in Chief of the Army and Navy of the United States, it is ordered as follows:

1. There is hereby established the position of Coordinator of Strategic Information, with authority to collect and analyze information and data, military or otherwise, which may bear upon national defense strategy; to interpret and correlate such strategic information and data, and to make it available to the President and to such other officials as the President may determine; and to carry out, when requested by the President, such supplementary activities as may facilitate the securing of strategic information not now available to the Government. The Coordinator of Strategic Information shall perform these duties and responsibilities, which include those of a military character, under the direction and supervision of the President as Commander in Chief of the Army and Navy of the United States.

2. The several departments and agencies of the Government shall make available to the Coordinator of Strategic Information such information and data relating to national defense strategy as the Coordinator, with the approval of the President, may from time to time request.

3. The Coordinator of Strategic Information may appoint such committees, consisting of appropriate representatives of the various departments and agencies of the Government, as he may deem necessary to assist him in the performance of his functions.

4.

THE WHITE HOUSE,

        June   , 1941.

Fig. 2. Budget Bureau's Draft Order.

knock out the "United States Army," as well as other military aspects of the Order. Indeed, the Army was to strip it of any military character.

To see how that happened, we must turn our attention away from the draftsmen to Colonel Donovan and some of the top people in the Army and Navy. On Friday, the 20th of June, Secretary of the Navy Knox informed Henry L. Stimson, the Secretary of War, that the President was "going to appoint Donovan as coordinator of all military, naval, and other intelligence," and that he, Knox, favored it. Stimson, an old friend of Donovan's, a person who enjoyed discussing the military strategy of the current war with him, noted in his diary that "I told him [Knox] that I was inclined to favor it because I trusted Donovan.[18] Two days later, on a Sunday afternoon, Donovan talked with Stimson about what the latter described as Donovan's coming appointment as "Coordinator of Intelligence." They talked for two hours; Donovan explained his plan; Stimson read "his analysis of what he intended to do," and noted that "I think there is a good chance of very useful service." Stimson further observed that he was "particularly glad that the President has landed on a man for whom I have such respect and confidence as Donovan, and with whom I think we can work so satisfactorily in respect to our own intelligence branches in the Army and Navy."[19] Trouble and doubt, however, lay just ahead—two days, in fact.

Marshall Objects

On 24 June, Stimson had an early conference with his Chief of Staff, General George C. Marshall, who then told him "about a subject which has evidently been worrying him very much and making him extremely angry." That, of course, was Donovan's appointment as "Coordinator for Intelligence." Here it must be interjected that for three months there had been considerable talk within the services, the FBI, State, and other agencies that Donovan was pushing such a project, and there was unanimity among the concerned agencies that such an eventuality ought to be sabotaged. It is, in fact, interesting to note that FDR, in making his decision to set up Donovan as COI, did not consult any of the interested parties, with the possible exception of Donovan's friend at court, Secretary of Navy Knox. Hence, when Marshall is described as having been "worrying very much," it is reasonably safe to assume that he had long been familiar with the rumors circulating in the corridors and that the announcement of the fact simply brought things to the proverbial head. Be that as it may, Stimson tried to re-assure Marshall that "the project did not seem to be so bad." He chewed the matter over in his diary:

> But it has come to Marshall evidently in the wrong end to, and he saw behind it an effort to supplant his responsibilities and duties in direct connection with the Commander-in-Chief. There is certainly a danger in this proposition in case both men are not tactful and fair to each other but I think it probably can be avoided—those risks I mean—and certainly the proposition of checking up the Intelligence which we get from our military G-2 and Navy Information Service [sic] ought to be accomplished. I mean there are many economics and other bits of information through the world which would bear directly upon the military intelligence and its accuracy which comes to us. I afterwards had a talk with Knox about it. He of course is a

---

[18] Henry L. Stimson Diary (Yale University, New Haven, Conn.), Vol. 34, entry for 20 June 1941.

[19] *Ibid.*, 22 June 1941.

close friend of Donovan and he is very hot for the project and thinks that it is all wrong to be suspicious of it."

Marshall must have gotten his point across, as is shown by the following quotation from Stimson's diary for 25 June; it is a long one, but the reader will surely find it interesting:

> Either this morning or yesterday Marshall came in to voice his objections to the Donovan proposition and they were very vigorous—relating to the danger of giving to any other military man than the regular channels access to the President with military information. I had been thinking of the matter myself and had come to the conclusion that, although the purpose of getting a collection of economic, political, and other information available to check off against our present G-2 information was a very laudable and fruitful project, yet this plan of Donovan's may be not the right way to do it. So, when a little later Benjamin V. Cohen came in to see me at the suggestion of the President with a draft Executive Order for my examination and criticism, I looked at it with care and worked the thing out in my own mind, with the result that I finally told Cohen that I thought it was such bad planning from the standpoint of military administration that I should not favor it unless Donovan was kept in a purely civilian capacity; that I disapproved wholly of having him made a Major General simultaneously with this assumption of this position of Coordinator of Information. The proposed draft was full of language treating the function as if it were a military one. I told Cohen that this plainly resulted in giving the President two Chiefs of Staff; one, the regular one and one, an irregular one, because no military man could go to the President with military information without giving at the same time some views in the nature of advice based upon that information. I told Cohen that I thought the thing might be worked out if the Coordinator were kept purely as a civilian. I told him also that I was a friend of Donovan's and that I sympathized with his ultimate ambition to get into the fighting if fighting came and that I would have no objection to recommending him at that time as a Major General; but that I was wholly against combining in his person the function of being a Major General and being a Coordinator of Information.
>
> Cohen seemed to realize the strength of my argument and said he would go over it and take the military phrases out. I suggested particularly that they should also add a phrase to the effect in substance that nothing in the duties and responsibilities of the Coordinator of Information should in any way interfere with or impair the duties and responsibilities of the regular military and naval advisers to the President as Commander in Chief of the Army and Navy.
>
> Later in the morning I called up Knox who had been very warmly seconding this project to put Donovan into this position and I told him of my views on the subject as thus expressed. Knox, who had been quite rampant on the subject in favor of immediate action on behalf of Donovan saw my point and cooled down."

The Navy Secretary may have "cooled down," but he did not remain quiet. The same day that he talked with Stimson—whether before or after is not known—he asked the President to send a letter to Secretaries Hull, Morgenthau, and Stimson and to Attorney-General Jackson "outlining just what the Coordinator of Strategic Information will do." He explained that all those regular departments "have their hackles up over the danger that somebody is going to take something away from them." He also indicated that he had "already encountered some misunderstandings in the Navy Department over the premature publicity given out concerning Bill Donovan's new job." Nor was he "able to completely convince the Navy people that the major project" the President had in mind "was one of coordination, analysis and digestion of information

---

[20] *Ibid.*, 24 June 1941.
[21] *Ibid.*, 25 June 1941.

procured from various Departments." Finally, he expressed the thought that the letter he proposed would "make it a good deal easier for Bill when he gets on the job." [22]

Three days later, FDR asked Harold D. Smith, the Director of the Budget, "to do the necessary for my signature." [23] But before pursuing that matter let us return to Ben Cohen as he left Stimson and went back to his office and the Budget Bureau to revise the military order to make Marshall and Stimson less unhappy with its character and provisions. (Figs. 3A, 3B.)

Ben Cohen's Revisions

First of all, it remained a Military Order, but eleven times Cohen struck the word "strategic" from the document, and replaced it, depending on the context, by "defense" or "national security." This changed Donovan's title to "Coordinator of Defense Information" and related his activity to "national security" rather than the "hard" subject of military strategy. He did retain the line that the Coordinator "shall perform his duties and responsibilities, which include those of a military character, under the direction and supervision of the President as Commander in Chief of the Army and Navy of the United States," but he added the sentence requested by Stimson, namely, that nothing in those duties would in any way interfere with "the duties and responsibilities of the regular military and naval advisers of the President as Commander in Chief..." As we shall see, only this last sentence actually survived.

The Budget Bureau cleaned up the paper, and on the 27th returned a copy to Cohen and sent other copies to both Stimson and Knox. In the letters to the Secretaries, Blandford said he understood that the drafts were to be used "as a basis of discussion with your associates . . . over the week end." He hoped that the order could be put in final form for the President when he returned from Hyde Park early the next week. He was, however, to be disappointed.[24]

For almost a week, Secretary Stimson, General Marshall, and Assistant Secretary of War John J. McCloy continued to chew over the subject. On Monday, the 30th, when FDR returned to Washington, Stimson was noting in his diary that the Donovan business was "a troublesome matter even with the best of luck. I am afraid of it." That evening he told the President on the telephone that he had decided "it would be a great mistake" to set up the COI with Donovan as a military man. As a civilian, yes, but Stimson asked the President to do nothing about it until they had a chance to discuss it.[25]

The next morning Stimson had a long talk with Marshall again—at least the third, possibly the fourth—and his brief account leaves us with unsatisfied curiosity. He said he explained to the General "how important it was for his own—Marshall's—sake that there should not be a sharp issue made on this." [26] May one not conclude that Marshall continued to express Army opposition to the very existence of COI? Certainly he remained very hostile to the idea.

Stimson spent "a good deal of the morning and afternoon" of the next day, 2 July, talking over the matter with both the General and Assistant Secretary

---

[22] Knox to Roosevelt, 25 June 1941, Roosevelt Papers, OF 4485(OSS) Box 1.
[23] Roosevelt to Smith, 28 June 1941, *ibid.*, PPF 6558 (William J. Donovan).
[24] Smith to Stimson, 27 June 1941, BOB Records, Folder 210.
[25] Stimson Diary, Vol. 34, 30 June 1941.
[26] *Ibid.*, 1 July 1941.

CONFIDENTIAL   Donovan

6-24-41

First Version

Master for 6/27/41

MILITARY ORDER
- - - - -
                        Defense
DESIGNATING A COORDINATOR OF ~~STRATEGIC~~ INFORMATION

By virtue of the authority vested in me as President of the United States and as Commander in Chief of the Army and Navy of the United States, it is ordered as follows:

1. There is hereby established the position of Coordinator of ~~Strategic~~ Defense Information, with authority to collect and analyse information and data, military or otherwise, which may bear upon national ~~defense~~ Security ~~summary~~; to interpret and correlate such strategic information and data, and to make it such information and data available to the President and to such other officials as the President may determine; and to carry out, when requested by the President, such supplementary activities as may facilitate the securing of ~~strategic~~ information important for national security not now available to the Government.

2. The several departments and agencies of the Government shall make available to the Coordinator of ~~Strategic~~ Defense Information such information and data relating to national ~~defense~~ Security as the Coordinator, with the approval of the President, may from time to time request.

3. The Coordinator of ~~Strategic~~ Defense Information may appoint such committees, consisting of appropriate representatives of the various departments and agencies of the Government, as he may deem necessary to assist him in the performance of his functions.

Fig. 3A. Ben Cohen's Revisions.

2

~~Defense~~

4. The Coordinator of ~~Strategic~~ *Defense* Information shall perform ~~his~~ those duties and responsibilities, which include those of a military character, under the direction and supervision of the President as Commander in Chief of the Army and Navy of the United States.

5. Within the limits of such funds as may be allocated to the Coordinator of ~~Strategic~~ *Defense* Information by the President, the Coordinator may employ necessary personnel and make provision for the necessary supplies, facilities, and services.

6. William J. Donovan, United States Army, is hereby designated as Coordinator of ~~Strategic~~ *Defense* Information.

THE WHITE HOUSE,
June   , 1941.

Nothing in the duties and responsibilities of the Coordinator of Defense Information shall in any way interfere with or impair the duties and responsibilities of the regular military and naval advisers of the President as Commander-in-chief of the Army & Navy.

Fig. 3B.

McCloy, and finally arranged to see Donovan the next morning at 8:30 in order to "settle the thing one way or another." It was surely bothering him: "It is a terrible nuisance to have this thrown on me at this time but it is so important that I have got to settle it in the right way." [27]

For a change, that was not going to be difficult. When Stimson and McCloy, but not Marshall, met at 8:30 with Donovan, "everybody was fair-minded." They "very quickly" agreed on "the general principles and what should be done." Donovan said he had thought from the beginning that his position was essentially and entirely a civilian one; that he had taken up the "point of rank of Major General because the President had suggested it." Either then or later in the conversation, Stimson offered to recommend Donovan for Major General any time he "wanted to fight"; indeed, if Donovan wanted to do it now and give up COI, he could have "one of the most difficult positions" in the Army, specifically, command of the 44th Division. The Colonel admitted that he was interested in developing a theory of guerrilla warfare which he had but that he preferred now to stay with the information job, "make something real out of it," and then turn to fighting and a commission later.[28] A lesser man than Stimson might, at this time, have been suspected of attempted bribery!

But back to the meeting. Donovan also agreed to a "diagram" which Marshall had drawn up and given Stimson and which McCloy had now brought forth; this showed "the relation of the different positions to each other in the hierarchy of the War Department." Stimson's diary is unclear, but apparently this diagram showed that "the routine channels for the recommendations as to intelligence and information were to be coordinated by Donovan as they came" from the collectors—the Army, Navy, etc.—"and then should go up through the channels, through the Joint Board and then through the Chief of Staff and the Chief of Operations of the Navy, the Secretary of War and the Secretary of the Navy, to the President." Even so, all agreed that Donovan had to have access to the President whenever he desired it, because it "was necessary to his position, and the President's temperament and characteristics" would make it inevitable.[29]

Agreement at last. Later the same day Colonel Donovan met with Ben Cohen and the Budget Bureau's trio—Blandford, Stone, and Gladieux—to finish the paperwork. The "final revised draft," however, had not been returned by Assistant Secretary McCloy, who apparently was still discussing it with Stimson. The Bureau had hoped to receive the paper in the afternoon, clear it, and "send it immediately to Hyde Park." [30]

Donovan Outlines his Plans

Pending the paper's return, Donovan elaborated on his needs and his plans, but only those remarks which bear on his orders will be noted here. The point has been made that, while the main thrust of Donovan's work was aimed at the foreign field, he did not think in terms of a clean distinction between foreign and domestic. Hence, his concept of a system for the coordination of informa-

---

[27] *Ibid.*, 2 July 1941.
[28] *Ibid.*, 3 July 1941.
[29] *Ibid.*
[30] Memorandum of "Conference with Colonel J. Donovan and Ben Cohen," 3 July 1941, BOB Records, Folder 212.

tion envisaged "various operating sections," apparently in Washington but also "apply[ing] in zones throughout the country," feeding information into "a central clearing section." Also in connection with this function, he planned to have the Librarian of Congress work in liaison with "all libraries and scholars of the country"; the University of Chicago was to be "the map-making unit of the Coordinator's Office."

On a second point, Donovan explained the offensive side of his work, broadcasting to Europe, in which incidentally Robert Sherwood and William Shirer were to be used because of—according to Gladieux' account of Donovan's remark—their knowledge of the grammar requirements! "Psychological warfare," said Donovan, "will be started on all fronts"; did he mean the domestic front also?

On a third point, "The President expressed his desire to Donovan," wrote Gladieux, "that he set up a Committee on 'economics of the future'." Donovan was not, however, to have easy sledding on this subject.

Some time later on the 3rd McCloy's draft was returned to the drafting crew. Some significant changes had been made. The "Military Order" was now just an "Order." So also, the "Coordinator of Defense Information" was now just the "Coordinator of Information." The COI, instead of making his information available "to the President and to such other officials as the President may determine," now sent his productions "to the Joint Planning Division of the Joint Army and Navy Board, and to such departments and officials of the Government and other officials as the President may determine." Surely, Donovan must have hit the ceiling when he saw that insertion! Again, the COI was to carry out his supplementary activities "when requested by the President, the Secretary of War, and the Secretary of the Navy. . . ." The sentence about the COI performing his duties, "which include those of a military character," under the President as Commander in Chief, was excised; and there was left standing in that paragraph only the guarantee that the COI would not interfere with the President's regular military and naval advisors. In the last paragraph a subtle difference must have been intended when "William J. Donovan, United States Army," was changed to "Colonel William J. Donovan" and "designated as Coordinator of Defense [sic] Information."

Donovan and the others apparently quickly went to work on these changes. The "Order" was now eliminated, so now there was no indication what was being issued! They accepted elimination of "Defense" from the title of the new post. They excised the wholesale insertion of reporting to the Joint Planning Division and responding to the requests of the President and the Service Secretaries. They accepted McCloy's Paragraph 4. (See Figure 3 above.) Finally, it was just "William J. Donovan" who was designated COI. The job was clearly not military.

The Final Version

The wrap-up must have gone quickly; for, still on the 3rd, Harold D. Smith, the Director of the Bureau of the Budget, sent to the President the finished product and a proposed statement for the press.[31] In his letter Smith observed that since the appointment rested on the President's authority as Commander

---

[31] Smith to Roosevelt, 3 July 1941, *Ibid.*, Folder 210.

in Chief, "it should be issued as a Military Order." Be that as it may, it appeared officially, and so it appears today, simply as an undenominated Presidential act "Designating a Coordinator of Information." (Appendix B)

On the second point raised by Smith there is no ambiguity or room for argument:

> While both the Army and Navy objected to our original title for Colonel Donovan of Coordinator of *Strategic* Information or Coordinator of *Defense* Information, I think *either of these titles is preferable to the one used in this Order as now presented.* "Coordinator of Information" is vague and is not descriptive of the work Colonel Donovan will perform.

The statement which Smith had readied for the press was a combination of three bland and one strong announcements. The first simply iterated the functions of COI as the collection, assembling, and collation of data bearing on nationl security and the fulfillment by Donovan of such extra activities as the President might from time to time request of him. The strong assertion was the assurance given the General Staff, the regular intelligence services, the Federal Bureau of Investigation, and all other government agencies that Donovan's work "is not intended to supersede or to duplicate, or to involve any direction of or interference with" their own activities. This was also intended to blunt the expected opposition of some Congressional critics of the Administration.

The line about the extra activities Donovan might be asked to render caught the attention of FDR's press secretary Steve Early before he passed it on, and so he wrote the President: "Is this sentence necessary? It won't be clear to many and will lead to much questioning." Harry Hopkins agreed "with Steve that [the sentence] should be eliminated from [the] release." [32]

Smith's letter to the President also stated that his Bureau was preparing letters to the various departments requesting their cooperation with Donovan, as Secretary Knox had asked several days earlier. This letter, which was sent to 16 departments on 14 July—three days after COI was officially established— reiterated the points made in the press release, that he was going to coordinate data and not going to upset anybody else.[33]

Although the work of drafting was completed on the 3rd, it was not until the 11th that the President actually signed the document. There is no indication of the reason for the delay, and it is assumed here that simply the press of the Presidential calendar accounted for it. There had of course already been some public expectation of a forthcoming announcement, and the coverage in the *New York Times* provides us with a contemporary view of what COI looked like. On 6 July the Associated Press reported that Colonel Donovan was "slated for a big post." The only clue to its character was "the reports for some time that . . . Donovan would head a new anti-spy agency." According to these reports, Donovan was to "coordinate a staff of investigators" in the Justice, Treasury, State, and military and naval departments. The rest of the article tied the expected job in with spies, the FBI case load, and Donovan's own investigations of the Fifth Column the year before.[34]

---

[32] Early's notation appears on the press release Smith sent the President, and Hopkins appended his note to Smith's letter.
[33] BOB Records, Folder 210.
[34] *New York Times*, 6 July 1941, p. 16, cols. 2-3.

On 9 July the *Times'* own staff had a better grasp on the shape of things to come. It had a name which had never been contemplated, however—"Coordinator of Intelligence Information." It did know that the new job was to be "without precedent in the government's operations," and was well-informed enough to know that his duties were "sufficiently elastic to take in such future possibilities as counterespionage operations and, perhaps, direction of some economic programs." His primary task, however, was to take other departments' reports and present them to the President in unified and manageable form.[35]

Even on the 12th, the *Times* could not get the new post properly titled; now it was the rejected "Coordinator of Defense Information." Donovan's "relatively small staff" was to "supervise" and "digest" reports for the President. He had told associates that "the scattered reports which came to his desk often were hopelessly confusing."[36]

In concluding this second portion of our inquiry, it must be clear that as far as clarifying the content of Donovan's original instructions from the President is concerned, the process of drafting the order of 11 July 1941 added nothing to the knowledge either of the drafters themselves or of us who now read the record. The decision to put nothing in writing meant, of course, that the resolution of many uncertainties and ambiguities would not take place in the drafting but would, in effect, simply be pushed under the rug to be turned up later as people went about the business of handling the many irons Donovan had in the fire: coordination of data, counterintelligence, subversive action, sabotage, all kinds of foreign and domestic propaganda, economic warfare, economics of the future, and a few sleepers which had not yet surfaced—planning military strategy, and "the writing of the peace!"

Organizing COI: July–September 1941

With the issuance of the 11 July order, Donovan could now intensify his organizational activity. He had, of course, already had numerous discussions with prospective colleagues on the job he was to do and the structure that would be needed. He was certainly in touch with the head of British Intelligence, William S. Stephenson, on organizing clandestine activities. He had already agreed with the dramatist, the presidential speechwriter, Robert Sherwood, on setting up what became the Foreign Information Service. He had met with officials of the Library of Congress on drawing on the resources of the American academic community for the research and analysis job.

It was not, however, until he and his associates had entered on a new phase of their negotiations with the Bureau of the Budget, that is, on setting up COI, that specific jurisdictional conflicts with other agencies began to take shape. This occurred on 16 July when Donovan and his colleagues—Sherwood, Atherton Richards, Thomas G. Early, and Ernest S. Griffith, the Director of the Legislative Reference Service of the Library of Congress—held three conferences with Budget officials to outline their plans and to obtain necessary guidance from the Bureau on organizational necessities.

These conferences began the laborious process of defining functions, drawing organizational charts, establishing budgets, fixing salaries, renting space, and

---
[35] *Ibid.*, 10 July p. 12, col. 3.
[36] *Ibid.*, 12 July, p. 5, col. 1.

purchasing equipment. Of course we are not going into these ramifications of the early history of COI; they would carry us well beyond our narrow concern with the content of the agreement reached on 18 June by Roosevelt and Donovan. This organizational development is but the context out of which we must pluck the indicators of Donovan's understanding of his assignment.

These indicators first show up in the reports of the 16 July conferences which were written by William O. Hall, the Budget officer who handled COI matters extensively and who will be quoted frequently in the next several pages.[37] We will single out from Hall's memoranda three topics which raise the question of Donovan's area of jurisdiction: "the morale function," postwar planning, and economic warfare.

The business of morale, as has been mentioned, had long been agitating many of Roosevelt's top advisors. For them some organization and activity were needed. La Guardia and the Office of Civilian Defense were finally settled upon, but the boundaries of activity were apparently clear in nobody's mind, least of all the President's. Hence it was that on the 16th the subject of morale came up in a discussion of COI's need for "country experts," and in that connection the name of Robert Lynd, the author of *Middletown* and *Middletown in Transition*, was mentioned. According to Hall, Griffith of the Legislative Reference Service then "stated that he (Lynd) was an authority on domestic sociological problems, but that he had no knowledge in the foreign field." Hall then adds:

> Donovan stated that this would fit very well into the President's plans. The President has told Donovan that he is to investigate the state of domestic (U.S.) morale and formulate plans for the domestic morale program. These plans will then be forwarded to Mayor La Guardia (civil defense) for execution. Accordingly, Griffith should plan to set up a Domestic Morale Unit and Lynd would be a good man to head that unit, according to Donovan.

So much for the time being for COI's morale function; let us turn to the second topic singled out: postwar planning. This is another large topic that had been agitating people inside and outside of the government. The thinking ran roughly like this: in 1919 Versailles had not ushered in a new world; instead, the settlement simply generated and aggravated economic conditions which made another war inevitable; now, in 1941, history must not be allowed to repeat itself; therefore, a start must be made on planning the economic rehabilitation of the world once Nazism has been destroyed. The big question was who should do the planning, and how he should proceed. Donovan clearly had thoughts on the matter. Hence, on the 16th, Atherton Richards, who was then apparently slated to head COI's economic division, a major component, was asked by Donovan "to state the needs of his unit for postwar planning." Richards, an Hawaiian-born businessman admittedly without experience in government research, was not too clear on his requirements; he did know that the chief of the division would get $9,000 per year, two assistants would each get $7,500, and nine special assistants would be hired at $6,500 each. What is most significant from our point of view is the fact, however awkwardly stated, that "these men would be assigned on the basis of general divisions of our economy to developments in the various departments and agencies in postwar planning and to coordinate the efforts of government, industry and labor."

---

[37] BOB Records, Folder 212. These reports are all dated 16 July 1941; it is possible, however, that one of the conferences occurred on 15 July.

The third topic, economic defense and economic warfare, was just as large as the other two, and Richards was no clearer on this than on postwar planning. "After discussion with Colonel Donovan . . . concerning the possibilities of economic warfare organization," wrote Hall, "Richards stated that further amplification of his estimates for the Economics Division would be necessary." Hall himself did not appear to be too clear on just what "economic defense" and "economic warfare" actually were, but this is not surprising inasmuch as there was considerable confusion on just what the government should do at one and the same time to aid Britain economically, deny economic resources to the Axis, sustain the American economy, and still mobilize the economy for preparedness and, if necessary, war. Hall, after hearing Sherwood's explanation of his propaganda activities and needs, thought immediately in terms of economic warfare because "any activities in propaganda warfare must be directed at economic objectives." As will be seen, Donovan's interests in economics was considerably broader than propaganda. Anyhow, Hall concluded that "Sherwood's activities must be closely coordinated with the economic warfare agency, whether it be OED [Office of Economic Defense] or State-Treasury-Commerce-Export control, Federal Loan or Federal Reserve." Hall had another worry on his mind: except for Sherwood, Donovan's staff did not strike him as "particularly able;" and Donovan had "a tendency to commit himself too quickly on personnel and financial arrangements"; worse still, found Hall, a 27-year-old administrative officer, the 57-year-old Donovan "probably lacks the general background which should be present in the person directing the propaganda and economic warfare activities."

Budget Bureau Concerned Over Conflicts

Within two weeks, the Bureau of the Budget was sufficiently concerned by the tendency of COI to "impinge so directly upon a variety of activities of existing agencies," that a memorandum for the President was prepared for the signature of the Director, Harold D. Smith.[38] While the document was apparently not sent, it still succinctly summarizes some Budget worries that were to persist. First of all, Donovan's request for $10,000,000 for the first year could not be reconciled with "the original proposal for establishing the office." Secondly, Vice President Henry A. Wallace, who was about to be named chairman of the newly-established Economic Defense Board, wanted Smith of the Budget to take up with the President the extent to which he wanted Donovan to "enter the economic defense field;" it was clear to Wallace that Donovan was "planning to carry on extensive economic defense activities . . . with particular reference to the assembly and correlation of information and plans." Thirdly, what about morale? Donovan "is planning a Public Relations Division to deal with problems of domestic information and morale as related to the coordination of strategic information and foreign propaganda;" so how does this square with La Guardia's authorization "to conduct domestic morale programs?" Fourthly, Donovan "is organizing a staff to develop original data on strategic situations in foreign countries," and this "will in some measure duplicate" State, War, and Navy activities. Smith then asked a question which seems to echo the *Times'* expectation that

---

[38] Memorandum for the President, *ibid.* Gladieux prepared this for Smith's signature on 30 July 1941. An illegible note written by Hall and dated 31 July makes the writer uncertain that the memorandum was actually sent.

Donovan was to "supervise" and "digest" other department's reports for the President: "To what extent should [Donovan] . . . develop such original research reports?"

Whatever the reason was for not forwarding this memorandum to the President, it certainly was not lack of concern on the part of the Budget Bureau. Before August was out, Hall wrote his boss, Bernard L. Gladieux, a memorandum on "Functional Confusion" in COI in which he outlined five areas of conflict with other agencies, cited the causes, and suggested some "correctives for the situation."[39] As might be expected, the domestic defense effort and postwar planning were two areas of conflict; here COI was seen to be running into the Reconstruction Finance Corporation, the National Resources Planning Board, the Office of Price Administration and Civilian Supply, the Office of Production Management, and, of course, the Economic Defense Board. A third area, research on propaganda and undercover activities in South America, wrote Hall, had been "assigned to Nelson Rockefeller," the Coordinator of Inter-American Affairs. A fourth area was "the coordination of domestic counter-espionage and counter-subversive activities programs" which had been "assigned" to the Federal Bureau of Investigation. It is the fifth area which may strike the reader as the most remarkable function which Donovan allegedly thought was his, namely, "the writing of the peace," which, wrote Hall, had been "assigned" to the Department of State and the EDB. On the margin of this memorandum Gladieux wrote and initialed this most interesting indirect quotation: "Milo Perkins [EDB's "most able, adroit, and energetic"[40] executive director] told me that Donovan claims the President told him to 'write the Peace' [sic], and he certainly is proceeding accordingly." We will see more of this function when we come to consider Hall's subsequent and much longer memorandum of 11 September on COI's conflicts with other agencies.

All this confusion was attributed by Hall to the "general character" of the 11 July order, to the "oral instructions to . . . Donovan from the President, with which we are not familiar," to the "conflicting newspaper reports and . . . rumors" about COI's functions, and to the use of the President's son James as the COI's Liaison Officer with the defense agencies. The 11 July order certainly was not helpful, and the "oral instructions" we do not know to this day. The President's son James was detailed by the Navy, run by Donovan's very good personal friend Frank Knox, to work with Donovan; just how this was accomplished we do not know, but Hall cannot be far wrong when he observed that the young Roosevelt made "it possible for Donovan's assistants to gain entre [sic] to any of the defense agencies." Certainly there was confusion both inside and outside the government; the press thought Donovan was going to "digest intelligence reports;" one Senator denounced COI as an Ogpu or Gestapo; Assistant Secretary of State Adolf Berle warned Under Secretary Welles against Donovan making foreign policy with his propaganda service; elsewhere in State, Secretary Hull was being warned that Donovan's activities in the field of postwar planning would result in "an intermingling of war and post-war problems;" and the Administrator of Export Control was telling his staff that "if rumors are true

---

[*] Memorandum from Hall to Gladieux on "Functional Confusion in the Office for Coordination of Information," 28 August 1941, ibid.

[†] Dean G. Acheson, *Present at the Creation: My Years in the State Department* (N.Y.: Norton, 1969), p. 41.

that he [Donovan] is going to take over the La Guardia office, he will be pretty busy."[41] This last comment reminds us that Donovan intended, indeed, to be "pretty busy," and that the vigor with which this dedicated man, armed with a Presidential mandate, embarked on a varied program dear to his thinking and heart undoubtedly sowed both confusion and apprehension among settled bureaucrats and able newcomers in other agencies.

Hall's "suggested correctives" for the situation were two: "a letter or confidential order from the President to Donovan setting forth in clear terms the area in which he is to function;" and "a competent administrative assistant" to end COI's internal confusion which Hall also found troublesome but with which we have not been concerned in this paper. Gladieux made a second note on this memorandum, and it is another "corrective" for the situation: "Consolidate him [Donovan] with the Economic Defense Board." This recommendation is, retrospectively, most significant as probably the first written suggestion that the newly-born COI be aborted; the suggestion was to recur, in one way or another, to such an extent that one can almost say that COI's major success was to have survived.

It may be appropriate here to stress the fact that COI was an unwanted child. The Army, the Navy, the Department of State, and the Federal Bureau of Investigation had made it quite plain to the President that they saw no need for such an organization.[42] There was also no rush on their parts to channel their information, per the 11 July order, into COI in-boxes.[43] This uncooperative attitude makes quite plausible Stephenson's claim that his organization provided COI, before Pearl Harbor and for several months after, with the "bulk" of its secret intelligence.[44] The other side of the coin of hostility to supplying Donovan with information was Donovan's own strong determination to get control of that information. His memorandum of 10 June, and indeed the very vagueness of the 11 July order—with its sweeping authorization "to collect and analyze all information . . . which may bear upon national security"—show how much stress this omnivorous reader, this corporation lawyer, this military strategist

---

[41] The reference to the unnamed Senator is in a memorandum from Early to Roosevelt, 1 August 1941, Roosevelt Papers, PSF (Donovan) (*Closed*). Berle's warning is in his memorandum to Sumner Wells, 25 July 1941, in Records of the State Department, National Archives, RG 59, File 103.918/2541. The warning to Hull is in a Memorandum from Pasvolsky, "Proposal for the Organization of Work for the Formulation of Post-War Foreign Policies," 12 September 1941; this can be found in U.S. Department of State, *Postwar Foreign Policy Preparation, 1939-1945* (Washington, GPO, 1949), pp. 464-67. The remark by the Administrator is found in the Records of the Economic Defense Board, National Archives, RG 169, Misc. File, Box 6, Information Division Minutes.

[42] "COI," Chs. VII and VIII.

[43] Here is a sample of this attitude: On 26 December 1941, Captain T. S. Wilkinson, USN, asked Secretary of the Navy Knox, in a memorandum, if Colonel Donovan should be allowed to see the "Daily Bulletin" issued by the Joint Intelligence Committee of the Joint Board.

Knox advised Wilkinson "to dig out the executive order" establishing COI and he would find therein "instructions for both Army and Navy to provide Colonel Donovan with all information in their possession. Under these conditions, it hardly seems necessary for me to instruct you to add his name to those who receive the bulletin. If you feel better about having such instructions, regard this as instructions to that effect." Found in Navy Records, CNO Central Classified File, Folder A8-3EF13, Secret.

[44] H. Montgomery Hyde, *The Quiet Canadian: The Secret Service Story of Sir William Stephenson* (London: Hamilton, 1962), p. 156.

placed upon a mastery of data. What is probably more relevant to some of the opposition encountered by Donovan is the fact that he did think of information in terms of strategy and was, perhaps, even more interested in the use to which information was put than in the possession of it for its own sake. Moreover, if information was the basis of strategy, strategy had meaning only when it was put into action; and Donovan really wanted to lead troops into battle. Donovan was an activist, and it is, therefore, not surprising that his eagerness to take the mass of new and old information pouring into Washington and convert it into meaningful intelligence which could give direction and strength to military, political, economic, and psychological warfare against the Nazis should bring him smack up against all the monarchs who reigned over domains of knowledge.

This comes out clearly in the memorandum which Hall wrote on 11 September; it is his longest—five pages, single space—and details no less than eleven areas in which Donovan is allegedly exceeding his Presidential authorization, and only two in which he is doing what is his to do! Again, we cannot go into the merits or the details of these issues; we can only single out the indicators of the Donovan agreement with Roosevelt.[45]

The first brings us back to the La Guardia situation; the Office of Civilian Defense was about to give birth to an off-shoot—the Office of Facts and Figures, which was soon to be headed by the poet and head of the Library of Congress, Archibald MacLeish. Until that situation became clear, however, Donovan, according to Hall, "proposes to report to the President and the public" on: production for military and civilian needs, American public opinion, the attitude of the American press toward the defense effort and the administration's foreign policy, the attitude of U.S. foreign press, and foreign press opinion.

The second is "writing the peace." Hall writes of Donovan "in his original plans stressing the preparation of 'the blueprints for a new world order'"; where Donovan did this, however, this writer has not discovered. On the same point, Hall wrote that Donovan's chief of research and analysis, James P. Baxter, III, "stated confidentially that Donovan would like to undertake another 'peace inquiry' like the one directed by Colonel Hause" [sic] at the end of the last war.

Next are four areas in which Donovan's research and reporting activities cause trouble. On Latin America, Donovan's plans caused Rockefeller's people to fear not only that their area was being usurped, but also that they were expected henceforth to obtain all their information from COI rather than directly from State, War, Navy, Justice, and Commerce. On the domestic defense production effort, Donovan planned a unit so as to be able to report "to the public and the President." On a related point, Donovan was described by Atherton Richards as feeling "that one of his responsibilities to the President is reporting on the status of organization for defense . . . on organizational and functional weaknesses;" Richards "anticipates that Donovan will at times recommend changes in the over-all defense organization." Despite conferences with Milo Perkins, wherein he and Donovan presumably reached agreement on their functions, "Donovan still speaks of providing the Economic Defense Board and the President with economic information" relative to postwar planning.

Hall sketched three areas in which Donovan was moving into policy-making and strategic planning. Indeed, wrote Hall "there has been some indication that

---

[45] Memorandum from Hall to Gladieux on "Scope and Function of the Office of the Coordinator of Information," 11 September 1941, BOB Records, Folder 212.

the Donovan group wishes to supplant the State Department in bringing together the military, naval, geographical, economic, and political information needed for the planning of basic foreign policy." Hall, echoing perhaps others' fears, saw this as Donovan insinuating himself between the President and the Department as did Colonel House in World War I. Next, Hall reported the belief on the part of members of COI's staff and of other agencies that "Donovan's hope is that he will be the planner of basic strategy." The mechanism for this leap to power was to be the coordination committees authorized by the 11 July order and calculated to operate at the highest level in the utilization of data in planning basic strategy. Hall threw in his, or others', estimate that Donovan's relationship with the President would tend to make him the "basic strategy advisor." Finally, Hall saw "some indications" that the Donovan organization hoped to develop as the "high strategy group," which many military and civilian people thought the defense program needed.

The last two of the eleven areas of conflict are relatively minor. Hall considered Donovan's tentative agreement with the military services to unify undercover activities abroad was "a primary accomplishment," but he feared this would interfere with Donovan's "informational strategy planning function." He also had fears about the COI section to produce propaganda motion pictures; "considerable question" could be raised, he said, about the usefulness of such films outside Latin America, and Rockefeller's organization found that such films were less appealing to Latins than commercial and informational films.

After detailing all these problems in four pages, two short paragraphs agreed that Donovan could make "definite contributions" in subversive activities and in psychological and propaganda warfare—radio broadcasting, underground messages, and leaflets—provided he stayed out of Rockefeller's Latin American preserve.

With these paragraphs we come to the end of this early organizational period in which there was so much discussion of and controversy about the legitimate functions of COI. Before trying to summarize these functions, however, it may be well to satisfy the reader's curiosity about how some of the controversies were resolved. First of all, it must be stated that the Bureau of the Budget continued for months to press for a Presidential re-statement of COI's funcions. Hall's last memorandum was sent to Director Harold D. Smith, apparently with the recommendation to take it up in substance with FDR. On 14 October there was written, probably by Hall, a draft of a memorandum for the President in which "a number of basic questions" about COI's function were raised for the President's decision.[46] Then, on 5 November Harold Smith, writing about COI's 1942 budget, suggested to the President that he write a letter or order "precisely defining the Coordinator's assigned area of activity."[47] Finally, on 28 February 1942, Smith advised the President that such an order was "becoming increasingly necessary" and that he, Smith, was ready to draft it.[48] That drafting, however, was caught up in another series of events which saw COI shorn of its Foreign Information Service and re-constituted, on 13 June 1942, as the Office of Strategic Services.

---

[46] Memorandum to the President, "1942 Allotment Request of Coordinator of Information," 14 October 1941 (draft), BOB Records, Folder 247.

[47] Harold D. Smith, Memorandum for the President, "Budget Request for the Coordinator of Information," 5 November 1941, Roosevelt Papers, OF 4485.

[48] Smith to the President, 28 February 1942, Donovan Papers, "Exhibits," Vol. II, Tab UU.

CONFIDENTIAL

Roosevelt Intervenes

In the meantime, Roosevelt—when forced to it—had taken steps to settle arguments. On 4 September 1941 he directed Ben Cohen—"I am not 'asking' you to do this! I am 'telling' you!"—he good-naturedly wrote—to "see that inconsistencies and conflicts do not arise" between Bill Donovan's organization and the new Office of Facts and Figures; the latter's establishment on 24 October ended Donovan's "morale function."[49] On 15 October, Roosevelt had to step in between Donovan and Rockefeller, and he did so on the side of the latter, telling Donovan to keep out of Latin America.[50] In economic defense activities, the appearance on the scene of Milo Perkins as executive director of EDB effectively closed that area to COI. As for subsequent developments in regard to "writing the peace" and postwar planning, with which State, EDB, and other agencies continued to wrestle, we must leave some loose ends lying about. Jurisdictional conflicts—involving not only COI but so many other wartime agencies—persisted throughout the war, but they are not our main interest here.

In reviewing this early history of COI's development we have been searching for indications of functions which Donovan thought or knew were his by right of the President's authorization of the memorandum of 10 June, the meeting on 18 June, and the order of 11 July. Now is the time to state some conclusions and cite sample pieces of evidence, and we will do so under the following headings:

1. Morale: This is the least troublesome area. Morale was not a part of Donovan's original plan, but the President was "struck by the thought that Donovan might take on the morale job temporarily . . ." The New Yorker apparently fell in very quickly with the idea, especially with the idea of reporting on the state of mind of the American public.

2. Economic defense: There is nothing in the record to show that Roosevelt authorized Donovan to study and report to him and the American public on the state of the American defense effort, but Donovan certainly moved early in that direction. Atherton Richards was quoted by Hall to that effect; and on 5 August, in a COI memorandum to the staff, the "Economics Branch" was authorized to conduct research bearing on "the economic problems of the United States during and following the termination of the war emergency," which the President had proclaimed in May; and at the same time the Branch was divided into three divisions: the domestic, the foreign, and the "Industrial, labor and agricultural economics division."[51]

3. Economic warfare: Donovan and Richards clearly discussed "the possibilities of economic warfare organization." This must have had reference at least to that passage in his 10 June memorandum wherein he wrote that "All departments should have the same information upon which economic warfare could be determined." Donovan, according to Hall, reached an agreement with Perkins whereby COI would provide the EDB "with the basic information which would be needed for postwar planning and for economic warfare." While this agreement was by no means the last word on the subject, there is no reason to doubt but that Donovan did expect that the provision of such data was within

---

[49] Roosevelt to Cohen, 4 September 1941, Roosevelt Papers, PPF 3509.

[50] Memorandum for the Coordinator of Information from F.D.R., 15 October 1941, BOB Records, Folder 239.

[51] "AR," presumably Atherton Richards, appear as initials of the originating officer on this memorandum, which was prepared for Donovan's signature.

his bailiwick. At this stage of development, the subject of operations in this field was not discussed.

4. *Postwar planning:* As just mentioned, Donovan intended to provide EDB with data relating to the postwar situation, and Richards was asked at the 16 July conferences to state the need of his unit for postwar planning. Also, an undated statement of the functions of the "Economic Branch" shows that it was to "formulate plans for the coordination of post-war planning activities" of the various agencies, to collect and "popularize" information on such planning for the President and department heads, and also to encourage such planning by industry, labor, and agriculture.[52]

5. *Writing the peace:* Milo Perkins is the indirect source of the Donovan claim that the President had told him to write the peace. According to Hall, writing on 8 September, Dr. Baxter was "disturbed by the rumors that Donovan has been commissioned to write the peace and believes that the State Department was also quite concerned." Baxter was further quoted as saying that some of his friends had been approached by Donovan, before the COI order came out, "asking them to serve with an organization similar to the House inquiry of the last war." Baxter was further quoted as saying that no such organization should be established and the function should be left with State, but that Donovan did not agree with him on this point.[53]

6. *Basic Strategy Planning:* There is no reason to doubt that Donovan aimed to influence basic political and military strategy. Others may have thought "policy" was not the field of COI, but Donovan did not think that way, at least, in the period under consideration. He aimed to gather and interpret the data "bearing on national security," and working through the "coordination committees" to make recommendations to the President. Again, an early but undated statement of functions shows that the "Research and Plans Branch" was to assist in the development of strategic plans, advise the Coordinator on national policy, prepare "popular" reports on strategic subjects for the President, and maintain such liaison as would insure the "full utilization of the expert facilities in the various departments and agencies in the determination of national policy."[54] Just how far Donovan expected to go in this direction is arguable, but it is not surprising if Hall and others thought the "Donovan organization" hoped to develop as "the secretariat of [a] high strategy group" within the defense organization.

Conclusion

By now it must be clear that there was anything but clarity in the listing of the functions that COI was to perform. First of all, we know only that the President approved Donovan's memorandum of 10 June which called for the establishment of an organization to collect information on enemy countries and to use the radio as an instrument of modern warfare and that the President also underwrote Donovan's plans for secret and subversive activities. Secondly, the order of 11 July authorizes Donovan to collect, analyze, correlate, and dis-

---

[52] This document appears in the BOB Records in company with Hall's reports of 16 July 1941, and there is no reason to doubt that it belongs there.

[53] Hall's Memorandum of Conference, 8 September 1941, on "Developments in the Office of the Coordinator of Information," BOB Records, Folder 212.

[54] Cf. Note 52 *supra*.

seminate information bearing on national security and also to carry out "supplementary activities" as requested by the President. We know also, from the drafting of the order, that Ben Cohen thought the new COI would not interfere with the "morale function" of La Guardia's office or the need for the projected Economic Defense Board. Thirdly, as just reviewed, Donovan was quickly involved in a whole host of activities which could not possibly have been touched upon, spelled out, and agreed upon in the conference that Donovan had with the President on 18 June.

The conclusion here is that Donovan was given a charter marked by vagueness, contradiction, and open-endedness. The vagueness is clear on the face of the 11 July order, and Smith had pointed this out to the President a week before it was issued. It was so vague even on the basic function of the Coordination of Information that some people concluded, honestly presumably, that his job was simply to "digest" others' reports to the President. The most patent contradiction contained in the order, although not spelled out, was the authorization to conduct world-wide radio broadcasts even though Nelson Rockefeller clearly had a monopoly on such activity as far as South America was concerned. The open-endedness—the coordination of data bearing on national security—Donovan was clearly quite prepared to exploit to the full, and it is not surprising that people like Breckinridge Long were soon accusing him of poking his nose "into everybody's business."

This conclusion raises the question of President Roosevelt's understanding of what he was doing when he issued such a charter to the Colonel. For an answer, the writer can only fall back on others' analyses of FDR's administrative principles and procedures, and here there are at least two schools of thought. James MacGregor Burns has described the President as ". . . avoiding commitments to any one man or program, letting his subordinates feel less the sting of responsibility than the goad of competition, thwarting one man from getting too much control. . . ," and it was this approach that "prompted him to drive his jostling horses with a loose bit and a nervous but easy rein." [55] On the other hand, Dean Acheson has rejected as "nonsense" the idea that Roosevelt liked "organizational confusion which permitted him to keep power in his own hands by playing off his colleagues one against the other;" instead, says the former Secretary of State, under FDR, "civil governmental organization . . . was messed up . . . for the simplest of reasons: he did not know any better." [56]

Let the last comment on the President's style go to William O. Hall, who, thirty years after the events narrated here, observed that "Donovan was a pusher, an empire-builder, a man with a sense of mission, whose activity had "the effect of stirring up the military and the State Department, and FDR was happy to see this." [57]

---

[55] James MacGregor Burns, *Roosevelt: The Soldier of Freedom* (Harcourt Brace Jovanovich, New York, 1970), p. 53. More recently, John P. Roche noted in his King Features Syndicate column (*Washington Post*, 22 May 1973) that: "[Roosevelt's] technique, to simplify, was always to give subordinates overlapping jurisdictions. Thus Jesse Jones of the Reconstruction Finance Corporation, Harry Hopkins, and Secretary of the Interior Ickes (to take one hypothetical case) would each be given the impression by FDR that he was in charge of some major aspect of domestic policy. Invariably the three would get into a fight on any significant policy question and—since it was impossible to settle it among themselves—the President would wind up as the arbiter."

[56] Acheson, *Op. cit.*, p. 47.

[57] William O. Hall, private interview, Washington, D.C., 16 September 1970.

Appendix A:

MEMORANDUM OF ESTABLISHMENT OF SERVICE OF STRATEGIC INFORMATION

Strategy, without information upon which it can rely, is helpless. Likewise, information is useless unless it is intelligently directed to the strategic purpose. Modern warfare depends upon the economic base—on the supply of raw materials, on the capacity and performance of the industrial plant, on the scope of agricultural production and upon the character and efficacy of communications. Strategic reserves will determine the strength of the attack and the resistance of the defense. Steel and gasoline constitute these reserves as much as do men and powder. The width and depth of terrain occupied by the present day army exacts an equally wide and deep network of operative lines. The "depth of strategy" depends on the "depth of armament."

The commitment of all resources of a nation, moral as well as material, constitute what is called total war. To anticipate enemy intention as to the mobilization and employment of these forces is a difficult task. General von Vernhardi says, "We must try, by correctly foreseeing what is coming, to anticipate developments and thereby to gain an advantage which our opponents cannot overcome on the field of battle. That is what the future expects us to do."

Although we are facing imminent peril, we are lacking in effective service for analyzing, comprehending, and appraising such information as we might obtain, (or in some cases have obtained,) relative to the intention of potential enemies and the limit of the economic and military resources of those enemies. Our mechanism of collecting information is inadequate. It is true we have intelligence units in the Army and Navy. We can assume that through these units our fighting services can obtain technical information in time of peace, have available immediate operational information in time of war, and on certain occasions obtain "spot" news as to enemy movements. But these services cannot, out of the very nature of things, obtain that accurate, comprehensive, long-range information without which no strategic board can plan for the future. And we have arrived at the moment when there must be plans laid down for the spring of 1942.

We have, scattered throughout the various departments of our government, documents and memoranda concerning military and naval and air and economic potentials of the Axis which, if gathered together and studied in detail by carefully selected trained minds, with a knowledge both of the related languages and technique, would yield valuable and often decisive results.

Critical analysis of this information is as important presently for our supply program as if we were actually engaged in armed conflict. It is unimaginable that Germany would engage in a $7 billion supply program without first studying in detail the productive capacity of her actual and potential enemies. It is because she does exactly this that she displays such a mastery in the secrecy, timing, and effectiveness of her attacks.

Even if we participate to no greater extent than we do now, it is essential that we set up a central enemy intelligence organization which would itself collect either directly or through existing departments of government, at home and abroad, pertinent information concerning potential enemies, the character and strength of their armed forces, their internal economic organization, their principal channels of supply, the morale of their troops and their people and their relations with their neighbors or allies.

For example, in the economic field, there are many weapons that can be used against the enemy. But in our government these weapons are distributed through several different departments. How and when to use them is of vital interest not only to the Commander-in-Chief but to each of the departments concerned. All departments should have the same information upon which economic warfare could be determined.

To analyze and interpret such information by applying to it not only the experience of Army and Naval officers, but also of specialized trained research officials in the relative scientific fields, (including technological, economic, financial and psychological scholars,) is of determining influence in modern warfare.

Such analysis and interpretation must be done with immediacy and speedily transmitted to the intelligence services of those departments which, in some cases, would have been supplying the essential raw materials of information.

But there is another element in modern warfare, and that is the psychological attack against the moral and spiritual defenses of a nation. In this attack the most powerful weapon is radio. The use of radio as a weapon, though effectively employed by Germany, is still to be perfected. But this perfection can be realized only by planning, and planning is dependent upon accurate information. From this information action could be carried out by appropriate agencies.

The mechanism of this service to the various departments should be under the direction of a Coordinator of Strategic Information who would be responsible directly to the President. This Coordinator could be assisted by an advisory panel consisting of the Director of FBI, the Directors of the Army and Navy Intelligence Service, with corresponding officials from other governmental departments principally concerned.

The attached chart shows the allocation of and the interrelation between the general duties to be discharged under the appropriate directors. Much of the personnel would be drawn from the Army and Navy and other departments of the government, and it will be seen from the chart that the proposed centralized unit will neither displace nor encroach upon the FBI, Army and Navy Intelligence, or any other department of the government.

The basic purpose of this Service of Strategic Information is to constitute a means by which the President, as Commander-in-Chief, and his Strategic Board would have available accurate and complete enemy intelligence reports upon which military operational decisions could be based.

William J. Donovan

Washington, D.C.
June 10, 1941

Donovan

CONFIDENTIAL

Appendix B:

DESIGNATING A COORDINATOR OF INFORMATION

By virtue of the authority vested in me as President of the United States and as Commander in Chief of the Army and Navy of the United States, it is ordered as follows:

1. There is hereby established the position of Coordinator of Information, with authority to collect and analyze all information and data, which may bear upon national security; to correlate such information and data, and to make such information and data available to the President and to such departments and officials of the Government as the President may determine; and to carry out, when requested by the President, such supplementary activities as may facilitate the securing of information important for national security not now available to the Government.

2. The several departments and agencies of the government shall make available to the Coordinator of Information all and any such information and data relating to national security as the Coordinator, with the approval of the President, may from time to time request.

3. The Coordinator of Information may appoint such committees, consisting of appropriate representatives of the various departments and agencies of the Government, as he may deem necessary to assist him in the performance of his functions.

4. Nothing in the duties and responsibilities of the Coordinator of Information shall in any way interfere with or impair the duties and responsibilities of the regular military and naval advisers of the President as Commander in Chief of the Army and Navy.

5. Within the limits of such funds as may be allocated to the Coordinator of Information by the President, the Coordinator may employ necessary personnel and make provision for the necessary supplies, facilities, and services.

6. William J. Donovan is hereby designated as Coordinator of Information.

(Signed) Franklin D. Roosevelt

THE WHITE HOUSE
July 11, 1941

* * * * * *

(Federal Register, Tues., July 15, 1941. p. 3422-23.
F.R. Doc. 41-4969; Filed, July 12, 1941; 11:53 a.m.)

INTELLIGENCE RIVALRIES IN WARTIME

Hoover versus Donovan

INTELLIGENCE RIVALRIES IN WARTIME

Dennis DeBrandt

On 11 July 1941, President Roosevelt signed a directive creating a Coordinator of Information (COI) with the authority to collect, analyze and correlate data pertaining to the national security and to carry out, as requested by the President, "... as may facilitate the securing of information important for national security not now available to the Government."[1] In authorizing this activity, which would be directed by William J. Donovan, the President instructed the "departments and agencies of the Government (to) make available any and all such information and data relating to national security as the Coordinator with the approval of the President may from time to time request." The COI also was empowered to appoint committees composed of whatever agency representation he deemed necessary. With this directive in hand, Donovan set about to create his agency.

Before the directive was signed, Donovan had prepared a "Memorandum of Establishment of Service of Strategic Information" that may have reflected the philosophical underpinnings of what he had in mind for his new agency.[2] He wrote that without the linkage of strategy to intelligence, strategy is helpless and intelligence is useless. He saw intelligence gathering as an attempt to predict what was going to happen and to take steps to gain the advantage. He believed the US lacked an effective service for analyzing, comprehending, and appraising the intentions and resources of potential enemies. In his view, the US had scattered through various departments information concerning the military, navy, air and economic potential of the Axis which, if gathered and studied by trained personnel, could yield valuable information. Consequently, he called for setting up a central intelligence organization that would collect directly or through existing departments information concerning actual or potential enemies.

On 14 July 1941, Roosevelt sent a letter to the Attorney General advising that he had appointed Donovan as COI.[3] Possibly to soften FBI Director Hoover's opposition, the letter stressed that Donovan's work was "not intended to supersede or duplicate or involve any direction of the activities of established agencies already obtaining and interpreting defense information." The letter ended with a request that the Attorney General and his associates extend the full use of their services and informational facilities to Donovan.

Creating a New Agency

The COI had to start from scratch. One of the President's sons, James Roosevelt, was appointed liaison officer for Donovan. By the latter part of August 1941, he had asked Edward Tamm, the Assistant to the FBI Director, to designate a liaison contact who would have daily contact with the COI.[4] Tamm extended the FBI's complete cooperation to the new agency.

On 5 September 1941, General Miles, the head of the Army's Military Intelligence Division (MID), wrote a memorandum to Army Chief of Staff George C. Marshall citing the fact that, while MID and the Office of Naval Intelligence (ONI) were performing "undercover work in a limited way," a single, civilian agency could do it better. ONI finally joined this position in October, when Vincent Astor, Roosevelt's coordinator of intelligence in New York, raised the issue of costs in supporting undercover intelligence, which involved sending agents into hostile or denied areas to organize resistance groups. [5] The fact that the US was not yet at war evidently was not considered in these discussions and in sorting out which agency would do what.

Tamm told Donovan that the FBI wanted to take a "middle-of-the-road approach," in that the Bureau did not want to be perceived as trying to get out of anything or of keeping anything it should not have. Donovan said that he wanted to do what Hoover wanted, and, if the FBI was more comfortable with the COI collecting intelligence, Donovan would accept the task. But he would still want the Bureau "down there," referring to South America.

This issue resurfaced in late December 1941, when Donovan again informed the FBI that the Army and Navy had asked him to take over and handle all of their intelligence work in the Western Hemisphere. Because Hoover believed that he had exclusive responsibility in the area, he asked that the issue be placed on the agenda for regular weekly conferences among the various agencies so that he could hear what the services thought.

Cracks in the System

The apparent reasonableness shown by the FBI in August may reflect bureaucratic parrying to size up a new opponent. Hoover would wait for the right opportunities to assert the FBI's interests. This surface calm broke in September 1941, when the New York Office of the FBI reported that a British Security Coordinator (BSC) official named "Stott" was worried because some of Donovan's men had been talking too much about "... sending men into Europe and that was just a common matter of round-table discussion among them." [6] "Stott" actually was William Stephenson, head of BSC.

Meanwhile, the question of the FBI's exclusive intelligence operations in the Western Hemisphere continued to fester. Ultimately, Hoover would aver that the FBI either would have total control over this function in the region or it would withdraw entirely and concentrate on domestic operations. Hoover probably was ambivalent about operating outside of the US because he had no personal experience abroad; he did not understand or trust an alien environment in which his authority could be severely limited. To Hoover, control was everything, and he viewed the establishment of the COI as a threat to that control. On the other hand, Hoover could not completely resist the allure of exerting his power worldwide. This issue would continue until the founding of the CIA in 1947.

The State Department also saw the COI as a threat and wanted it dissolved. It claimed Donovan was meddling in the business of others. [7] When Assistant Secretary of State Adolf Berle inquired as to whether or not the FBI had any knowledge of "Donovan's group" infringing on the responsibilities of the FBI, Tamm told him that it did not. [8]

The Rockefeller Connection

In contrast with the suspicion Hoover felt for Donovan, Hoover immediately worked out a cordial relationship in 1940 with Nelson Rockefeller, head of the Office of Coordinator of Inter-American Affairs, a US propaganda agency aimed at Latin America. Rockefeller quickly won Hoover's approval by expressing an early interest in working in the region with the FBI, which was organizing its Latin American Special Intelligence Service (SIS).

The SIS was to conduct investigations to develop information dealing with financial, economic, political, and subversive activities. Rockefeller thought that information developed by his organization might materially assist the FBI. He also thought that the FBI could help him to learn what propaganda individual countries were spreading, thereby allowing the US to formulate its own. As a result of Rockefeller's request, Hoover designated P.E. Foxworth of the FBI to be named to an "economic commission" to travel to Latin America to assess the situation there.

By October 1941, the matter of distributing pro-American propaganda had been divided between Rockefeller and the COI, with the latter responsible for all areas outside the Western Hemisphere. Rockefeller reiterated that propaganda could be predicated only on information provided by an intelligence service operating in the area. Berle had recommended to Rockefeller that his organization review FBI reports for this purpose, but Rockefeller demurred until he got Hoover's approval. [9]

Increasing Suspicion

On 17 October 1941, Colonel Robert A. Solborg, COI Chief of Operations for Special Activities, and his Deputy, Major M. Preston Goodfellow, advised Tamm that they were setting up "strongarm squads" to organize groups of saboteurs, propagandists and others to "... operate affirmatively in Axis-dominated countries." [10] Solborg avoided specific reference to Latin American operations. In terms of the FBI's role in Latin America, Solborg noted that the FBI was to operate as an intelligence agency there, while the COI would operate as a "counter" agency to offset fifth columnists and the like. He promised to keep the FBI advised of what he was doing.

FBI suspicion of the COI increased in November 1941, when the Bureau learned that BSC was trying to get information about the US Army and other internal US matters through the COI. The FBI also learned that ONI had complained that BSC was making similar inquiries through ONI. BSC denied the charge, saying that the COI had requested "mountains of stuff" from BSC concerning military and naval operations throughout the world. [11] In an internal document, William Stephenson had said that BSC's existence was based on liaison with Hoover but not just as an SIS function. Stephenson was using BSC to assure aid to the UK and to get the US into the war. [12] Hoover could not help much in these two areas, but Donovan played a key role in assisting the British in accomplishing these objectives.

The West Coast Issue

In December 1941, Hoover learned directly from Donovan of the latter's appointment of a Colonel Buxton to be COI representative on the West Coast. [13] Hoover asked if Donovan intended to establish an area comptroller or coordinator, similar to the one in New York City. Donovan replied that it was not his intention, but Hoover later indicated that he did not believe the disclaimer. Citing the harmonious relations on the West Coast among government agencies, Hoover told Donovan that any such setup was not necessary or desirable. If an area comptroller were to be established, however, Hoover said he hoped that a well-qualified man would be selected.

Representation in London

Hoover's distrust and dislike of Donovan manifested itself in other ways. In a conversation Donovan had with H.H. Clegg, a ranking official with the FBI, who in the previous year had conducted a survey in London on Hoover's behalf, probably about assigning FBI representatives there, Donovan reported that the British were pleased that the FBI was not pushing them to speed up their discussions of intelligence problems and the issue of FBI representation in

London.[14] According to Clegg, Donovan thought one of his main accomplishments was helping to pave the way in the UK for an FBI representative to obtain valuable information on most confidential matters. Hoover noted at the bottom of this memorandum, "If I recall correctly, I think we were there before the Colonel (Donovan) arrived." Clegg informed Hoover, however, that Donovan did precede the FBI to London and that his trip resulted in a series of articles on fifth column activities.[15] According to Clegg, these articles distressed the British and initially complicated the ability of the first FBI representative to deal with authorities in London. Clegg, however, was unaware of the vital role Donovan played in sending US destroyers to the UK in exchange for bases in the Caribbean basin and of the British view that Donovan's mission was crucial to their war effort.

The Breaking Point

The polite but wary relations between Hoover and Donovan came undone two days after the attack on Pearl Harbor, when Roosevelt issued a directive ordering Donovan to coordinate "North American agencies," meaning Canadian, British and US agencies. Hoover countered on 23 December with a suggested presidential directive that stipulated that the FBI was and should be the coordinating authority within the US and the Western Hemisphere. Roosevelt signed this Hoover-inspired directive without reading it. When Donovan protested, Roosevelt admitted his inattention and asked his intelligence chiefs to sort things out. In a five-page memorandum personally delivered by Hoover to the Attorney General, Hoover issued an ultimatum that the FBI should either have single control of intelligence operations in the Western Hemisphere or that it should operate only within the confines of the US and its territories.[16] The directive in question was not available for review in this article. According to Hoover, however, it formalized the FBI's relationship with the British and Canadian intelligence services. It must have asked for exclusivity in these relationships on issues and operations pertaining to the Western Hemisphere. Hoover portrayed the FBI as a "service agency" for State, Rockefeller's organization, MID, and ONI. Pointedly, he left out the COI, which, under the President's directive founding that organization, should have been a primary recipient of FBI intelligence.

In the memorandum, Hoover briefly reviewed the history of the Bureau's involvement in foreign intelligence operations, saying that in 1940 he was instructed to establish an informal but close relationship with the British and Canadians. He added that, at the same time, the FBI was directed to set up the SIS in Latin America. He cited the fact that, in the early part of 1941, MID and ONI had asked the COI to take over intelligence collection in the areas abroad where it was previously agreed they should have primary responsibility. But Hoover also acknowledged that the COI had not undertaken operations in the Western Hemisphere and that Donovan had said he would not send anyone there without first consulting Hoover.

Zeroing in, Hoover advised the Attorney General that, after the directive of 23 December had been issued, he received a call from Donovan, who seemed "... considerably put out ..." Donovan said that he thought it necesary for him to send COI agents (officers) to Latin America because the FBI could not gather the information the COI needed. According to Hoover, Donovan thought his agents should work together with Special Agents of the FBI. Hoover disagreed. He said that, because of the delicacy and danger of operating in Latin America, one agency should be responsible. Hoover saw confusion and embarrassment flowing from such an arrangement. He then asssterted that if Donovan were to operate in Latin America, the FBI should get out. Hoover concluded that, unless Donovan were to take over intelligence work in the US, the FBI should have a formalized relationship with British and Canadian intelligence concerning civilian intelligence matters in the US.

Several days later, on being informed by the FBI's Foxworth in New York that BSC said it could give information only to Donovan, Hoover reviewed for Foxworth the events of the month before, citing the fact that Donovan had held up the Hoover-inspired Presidential directive and that a meeting was to be held soon to sort things out. [17] Hoover said that ONI, MID, State, and the FBI agreed that SIS in Latin America should be run by the FBI. Hoover related that the new MID Commander, General Lee, had never asked Donovan to take over anything in the Western Hemisphere and that Donovan's group was not capable of it. (General Miles, Lee's predecesor, was the one who made the request.) Admiral Wilkinson of ONI and Adolf Berle of State, Hoover said, were of the same opinion.

Continued Maneuvering

The conference to resolve these differences took place on 6 January 1942, with Hoover, Donovan, Berle, General Lee, Admiral Wilkinson, and Colonel Bissel of the War Department attending. [18] The conference revised the directive of 23 December. The new directive gave all responsibility for intelligence gathering in Latin America to the FBI, and it required other agencies to clear with the FBI any intelligence work they intended to conduct in that region. The directive was approved by Donovan, Wilkinson, and Lee. On 14 January 1942, however, Berle told Tamm that Donovan had written a letter to General Lee and possibly to the Attorney General indicating that the directive was not based on a real agreement. [19] The next day Berle told Tamm that he had received a letter from Donovan transmitting the directive drawn up at the Justice Department. [20] While Donovan said he approved the directive, he set forth in considerable detail his desire to set up a "Board of Strategy" in Canada and in other countries.

Berle characterized Donovan's letter as agreeing to the directive in the first place and then going ahead with plans to ignore it. Berle added that he thought that it was a waste of time to try to get Donovan to agree to anything and that the only thing Donovan would understand would be a "big switch" wielded by the President. Hoover, in recounting a telephone conversation he had with Admiral Wilkinson, told his assistants on 16 January 1942 that the President had approved the directive. [21]

"Refuse Any Request"

Now that Hoover had the President's directive behind him, BSC representatives approached the FBI concerning radio intercepts. [22] No mention was made of where the intercepts occurred or of their substance. BSC thought all of these intercepts should be handed over to the FBI, with the exception of specific ones they thought of interest to the COI, and these would be so marked on the copies sent to the FBI. The issue of direct COI contacts with BSC also came up in this exchange, causing the FBI to suggest that BSC should cite the President's directive that had been the subject of sharp dispute between Donovan and Hoover. Hoover wrote at the bottom of the memorandum, recounting this conversation, "Tell them (BSC) to flatly refuse any request of this kind and it can be said it was on orders of the FBI."

At this point, the real fear was that BSC was playing the COI and the FBI off against one another. Berle spoke with Tamm in March 1942, recounting a meeting he had with the Attorney General and the British Ambassador, Lord Halifax. [23] The issue was whether BSC was an operations or liaison group, with Halifax contending it was the latter. Up to this point, BSC had been very much an operational organization in the US, working both with and without the knowledge of US authorities.

Berle thought there had been recently a shift in operations with the transfer of men and operations from BSC control to the COI. Berle added that he thought the FBI should be aware of this activity. Tamm confirmed that there had been a change in the tempo of activity by BSC in the previous 10 days, although he did not specify what that was. Berle cautioned that the FBI probably was not entitled to a list of names of operatives shifted to the COI from BSC but that it was entitled to the names of British operatives transferred to the US under BSC control.

Some Cooperation

The estrangement between Hoover and Donovan did not prevent some sensible collaboration at the working level between the two agencies. In March 1942, the COI established a section to maintain contact with foreign political groups in the US. The State Department had performed this work, but it thought that it could no longer do so because it was also dealing with foreign missions of the same nationalities. The COI advised that it would ask the FBI to investigate these groups, as needed. The FBI representative agreed to this action, and he recommended that a special liaison be established to accomplish this work.[24] Hoover apparently did not see these contacts between the COI and foreign political groups in the US as encroachment on his responsibilities.

Later that month, an FBI representative met with David Bruce, Donovan's deputy, and David Williamson, head of the Geographical Section of the COI. Williamson acknowledged that the men they were sending abroad were not the best but that Donovan believed inefficient coverage was better than no coverage. In this meeting, Bruce and Williamson stressed the fact that they were not operating in Latin America, bowing to the reality that the issue had been settled.[25]

Origins of the OSS

In April 1942, Hoover wrote a confidential memorandum to the Attorney General stating that the British were conducting schools to train saboteurs, one of which was attended by an FBI Special Agent and another by seven of Donovan's men.[26] Hoover said that the President and the War and Navy Departments had approved a new organization in March 1942, which would be similar to the British commandos. It would be headed by Donovan, who had authority to employ 2,000 agents (officers). In addition, according to Hoover, Donovan had authority to set up his own air force to place agents in enemy-occupied areas. These new agents were to be trained at three large estates in the Washington, D.C., area, and they were being offered commissions as captains with rapid advancement to follow. Hoover reported that the President by Executive Order could remove any individual from any department in the government and place him in a pool from which Donovan could draw personnel, an idea that must have horrified Hoover. He noted that all of Donovan's people acted as recruiting agents and that they had tried to recruit the only FBI agent at the British school.

These training facilities and paramilitary missions preceded the creation of the Office of Strategic Services (OSS), which the COI was renamed after being placed under the control of the Joint Chiefs of Staff (JCS) in 1942. Hoover expressed alarm, as he had in the past, that this new organization would "... take over the legitimate functions of the FBI, particularly those relating to the (FBI's) SIS operations."[27] Hoover reiterated his desire to withdraw completely from South America, if Donovan intended to operate there. Berle assuaged Hoover, saying that Donovan was to operate under the Joint Intelligence Committe (JIC). Berle was the ranking member of the JIC, and he promised to keep a close check on Donovan's activities. He also offered the FBI representation on the committee, which the FBI accepted. Admiral Wilkinson, who chaired the first meeting, said that, while the JIC lacked a formal charter, it would serve as a gatekeeper for all papers prepared for the JCS or the Combined Chiefs of Staff.[28]

Berle thought this approval authority would curb Donovan. In one view, the creation of the JIC was based on the false assumption that coordination itself was sufficient to meet the different intelligence requirements of the services, a theme Hoover and the services had been playing since 1939. In actuality, the JIC represented a systemic failure of the US to translate an acknowledged need for intelligence into a valid organizational response. Within a month, Donovan became convinced that the JIC was useless.

Conclusion

Donovan often was his own worst enemy as a result of his zealous disregard for the bureaucratic sensitivities of the other intelligence chiefs, particularly Hoover. The attack on Pearl Harbor, which should have caused the intelligence chiefs to look beyond their parochial interests, did not appear to have changed a thing. Hoover maintained that the principle of cooperation among the existing agencies, mostly on his terms, was all that was necessary to fulfill US intelligence requirements.

And then there is the role of the President. The war forced him to take action he probably would have preferred to avoid in appointing Donovan as an intelligence coordinator. The action was a typical Roosevelt half-measure, because the established agencies' activities and responsibilities were not to be affected by this appointment. He invested Donovan with considerable power, but he evidently did not back it with much support when the other intelligence chiefs balked or withheld cooperation. Roosevelt had no firm intelligence strategy and that, combined with his inattention to or encouragement of the bureaucratic infighting, hindered Donovan's ability to put together a coordinated intelligence capability.

NOTES

1. Undated directive "Designating a Coordinator of Information" signed by Franklin D. Roosevelt.
2. Signed, William J. Donovan, 10 June 1941, at Washington, D.C.
3. Signed, Franklin D. Roosevelt, 14 July 1941, at the White House.
4. Edward A. Tamm, FBI Assistant to the Director, memorandum to Hoover, 20 August 1941.
5. William R. Corson, *The Armies of Ignorance, The Rise of the American Intelligence Empire*, The Dial Press/James Wade, NY, 1977 p. 145.
6. P.E. Foxworth, Special Agent in Charge, FBI, New York, memorandum to Hoover, 13 September 1941.
7. Philip Knightly, *The Second Oldest Profession, Spies and Spying in the Twentieth Century*, W.W. Horton Co, NY, 1986 p. 223.
8. E.A. Tamm memorandum to Hoover, 2 October 1941.
9. E.A. Tamm memorandum to Hoover, 2 October 1941.
10. E.A. Tamm memorandum to Hoover, 17 October 1941.
11. P.E. Foxworth memorandum to Hoover, 5 November 1941.
12. William Stevenson, *Intrepid's Last Case*, Villard Books, NY 1983, p. 138.
13. Hoover memorandum to Assistants to the Director, Clyde Tolson and E.A. Tamm and Assistant Director D.H. Ladd, 2 December 1941.
14. H.H. Clegg, FBI Assistant Director, memorandum to Hoover, 29 November 1941.
15. H.H. Clegg memorandum to Hoover, 10 December 1941.
16. Hoover memorandum to the Attorney General, marked personal and confidential, 31 December 1941.
17. Hoover memorandum to Tolson, Tamm and Ladd, 2 January 1942.
18. Hoover memorandum to the Attorney General, 6 January 1942.
19. E.A. Tamm memorandum to Hoover, 14 January 1942.
20. E.A. Tamm memorandum to Hoover, 15 January 1942.
21. Hoover memorandum to Tolson, Tamm and Ladd, 16 January 1942.
22. D.M. Ladd memorandum to Hoover, 16 January 1942.
23. E.A. Tamm memorandum to Hoover, 12 March 1942.
24. G.C. Burton memorandum to Hoover, 6 March 1942.
25. R.R. Roach memorandum to D.M. Ladd, 26 March 1942.
26. Hoover memorandum to the Attorney General, marked personal and confidential, 4 April 1942.
27. E.A. Tamm memorandum to Hoover, 15 June 1942.
28. Corson, op. cit. p. 164.

THE OSS ASSESSMENT PROGRAM

How CIA's predecessor separated sheep from goats and launched a modern management technique

THE OSS ASSESSMENT PROGRAM *

Dr. Donald W. MacKinnon

During the first year of its operation, there were three channels of entry into OSS: recruitment of military personnel by the Personnel Procurement Branch, recruitment of civilians by the Civilian Personnel Branch, and recruitment of both military and civilian personnel through the initiative of individual OSS members—all of this without benefit of any professional or uniform screening process. Nobody knew who would make a good spy or an effective guerrilla fighter. Consequently, large numbers of misfits were recruited from the very beginning, and this might have continued had it not been for several disastrous operations such as one in Italy for which, on the assumption that it takes dirty men to do dirty works, some OSS men had been recruited directly from the ranks of Murder, Inc., and the Philadelphia Purple Gang. The need for professional assistance in selection was obvious, but resisted by many in the organization.

In October 1943 an OSS official back from London suggested that a program of psychological-psychiatric assessment similar to that in the English War Office Selection Boards be set up in the OSS. This idea was picked up and pushed by Robert C. Tryon, psychologist on leave from the University of California, who was Deputy Chief, Planning Staff, OSS. He recommended that an assessment center be set up in the Schools and Training Branch and in collaboration with three other California Ph.D.'s, James A. Hamilton, John W. Gardner, and Joseph Gengerelli, he set about planning the first assessment center in the United States.

By November a physical facility had been acquired: the Willard Estate, the spacious residence and grounds of the owners of the Hotel Willard in Washington which was to become Station S (for Schools and Training, though most preferred to think the S stood for Secret) in Fairfax, Virginia, some 18 miles from Washington.

The first planning conference for the program of Station S was held in early December with Henry A. Murray (Harvard) and Donald Adams (Duke) joining the California psychologists. Shortly thereafter, the director of OSS authorized the establishment of an assessment unit, and 15 days later the first assessment was held with a skeleton staff.

Although the push for an assessment program in OSS came from the California psychologists, the ultimate form and nature of the program was most importantly shaped by Henry A. Murray.

In addition to the speed with which it was initiated, the assessment program suffered from other handicaps. Although backed by General Donovan and some of the bureau chiefs, it was opposed by others and especially by the military. We lacked

---

* Adapted from "How Assessment Centers Got Started in the United States: The OSS Assessment Program," copyright 1974 Development Dimensions, Inc., Pittsburgh, Pa. Reprinted by permission.

The OSS Assessment Program

knowledge about the assignments, most of them novel, to which our assessees would be sent. Without job analyses, we did not know what specifically we were assessing for. We needed experts to write job descriptions, but there were none in the field. At best, job assignments were described by single terms: language expert, cartographer, news analyst. Had we known what specific skills would be required there would have been so many of them as to preclude a testing of them all.

Later we would learn more about what was required for successful execution of OSS assignments from branch chiefs who had by then received more specific job descriptions, from reports of returnees, from assessors who had received training in the OSS schools, and from assessors who had traveled abroad for firsthand observations.

In the beginning it was the lack of specific knowledge that led us to conclude that our assessments could not be of the specific skills of a given candidate for a specific job but rather in each case an assessment of the "man as a whole," the general structure of his being, and his strengths and weaknesses for rather generally described environments and situations. As it turned out, there were some advantages to our having taken this stance toward assessment, for we soon discovered that very often assessees were never assigned to the job for which they were recruited. Typically, two to eight months elapsed between assessment and job assignment overseas. The candidate had first to be trained and by the time that had been accomplished, the war had moved on and the job for which he had been recruited no longer needed to be done.

Only those destined for overseas assignment were assessed; those who remained in the States were exempt. At first our assessment reports were only for the information of bureau chiefs. They were free to accept or reject our recommendations as they saw fit. After two months all that changed. By order of General Donovan only those who received a positive recommendation from Station S could be sent overseas. This was personally flattering, but very frustrating to our scientific egos since it meant that anything like pure validity studies of our assessment operation could not be made. This order meant that Station S with its three-and-a-half-day program would not be able to assess all those destined for overseas duty. Thus it was that in late winter 1944, a one-day assessment center, Station W, was set up in Washington to assess a large number of candidates, many of whom were to be assigned to headquarters and rear bases overseas rather than to operations in the field. Two months later a center to assess candidates recruited on the West Coast was established at Laguna Beach, California. This was Station WS. Later assessment stations to screen native agents were set up in Ceylon, Kunming (Yunnan Province), Calcutta, and Hsian. During the period of their operation, Stations S and W assessed 5,391 recruits.

The program for Station S, set up hurriedly and with little knowledge of what OSS assignments would entail, was bound to undergo many changes. There were seven periods in the history of Station S, but there were no radical changes in the program during the last six periods (June 1944 to V-J Day, September 1945) during which time I served as Director of Station S, and this is the program I shall describe.

I have spoken of some handicaps under which the assessment program had to operate. Let me mention two others. From its inception, the OSS had to guard against infiltrations by foreign agents, and, of course, if its operations were to succeed they had to be kept secret. But these concerns hardly justified the extreme secrecy which was maintained and which merely added to the atmosphere of cloak-and-dagger mystery that enshrouded the organization. This was nowhere more obvious than in the recruitment of OSS personnel. Barred from mentioning the OSS by name but free to talk about mysterious, exciting overseas assignment with a government agency, the

The OSS Assessment Program

pitch made by OSS recruiters was especially attractive to the bored, to the pathologically adventuresome, to those neurotically attracted to danger, and to psychopaths in general. Thus, we had more than our share of misfits to weed out, and of course it is psychopaths who have a special talent to make a good impression over brief periods of time. Under the given circumstances, the branch representatives who briefed candidates for their visit to Station S were wary about telling them much about the work for which they had been recruited. Many, when seen in assessment, had no idea of what their assignment would be, and some even thought they were in the State Department!

The other handicap we faced, or so it seemed at first, was that we would not know whom we were assessing. That is, they would not be allowed to reveal to us or to the other members of their assessment class their true names. In December 1943 when Station S was established, many of the recruits into OSS were refugees from Europe, often with families and relatives in occupied territory. If their true identity were to become known to others in the organization who had infiltrated it they might become subject to blackmail through threats to relatives abroad.

Not knowing who our assessees were, was not, however, entirely disadvantageous. Quite innocently we could be a check on the misuse of nepotism, turning down even a Roosevelt or a Donovan if his performance at Station S left something to be desired.

In any case, we had to live with the anonymity of our assessees, so what we did was to turn it into an assessment exercise!

Assessment at Station S ran in two-week cycles, during which three groups of 18 candidates would be assessed: the first group would arrive on a Sunday afternoon and leave the following Thursday morning; that afternoon a second group would arrive and, assessed over the weekend, would leave Monday morning; that afternoon a third group would arrive and leave Friday morning. That weekend the staff would draw its breath and prepare for the next two-week cycle which would begin again on Sunday afternoon.

Each recruit for OSS, upon arrival in Washington, would report to the Branch representative who would supervise him throughout training and who had authority then and there to reject the candidate if he was obviously unsuitable. Otherwise and usually, the recruit would be told something, but not much, about the type of work for which he had volunteered, and he would fill out a Student Information Sheet.

He was then informed that he would spend the next three and a half days at an assessment school in the country, where he would be asked many questions and given many tests by a group of psychologists and psychiatrists. He was told there was no reason to feel apprehensive, that most who had gone through the school had enjoyed it. He was urged to do his best. He was also told he would go incognito for his own protection. And finally he chose a name by which he would be known during assessment.

During that day in Washington he was given a medical examination, and that afternoon he would report to Schools and Training Headquarters, an old brick school house that stood where Watergate now stands. He would report at 3:30 if he was an enlisted man, at 4:00 if a civilian, and at 4:30 if an officer. Reporting was staggered in this fashion so that each might know the status of some of the men in his own group, the fewer the better, but not the others, e.g., no officer would know who were enlisted men and who were civilians, et cetera.

Upon arrival at Headquarters, the candidate would be taken to a room, stripped of his clothing and anything else that might identify him, issued army fatigues and boots, and ushered into a waiting area. At 5:00 the group would be put in a completely closed army van and driven over the eighteen winding miles to Station S.

After a brief welcome and orientation to the program, the candidates were told that during their stay at S each would have to build up and maintain as completely as possible a cover story for himself, claiming to have been born where he wasn't, to have been educated in institutions other than those he had attended, to have been engaged in work or profession not his own, and to live now in a place that was not his true residence. The cover story was to be maintained with staff and students alike at all times except under "X conditions," at which time candidates could reveal anything about themselves except their name and true identity. X conditions prevailed when filling out a Personal History Form, in a Life History Interview, when a staff member established X conditions, and when in case of need a student asked for X conditions and a staff member granted them.

Thus, Station S was one grand simulation, each candidate having the task of consistently simulating a person he was not. Since many of the candidates would eventually be living abroad under cover, the relevancy of the cover story task seemed clear enough.

The variables rated on the Station S report for each candidate offer a rationale for the assessment exercises which were developed for the program. The rated dimensions were these: Motivation, Practical Intelligence, Emotional Stability, Social Relations, Leadership, Physical Ability, Observation and Reporting, Propaganda Skills, and Maintaining Cover. Each variable was rated on a 6-point scale: Very Inferior, Inferior, Low Average, High Average, Superior, Very Superior. Note that to force a spread of ratings, using more of the whole scale, no rating of Average was given. If the dimension was not measured, that fact was indicated in the final report.

Components of each of the dimensions were printed on the face sheet in the following manner:

Motivation: energy, zest, effort, initiative, war morale, interest in assignment.

Practical Intelligence: speed and accuracy of judgment, resourcefulness in solving problems.

Emotional Stability: emotional control and maturity, absence of neurotic symptoms.

Social Relations: social awareness, goodwill, teamwork, tact, absence of annoying traits.

Leadership: social initiative, organizing ability, ability to evoke cooperation.

Physical Ability: agility, daring, ruggedness, stamina.

Observation and Reporting: ability to search, question, observe and recall, infer, report.

Propaganda Skills: ability to affect others through acts, words, or displays.

Maintaining Cover: caution, ability to remain inconspicuous, bluff, mislead, keep a secret.

If one of the components of a variable was especially high, let us say tact, it would be underlined; if especially low it would be crossed out.

The OSS Assessment Program

The core of the assessment program was a rather detailed life-history psychiatric Interview conducted by a senior staff member. In preparation for the interview, the interviewer read a Personal History Form which the candidate had filled out as well a Projective Questionnaire, a Sentence Completion Test, a Health Questionnaire, and a Work Conditions Survey which described 43 conditions that the candidate rated on a six-point scale, ranging from (1) "Highly desirable" to (6) "Would make job impossible." In the light of all this material the interviewer had some impression of the candidate and knew the areas in which he would want to get more information in the interview.

Two conventional measures of intellectual ability were administered, the *Otis Self-Administering Test of Ability* and a Vocabulary Test, plus two tests of special aptitudes, the *Bennett Mechanical Comprehension Test* and the *Signal Corps Code Aptitude Test*, but we were less interested in our candidates' scores on intelligence tests than in the effectiveness with which they used whatever intelligence they had. And this, as well as most of the dimensions of behavior which we rated, was more clearly to be seen in the most novel aspect of the OSS program—the situational tests which we developed, tests which today would be more often referred to as simulations or simulation exercises. Our objective was to observe as much of our candidates' behavior in situations which simulated as realistically as feasible the kinds of situations they would be likely to encounter in OSS assignments.

For those destined to work in Secret Intelligence, the abilities to search, to question, to observe and recall, to infer, and to report would be of crucial importance and a variety of tests (some situational) to tap the dimension we called Observation and Reporting were devised. Examples of such tests in which, of course, other variables could also be observed and rated were:

Belongings Test. In this test the candidate would be taken to a bedroom in which 26 items such as articles of clothing, written materials, a time table, newspaper clippings, a ticket receipt, etc., were placed openly on the bed, chairs, and tables. His task was to examine them, to size up the man who left them, to learn all he could about the person, what he was like, etc. Objects could be picked up and examined, but had to be replaced. After four minutes the candidate was taken to another room to answer a 36-item questionnaire, a test of the candidate's ability to observe and draw correct inferences.

Map Memory Test. Here the candidate is to assume that he is an agent operating in the field and that he has just made a secret rendezvous with a courier who has a map of the territory that the agent will be covering. After a few minutes the courier must leave with the map and since it would be dangerous for the agent to have it, he must memorize it. After eight minutes to examine the map, it is taken away and the candidate answers a set of multiple-choice statements about the terrain of the map.

Interrogation Test. In this situational test a junior staff member plays the role (a standardized one) of an escaped prisoner of war who is interrogated by the candidate. Background material for the interrogation is supplied in the form of a map and some general information about the imprisonment and escape of the prisoner, who had served as a tail gunner of a B-29 before its crash landing. Another staff member sits by and rates the candidate's skill in Developing Rapport, Asking Productive Questions, Following Up Leads and Hints by the "Prisoner," etc.

For those destined to work in Morale Operations (MO), the ability to affect others through acts, words, or displays would be crucial, and special tests were devised in

The OSS Assessment Program

which these skills might be displayed, thus providing the assessors with some estimate of the Propaganda Skills of candidates. Two examples of this type of test of propaganda skills would be the *OWI Test* and the *Manchuria Test*. In the former, a test of one's sensitivity to cultural differences, the candidate was to assume that he was working for OWI in Korea and knew nothing about the country. He had 20 minutes to indicate the kind of information he would want to have in order to work up a propaganda program designed to win Koreans to our side. In the *Manchuria Test*, the candidate, given some background facts, was, over a day and a half, to prepare two pieces of propaganda to lower the morale of Japanese railway workers and guards on the South Manchurian Railway. In this task candidates were urged to use whatever graphic skills they had.

One of the better known of our situational tests was the *Brook Test* (a Leaderless Group Situation), in which a group of six candidates would be taken to a shallow, quiet stream whose banks were eight feet apart. On one bank was a heavy rock, on the other a log. There were trees on both sides and scattered on the side where the group stood were a number of boards, none long enough to reach from bank to bank, three lengths of rope, a pulley, and a barrel with both ends knocked out.

The candidates were told: "In this problem you have to use your imagination. Before you, you see a raging torrent so deep and so fast that it is quite impossible to rest anything upon the bottom of the stream. The banks are sheer, so it will be impossible to work except from the top of them.

"You are on a mission in the field, and having come to this brook you are faced with the task of transporting this delicate range finder, skillfully camouflaged as a log, to the far bank, and of bringing that box of percussion caps, camouflaged as a rock, to this side. In carrying out this assignment, you may make use of any materials around here. When the job is done, all of you, as well as any material you used, are to be back on this side."[*]

The group was to work in an area about 15 feet along the bank marked by two white stakes.

In this exercise one could easily note the difference between asserted leadership and effective leadership, and ample opportunity was given to observe differences among the candidates on such variables as Energy and Initiative, Effective Intelligence, Social Relations, Leadership, and Physical Ability.

A second Leaderless Group Situation was *The Wall*. Here the candidates were led to a wall 10 feet high by 15 feet long. Behind the wall which the candidates could see was another wall of the same height and length, parallel to it, the two walls being eight feet apart. On the candidates' side of the wall there were a heavy log, an old board a few inches longer than the log, and a couple of 2 × 4s, two feet and three feet in length.

The candidates were informed (fancy being mixed with fact as in all situational tests) that although they could not see it, the barrier before them actually consisted of two walls (fact) separated by a 200-foot canyon (fancy). They were escaping from some Japanese soldiers. In order to save themselves they would have to get to the other side of the far wall and to fulfill their mission they would have to take their king-size bazooka (the log) with them. They might get across the wall in any way they wished, but they must not walk around the ends of the wall, and, of course, whoever or whatever fell into the canyon would be counted as lost.

---

[*] "Assessment of Men," OSS Assessment Staff, Holt, Rinehart and Wilson, 1948, pp. 95-96.

The OSS Assessment Program

The same variables observed and rated at *The Brook* were observed and rated at *The Wall*.

The Brook and *The Wall* gave some advantage to men with marked initiative and assertiveness. To discover real ability when leadership was assigned, five other field tests were employed. The task of the leader in the *Mined Road* was to get his group across a mined road in 10 minutes; in the *Sentry* to get his group, with one man wounded and unable to walk, across a road guarded by a sentry (played by a junior staff member in uniform) whose regular beat meant that for about 45 seconds of each of his tours he could not see the section of the road where the group would try to cross. In the *Agent's Room*, the leader has just received a radio message that a friendly agent had in a hurried getaway left some important papers behind; the task would be to recover the papers. The instructions were given at the entrance to a large, unused carriage house on the second floor of which was a crude living room (the agent's room). Members of the group were told that they had been passing as natives, had forged credentials, were dressed in native costume, and could speak the native tongue. Midway through this exercise a German guard armed with a rifle approached the carriage house.

The other two assigned leadership exercises, the *Blown Bridge* and *Killing the Mayor*, like the three just described, provided good opportunity to observe each candidate's leadership skills as well as other variables: Practical Intelligence, Emotional Stability, Social Relations, and Physical Ability.

An indoor, verbal counterpart of the outdoor, physical *Brook* and *Wall* exercises was a Leaderless Group Discussion. The topic was "What are the major postwar problems facing the United States and (if you have time) along what lines do you think they should be solved?" The dimensions observed and rated in this situation were Leadership, Effective Intelligence, Energy and Initiative, and Social Relations.

To measure resistance to stress and frustration tolerance, important facets of Emotional Stability, two situational tests were devised. *Construction*, which came to be known as *Behind the Barn*, for that was where this exercise was held, required the candidate to direct two helpers in the task of building a five-foot cube structure with seven-foot diagonals on the four sides, using a huge "tinker toy" set of materials. The candidate had 10 minutes in which to accomplish the task. All the physical work was to be done by the helpers, junior staff members who played the role of Kippy (passive, sluggish, and something of a stumblebum) and Buster (aggressive, critical, constantly making impractical suggestions). Both were insulting, faultfinding characters. In the history of Station S, this job was never completed in the allotted time. Some candidates gained insight into the problem, but more often they became so involved and so frustrated that they had difficulty in handling their frustration and controlling their anger. A few physically attacked their helpers, and some asked to be relieved from the program after this exercise.

After the *Construction* test, the candidate was taken aside by a senior staff member who in a *Post-Construction Interview* provided the candidate an opportunity for catharsis. Some admitted their anger and confessed to having almost hit their "helpers" while others, with quivering lips and trembling hands, denied they had been in any way emotionally upset in the exercise. This interview was also used to test the candidate's ability to maintain cover. Since a person is particularly inclined to break cover in moments of relaxation following stress, the interviewer would inquire about earlier similar experiences which the candidate had had and how he had acted then. If the candidate was not on guard he would be led into talking about past experiences of a similar kind in which he had performed better and this, of course, was a breaking of cover since X conditions had not been established.

In the *Stress Interview* proper, candidates, one at a time, were instructed that they have just been found by a night watchman in a government building in Washington going through papers in an office. The candidate is not an employee of the agency, nor does he have any identification papers. The night watchman is bringing him to the security office for questioning. The candidate was given 12 minutes in which to think up an innocent cover story that would explain his being in the building, after which he was to knock on a designated basement door. Upon being ordered to enter, he was seated in a dark room, the only light being a blinding spotlight directed at his face. For ten minutes he would be questioned about his presence in the building. At first quietly and in an understanding, sympathetic manner, he was encouraged to give more and more detail, then suddenly the questioner would turn sadistic, confronting him with inconsistencies and implausibilities in his story with ever-increasing tempo and crescendo of voice. The staff member who questioned the candidate was a New York trial lawyer skilled in techniques of cross-examination. Suddenly the examiner would break in with, "We now have abundant evidence you have not been telling the truth. That is all." Then after whispered conversation among the staff who had been sitting behind the examiner observing the candidate but not seen by him except as dim forms, the examiner would announce, "It is our decision that you have failed this test." After five seconds, during which his reactions were observed, he was told to go to a room on the third floor. There he found a staff member, feet on the desk, reading a paper, who would inquire, "How are things going?" and in this *Post-Stress Interview* many a candidate would break cover when sympathetically asked if he had ever been in a comparable situation. The *Stress* and *Post-Stress Interviews* provided ample opportunity to observe and to rate Emotional Stability, Maintaining Cover, and Motivation for assignment in OSS.

Late afternoon of the second day all candidates under 45 who had passed the physical examination before coming to Station S ran an *Obstacle Course* especially designed to test physical agility and daring.

That evening candidates were assigned in pairs to act in *Improvisations*. These were role-playing dyadic situations dreamed up by the staff in sessions referred to as "Brain storms" and tailor-made for each candidate to help resolve doubts which the staff might still have about him. For example, there might be some question left as to how Candidate A takes criticism or rejection, and how much tact Candidate B can muster. The situations they might be called upon to improvise, the emphasis being put upon what they would actually do if confronted with such a situation rather than acting it out, could be the following:

"A. moved to a small city about three months ago and opened a business there. He has been doing quite well and one month ago sent in an application for membership in a club in the town. He has heard nothing in response to his application and goes to the home of B., a prominent member of the club, with whom he is pleasantly acquainted. (A. is then sent out of the room and B. is told that A. has received several blackballs.) A. is then called back into the room" and the improvisation begins.*

After each improvisation the participants' reactions were questioned, commented upon, and criticized by the participants, and also by the other candidates and staff.

---
* OSS Assessment Staff, 1948, p.170

The OSS Assessment Program.

Each candidate was observed in two improvisations. At a halfway break, liquor was brought in and continued to be available throughout the evening and as long into the morning as anyone wanted.

After *Improvisations*, candidates were divided into two teams to debate the question: "What Shall We Do with Germany After the War?" *The Debate* provided opportunity to observe and rate the dimensions of Energy and Initiative, Effective Intelligence, Social Relations, Leadership, and especially since liquor was still flowing, the Ability to Maintain Cover.

The unmentioned and never named *Liquor Test* led to much behavior which otherwise would not have been observed. During the last month of OSS we were grateful for an OSS operator, an Army captain who had parachuted into France to work with a resistance group, who, staying up as long as any of the candidates wished, relieved the professional staff of this duty.

On the morning of the last full day of assessment the candidates' opinions of and attitudes toward each other were collected. The *Sociometric Questionnaire* asked candidates "With whom would you enjoy continuing your acquaintance?", "Which men expressed the most realistic and convincing opinions in the debate last night?", "If you were a member of a group on a dangerous mission, whom would you prefer to have as your leader?", and other questions of the same sort. The *Judgment of Others* test required the candidates to write five personality sketches for the five assessees whom they felt they had come to know best. Data from these two exercises were available to the staff in forming their final impressions of the candidates.

During the rest of the day, while the staff was preparing its S Report on each of the candidates, the assessees were involved in solving the *Murder Mystery*. For this exercise they were given copies of the mythical *Fairfield Chronicle* which reported the finding of the dead body of a woman on a road near S. Working in competing groups of six, their task was to wring from three junior staff members (standard role players), who were designated as possible informants, the information necessary for them to make proper inferences and thus to solve "the murder."

Athletic Events—broad jump, high jump, and shot-put—more in the spirit of a game than as a serious test, and a *Baseball Game* between the candidates and junior staff members not involved in the staff conference engaged the interest of the assessees during the last afternoon.

Reports on the candidates' performance in these last day simulations and games were available to the staff before their deliberations ended.

For each assessment class, usually consisting of 18 assessees, the staff was divided into teams of two senior staff member (professionals with Ph.D. or M.D. degrees) and one junior staff member (enlisted men who had had some training in psychology). Each team was assigned to a group of five to seven candidates. The senior members conducted the life history interviews; the junior member administered special individual tests and interpreted the projective test protocols. Otherwise, the work of both senior and junior members was the same, namely, to develop as a group as complete a conception as possible of each candidate in the subgroup assigned to them.

During the various situational tests the behaviors of each participant were carefully noted by both senior and junior members of the responsible team, each staff member rating each assessee on the variables relevant to the particular exercise. Usually immediately following each situational test, the staff team met to discuss their impressions of the candidates and the ratings they had assigned to them. The purpose of the meeting was to come to agreement upon the ratings to be assigned to each assessee on each of the rated variables.

The staff meeting for the preparation of the Station S Report on the candidates ran from after lunch on the last full day of the assessment until all reports had been finished, which was often close to midnight.

Before the staff meeting each interviewer had written a first draft of his section of the reports on the men he had interviewed and for whom he was the primary assessor. This was a description of the candidate as a person and of the major events of his past history that seemed to shed light on his present personality, with special emphasis being given to picturing how the candidate might be expected to behave in a variety of situations and circumstances in the future. Also before the staff meeting the member of the staff who was responsible for reporting on the behavior of the candidate at Station S as revealed in the various situational tests, the situationist, as he was known, had written his section of the final report, which not only described the behavior of the candidate at S but offered specific support for the statements and predictions made in the first part of the report written by the interviewer.

A huge board which covered one wall of the staff room offered a graphic display of how each candidate had been rated by the staff team assigned to him on each of the variables in each of the relevant tests and situations. Ratings were represented by thumb tacks, red if above average, blue if below. While the interviewer and the situationist read their reports, staff members looked at the board and the thumbtacks to see if the reporters' statements were supported by the ratings. If not, there was discussion until general agreement was reached about the changes that would have to be made in the overall rating of the variables on the Station S Report or in the statements in the written report. Sometimes the reports could be revised in the staff meeting. If not, they would be rewritten by the report writer after the meeting.

The final report consisted of a face sheet on which the candidate was rated on the nine variables already described, plus other sheets which carried a character sketch of the candidate based upon the interviewer's insights and the staff's obsevations of the candidate at S, and recommendations concerning overseas assignment made on a 5-point scale: Not Recommended, Doubtful, Recommended with Qualifications, Recommended, Highly Recommended. A similar scale (Not Recommended to Highly Recommended) was used to indicate candidate's fitness for work at (1) a rear base, (2) an advanced base, and (3) at or behind enemy lines; his fitness for (1) higher, (2) middle, or (3) lower level of authority and responsibility; and finally his fitness for different types of assignment, e.g., administrator, intelligence officer, operational agent, etc.

And these Station S reports, sometimes worked over long past midnight of the last day of assessment, were already at OSS Headquarters in Washington when the candidates arrived back there the next morning.

How effective was the OSS assessment program? We cannot say with certainty, but accepting our validity figures at face value we were forced to conclude that we were not very successful in predicting performance overseas. But were errors mainly in the assessment process, or in the appraisal process, or in both? Again we cannot say with certainty, but we do know that the appraisal process as carried out left very much to be described. Our appraisal data were of four types:

1. *Overseas Staff Appraisal.* These were appraisals made by OSS assessment staff members on the basis of interviews with the immediate chief or commanding officer and, if possible, associates of our "graduates" overseas.

The OSS Assessment Program

Footnote from a Guinea Pig

I can't resist a brief personal footnote to Donald MacKinnon's fascinating account of how OSS assessed its recruits. Having been one of those assessed in this imaginative experiment, I can provide a glimpse or two of the process as seen from the other end of the microscope.

The assessment process at Station "S", described so well in MacKinnon's *OSS Assessment Program*, was to many of us assessed a splendid lark—sort of an English country house party except for the phalanx of psychologists scrutinizing our every move. And even they seemed more like recreation directors on a cruise ship than inquisitors. On arrival at the old Willard place in Fairfax I had a fleeting moment to admire a magnificent stand of English boxwood before I was swept into the swirl of activity calculated to take my measure. We were sternly admonished to stick to our cover story and keep our identities secret. We were warned that efforts would be made by the staff to trick us into giving our true selves away so we must be eternally vigilant. This kind of enforced anonymity was in a way exhilarating—like taking a vacation from one's old self.

We were split into teams. Only with considerable research much later did I discover that my colleagues in real life were the president of a prominent bank in Paris, a ballet dancer, a disc jockey, a college professor, and a giant who had played pro football before the army inducted him. They had all adopted cover identities—most of which struck me as implausible. Hiding my real Foreign Service background, I chose to masquerade as a lumberjack since I had once had a summer fling at that and could more or less talk the jargon. But I, too, didn't fit my new role very well.

The battery of written aptitude tests was tedious, as always. But the live exercises were great fun even though we knew we were being watched carefully and rigorously graded. The "Brook Test" was my favorite. As described in MacKinnon's article, our team was indeed faced with a large boulder sitting heavily beside a small stream. It was explained that we would be timed while we sought to organize ourselves and make the best use of the boards and pulleys strewn about to move the rock to the other side of the stream. But before the earnest mentor could finish his instructions, our football hero grabbed the rock, hugged it to his chest as he would some sort of outsized, overweight football, and leaped nimbly to the other side of the stream for a touchdown. How our team was graded on leadership, effective intelligence, incipient bravery, or whatever, I had no way of knowing. But we had at least broken a time record.

In the "Behind the Barn" test each of us, with the help of two assistants provided by management, took turns at trying to erect a giant tinkertoy cube. It soon became clear that the two "helpers," known as "Kippy" and "Buster," were intent on sabotaging the effort. Never one to fight a hopeless problem, I used my allotted ten minutes to relax in a hayloft. As MacKinnon wrote, this test evoked a variety of responses. Some well-adjusted persons took it in the spirit of high humor—even joined in the highjinks, turning it into a sort of impromptu "Three Stooges" routine. Others, of course, let their frustrations show. Rumors were rife at the time that the only student to complete the tinkertoy had been a strapping Texan who flattened Kippy and Buster with two well-aimed blows. As a result, the Texan became a sort of folk hero at the station—perhaps a symbol that we could win the war after all so long as we had problem-solvers like that.

The "Liquor Test," rather gingerly touched on by MacKinnon, was presumably based on the old saw, *In Vino Veritas*. Under the guise of a relaxing farewell party we were plied with liquor, presumably so that our testers could catch us with our guards down. This is an interesting approach but I don't think it worked very well with our team. The college professor announced that he never touched the stuff. The linebacker poured more than his share into his generous stomach without its appearing to have any effect. The disc jockey, exhausted by his weekend, fell asleep promptly, while the Paris bank president shrewdly switched to French which went over the heads of our observers. Playing my woodsman cover to the hilt, I recall talking expansively to my observers about buying the Willard's prize boxwood after the War. So the evening passed. I doubt if it all proved much.

OSS's membership list was long. It read like a cross between *Who's Who* and the *Social Register*. Many of the young and untried later rose to positions of talent and prominence. It would be interesting to know how the assessment profiles of the like of Arthur Goldberg, David Bruce, Julia Child, Ralph Bunche, Walt Rostow, Sterling Hayden, Stewart Alsop, John Gardner, Douglas Dillon, and Paul Mellon read after they had paraded anonymously through Stations W or S.

Not that our team was a typical microcosm, but it acquitted itself well in real action as far as I could later determine. The disc jockey with no apparent talents distinguished himself behind the lines in France and Norway. The somewhat musty professor did magnificently in North Africa. The pro-ball star never surpassed his accomplishment of getting the rock across the stream, but I'm told he did his best in the Far East. The Paris banker served gloriously with the French undergound and re-entered liberated Paris in triumph.

MacKinnon's conclusion that the OSS assessment program had not been very successful in predicting overseas performance is discouraging. All these years I have cherished the illusion that by surviving the Station S trial I had been permitted to join an elite corps, pre-determined by scientific testing to win the war. Now I discover that the Station S assessment record was only 14% more accurate than what could have been done by a roulette wheel. Still, the experiment was a brave effort and perhaps contributed to the science of testing. I shall try to find at least a measure of satisfaction in having been a cheerful guinea pig.

John W. Waller

Table 1

Correlations between S and W Assessment Job Ratings and Appraisal Ratings
(After OSS Assessment Staff, 1948, p. 423)

Type of Appraisal	S Job Rating (Classes S-45 on) r	N	W Job Rating (All Classes) r	N
Overseas Staff Appraisal	.37 [a]	88	.53 [a]	83
Returnee Appraisal	.19 [a]	93	.21 [a]	173
Theater Commander's Appraisal	.23	64	.15	158
Reassignment Area Appraisal	.08	53	.30 [a]	178

[a] Cases in which correcting r for restricted sample made a significant difference: r given in each case is the corrected one.

These recommendations are reproduced below with the thought that the readers of this monograph may find it both interesting and informative as they review them to ask themselves such questions as these: How many of these recommendations have been carried out in the setting up of assessment centers in business, in industry, in government, and in education? If adopted have they proved helpful? And, if they have been ignored, were they rejected for good reason? And finally, what further recommendations should now be made for the improvement of assessment centers?

The recommendations follow:

1. Select a staff of suitable size and competence, diversified in respect to age, sex, social status, temperament, major sentiments, and specific skills, but uniform in respect to a high degree of intellectual and emotional flexibility (p. 473).

2. Before designing the program of assessment procedures, conduct a preliminary study of the jobs and job holders of the organization (p. 475).

2.1. Make an adequate functional analysis of each of the roles for which candidates are to be assessed as well as an analysis of the environments in which each role must be fulfilled (p. 476).

2.2. Obtain from members of the organization a list of attributes of personality which, in their opinion, contribute to success or failure in the performance of each role (p. 476).

2.3. After a careful survey, analysis, and classification of the information obtained by these obsevations and interviews (recommendations 2.1 and 2.2), make a tentative list of the personality determinants of success or failure in the performance of each role. These determinants will constitute the variables which, if possible, will be measured by the assessment procedures (p. 477).

2.4. Define, in words that are intelligible to members of the organization, a tentative rating scale for each personality variable on the selected list as well as for the overall variable, Job Fitness (p. 479).

2.5. Devise a satisfactory system for appraising the performance of members of the organization both at this time and later (p. 481).

2.6. Obtain appraisals of a properly distributed sample of the present members of the organization (p. 484).

The OSS Assessment Program

2. *Theater Commander's Appraisal.* From Spring 1944, each returnee was reported on and his personality traits were rated by his immediate superior.

3. *Reassignment Area Appraisal.* From Fall of 1944 a center was set up (Area F) for the re-assessment or re-evaluation of personnel who had completed a tour of duty in Europe or the Middle East for reassignment in the Far East.

4. *Returnee Appraisal.* Beginning in the summer of 1945, each returnee was asked to report on others known to him, rating their performance Low, Medium, or High.

When assessment job ratings were correlated with appraisal job ratings for Stations S and W, validity coefficients were all positive but disappointingly low, ranging from .08 to .53, depending upon the source of the appraisal data, as shown in Table 1. And, much to our surprise, the one-day assessments at W appeared to have been more effective than the three-and-a-half-day assessments at S.

We of the OSS staff are indebted to Jerry S. Wiggins (1973) who, making certain assumptions and using improved principles for estimating outcomes of predictions, worked over our data and came up with a more favorable picture than the one we had drawn.

His estimate is that at S, if we had used only random selection, our percent of correct decisions would have been 63%, but actually 77% were correct. Corresponding estimates for Station W are that by random selection 66% would have been correct, but actually 84% were correct. This means that at S, assessment effected a 14% increase in correct decisions over random selection and at Station W an 18% increment. Considering the crucial nature of the assignments, increments of 14% and 18% of correct decisions are not unimportant.

It is interesting to speculate as to why the briefer (one day) assessments of Station W were more accurate than the longer (three-and-a-half-day) assessments of Station S. It may have been that the procedures used at W were more efficient than those employed at S, although this seems unlikely. Perhaps the Staff at W was more competent than the one at S: more psychiatrists served on the staff at W and less use was made of junior assessors than at S. Differences in the populations assessed at the two stations could also have been a determining factor. Those assessed at W were more often high echelon executives in the organization, women secretaries, and office workers many of whom had already spent some time in the Washington headquarters, while those sent to S for assessment were either the more difficult cases who were already presenting perplexing problems or were men destined for more hazardous duty under more stress and danger than would be experienced by the W assessees. Indeed, of those assessed at W, 74% received rear base assignments with only 15% serving behind enemy lines. In contrast, only 29% of Station S graduates received rear base assignments while 43% operated behind enemy lines. Among possible explanations of the differential success rates of the two assessment centers the one that seems least plausible is the notion that the staff at Station S suffered from a superabundance of information about their assessees, while the staff at Station W, with less information, had just what they needed and no more to make the kinds of decisions called for in the OSS assessment program. But the fact remains that we cannot say with certainty why the assessments at W surpassed those at S. Indeed, still today the optimal length of assessment center programs remains an unanswered question, one which should long since have been subjected to empirical investigation.

At the end of their report on the OSS program, *Assessment of Men*, the OSS staff made a number of recommendations which it was hoped would remedy some of the defects of assessment as practiced in the OSS.

2.7. Examine the defects of the appraisal system as revealed in practice (recommendation 2.6), and correct these by revising, where necessary, the lists of variables, the definitions, the rating scales, or the other elements.

2.8. Obtain the figures necessary for a brief numerical statement of the personnel history of the organization over the last four or five years (p. 485).

3. Design a program of assessment procedures which will reveal the strength of the selected variables; for assessing these variables set up scales which conform to the rating scales that were defined for the purpose of appraisal (p. 485).

4. Build a conceptual scheme in terms of which formulations of different personalities can be made (p. 488).

5. Set up an efficient punch-card system which will permit periodic statistical analyses of assessment findings (p. 490).

6. Assess candidates for a long trial period without reporting ratings or decisions to the organizations (p. 491).

How far and in what directions the state of the art of assessment has moved beyond that which obtained in the assessment program of the OSS is a fascinating chronicle, but that is another story for another time.

References

OSS Assessment Staff. *Assessment of men.* Rinehart and Company, New York, 1948.

Smith, R. H. *OSS: The secret history of America's first central intelligence agency.* University of California Press, Berkeley, California, 1972.

Wiggins, J. S. *Personality and prediction: Principles of personality assessment.* Addison-Wesley Publishing Company, Reading, Massachusetts, 1973.

(*The foregoing article is* Unclassified.)

VIRGINA HALL AN AMERICAN SPY

One of American's most accomplished World War 2 spies

Ms. Virginia Hall receiving citation for her undercover OSS activities

SECRET

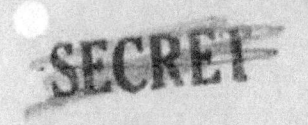

12 May 1945

MEMORANDUM FOR THE PRESIDENT:

Miss Virginia Hall, an American civilian working for this agency in the European Theater of Operations, has been awarded the Distinguished Service Cross for extraordinary heroism in connection with military operations against the enemy.

We understand that Miss Hall is the first civilian woman in this war to receive the Distinguished Service Cross.

Despite the fact that she was well known to the Gestapo, Miss Hall voluntarily returned to France in March 1944 to assist in sabotage operations against the Germans. Through her courage and physical endurance, even though she had previously lost a leg in an accident, Miss Hall, with two American officers, succeeded in organizing, arming and training three FFI Battalions which took part in many engagements with the enemy and a number of acts of sabotage, resulting in the demolition of many bridges, the destruction of a number of supply trains, and the disruption of enemy communications. As a result of the demolition of one bridge, a German convoy was ambushed and during a bitter struggle 150 Germans were killed and 500 were captured. In addition Miss Hall provided radio communication between London Headquarters and the Resistance Forces in the Haute Loire Department, transmitting and receiving operational and intelligence information. This was the most dangerous type of work as the enemy, whenever

-2-

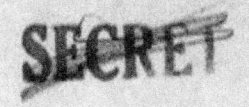

two or more direction finders could be tuned in on a transmitter, were able to locate the transmittal point to within a couple of hundred yards. It was frequently necessary for Miss Hall to change her headquarters in order to avoid detection.

Inasmuch as an award of this kind has not been previously made during the present war, you may wish to make the presentation personally. Miss Hall is presently in the European Theater of Operations.

                                        William J. Donovan
                                            Director

Declassified by 007622
date 15 May 73

THE WHITE HOUSE

WASHINGTON

CITATION FOR DISTINGUISHED SERVICE CROSS

     Miss Virginia Hall, an American civilian in the employ of the Special Operations Branch, Office of Strategic Services, voluntarily entered and served in enemy occupied France from March to September 1944. Despite the fact that she was well known to the Gestapo because of previous activities, she established and maintained radio communication with London Headquarters, supplying valuable operational and intelligence information, and with the help of a Jedburgh team, she organized, armed and trained three battalions of French Resistance Forces in the Department of the Haute Loire. Working in a region infested with enemy troops and constantly hunted by the Gestapo, with utter disregard for her safety and continually at the risk of capture, torture and death, she directed the Resistance Forces with extraordinary success in acts of sabotage and guerrilla warfare against enemy troops, installations and communications. Miss Hall displayed rare courage, perseverance and ingenuity; her efforts contributed materially to the successful operations of the Resistance Forces in support of the Allied Expeditionary Forces in the liberation of France.

/s/ Harry S. Truman

A true copy:

Frank L. Ball, Jr.
Major, AUS

THE LIFE AND WORK OF STEPHAN HALLER

THE LIFE AND WORK OF STEPHAN HALLER
Patrick R. Beller

This true biography of an intelligence officer is doubly a study in intelligence: it shows how a goodly endowment of intellectual equipment, the honing of scholasticism, and a catholic diversity of interests and experience provide none too elaborate a base for intelligence work, but indeed create the potential for extraordinary success. Haller's contributions to U.S. intelligence began in war, with the OSS. Often unorthodox in his methods but always effective in his stubborn onslaught on the work assigned him, he lived a career that is now part of the tradition of the U.S. intelligence service, a tradition that he and many of his colleagues have been building since the days of World War II.

Stephan Haller—scholar, mathematician, and political activist—was not the model intelligence officer, because there is no such thing. The job is so vast that in addition to that first requisite—brains—all kinds of persons and talents are needed. But Haller combined more talents than most men—combined them and controlled them, so that even seemingly disparate traits were fitted together. He was a thoughtful and sensual, purposeful and humane man.

But trying to measure him is like trying to measure other natural forces, like explaining a storm as so many foot-pounds of wind-thrust. He was more than a sum of attributes.

Stephan Haller was not his real name.[1] He did not want publicity or acclaim; he wanted to do his job. Those of us who knew him know that he would not only have chosen anonymity; he would have insisted on it for operational reasons. His identity and character merged with the work to which he was devoted, shaping it and shaped by it. The work is his memorial. And because we share in the work, we also share in his story.

R. Helms

---

[1] A pseudonym is used here because his contacts are still active and several of his operations continue to be of a sensitive nature.

Stephan Haller was the second of two sons born to a middle-class family of German Jews. Manfred and Margarete Haller were living in Frankfurt am Main with their three-year-old Emil in 1906, the year of Stephan's birth. Later a daughter, Sara, was born. Manfred Haller was a Rabbi. In 1916, after Stephan had finished grammar school, the family moved to Kassel. Graduation from *Mittelschule* at the age of ten is unusual in Germany; young Stephan was a good student. From 1916 to 1924 he continued his studies in Braunschweig, and two years later he took his first degree, a BS, at Marburg/Lahn. The next five years were spent at a number of universities inside and outside Germany. The young man's studies showed the breadth of his interests. He became skilled in mathematics and statistics, physics, psychology, sociology, and political science; and he read widely in other subjects.

His father was lean, bearded, and strictly orthodox, whereas Stephan's broad interests and his studies in the sciences had increased his natural curiosity and his scepticism. The result was frequent clashes between father and son. But although Stephan argued from materialistic concepts, one of his closest friends has said that later in his life he was deeply religious, a fact he tried to conceal. In any event, the Rabbi and his younger son were never intimate in their association.

Margarete Haller died in 1923, when Stephan was seventeen. Ten years more, and the Nazis were to put his father in a concentration camp. Later the Rabbi, his daughter, and his older son all managed somehow to reach South America. Stephan found a different course.

Politician and Propagandist

European students have always been more precocious in political life than their American counterparts. Young Haller associated himself with the Social Democratic Party when he was nineteen, and soon became very active in its student groups. From 1925 until 1933, when he was forced to flee Germany, he was much occupied with politics and the educational programs of the German labor movement. For several of those years he was chairman of the Social Democratic Students' Movement at the University of Frankfurt and a member of the movement's national board of chairmen. He was also

Stephan Haller

district leader of this movement for southwest Germany, which included the Universities of Marburg, Frankfurt, Giessen, Heidelberg, and Munich, as well as the Polytechnic Institute at Darmstadt. At the same time he took part in the educational program of the German labor unions, serving both as educational director and as teacher at various large plants, including I. G. Farben, throughout Hesse.

Haller also became intensely and practically interested in the theory and uses of political propaganda. It was this interest that brought him into intimate contact with Kurt Schumacher, Ollenhauer, and other leading Socialists. He became a member of the SPD Propaganda Committee for Hesse, which worked under the direction of Reichstag Deputy Dr. Carlo Mierendorff. For three years, from 1930 to 1933, this committee maintained a continuous survey and analysis of the effect upon the German people of the propaganda of all the political parties. The purpose of the survey was to improve SPD propaganda and reduce the effectiveness of that of all opponents. Stephan Haller's education thus drew a little closer to his future work.

During the same period he put his analyses to use, appearing as the SPD speaker at nearly a thousand political rallies held all over Germany. About half of these were meetings of nationalistic groups: the Stahlhelm, the German National Party, and of course the NSDAP, the Nazis. He sharpened his wits and skills in debate against men whose names were later heard in intercession and anathema—Goebbels, Hitler's propaganda chief; Baldur von Schirach, Nazi youth leader; Dr. Franz Seldte, founder of the Stahlhelm. Selected as a delegate to the SPD's national convention, he twice ran unsuccessfully for office, once for the Hessian Landtag and once for the Reichstag. Politics is not an easy life anywhere; it was a hard and rewarding school for a young Jew in the turbulent pre-Hitler Germany.

A statement written by Haller for the OSS in early 1944 includes this comment:

> I shall not dwell upon the fact that in the course of the above mentioned activities, I could not fail to acquire a rather thorough knowledge of the German party system as a whole, of the structure, history, methods of propaganda and action of the German national parties, particularly the Nazi Party,

the German National Party, and of the leagues and associations either connected to or collaborating with them; as well as, to a certain extent, a personal knowledge of many known leaders of these organizations.

He also learned how to assess people and how to deal with them, when to be friendly and kind and when to be hard or austere, whom to praise or reassure and whom to treat with just the right degree of that superciliousness so effective with certain Germanic types. His convictions gave him reason to act; his studies and political research had taught him how; and now experience was teaching him the hardest lesson, when to act.

Adolf Hitler became Reichschancellor on 30 January 1933. The night before the Reichstag fire, on 27 February, Haller made a pungently anti-Nazi speech at Darmstadt. Two days later the SS storm-troopers came to the Haller home. They did not find Stephan. A young student of his, a girl, had somehow learned what was coming and had warned him. The troopers smashed up the household, arrested the Rabbi, and hauled him off to the *Sammellager*.

The Wandering Jew

For six months Haller lived and worked underground with anti-Nazis in southwest Germany, the Ruhr, and Berlin. In September he escaped into Luxembourg. Here he continued his anti-Nazi work until the German government pressured the small duchy to arrest him and return him. A warrant for his arrest was issued, but he escaped again, to the Saar, which was then administered by the League of Nations. (Much later, at the war's end, Haller went back to Luxembourg with the American forces. He looked up the chief of police and identified himself: he understood, he said, that a warrant for his arrest and extradition was outstanding.)

He stayed in the Saarland until 1935, when it was returned to Germany. When the Nazis marched in he walked out, to Paris. There he resumed, at the Sorbonne, his studies in statistical mathematics, sociology, and political science. He became a volunteer statistician for the Pasteur Institute and a member of the National Center of Scientific Research, a branch of the French Ministry of Education. He was offered an assistant's post at the Institute of Atomic Physics of the

Stephan Haller

University of Lyon, despite the fact that in 1934 and 1935 France was suffering from unemployment, employed aliens were required to have work permits, and there were many times more refugees than permits.

When World War II started, all German aliens in France were arrested and confined in a detention camp. Soon thereafter Haller and some fifty other German and Austrian scientists were released and formed into a curious organization known as the *Prestation Savante* (Service of Scientists), organized by the French Ministry of War and attached to the University of Montpellier, where they worked under the orders of the Ministers of War and Education. The organization was semi-military, and the scientists were dressed in a compromise between soldiers' uniforms and the garb of monks. During this period Haller made friends with a number of fellow-scientists whom he later recruited and used as agents. Precisely what work was done by the *Prestation* until the fall of France is not clear now.

When France went under, Haller fled again. Both the Gestapo and the Vichy militia were looking for him. There was a price on his head. He went south, to the unoccupied zone. During his long sojourn there he became fluent in French and improved his accent sufficiently to pass as a Belgian. After the Franco-German armistice, the French set up numerous depots at which French military personnel could be demobilized upon request. Their proof of bona fides was the uniform; upon discharge they were given a few thousand francs and a civilian suit. Haller managed to go through the process three times in three different towns, living in each on his severance pay.

Finally picked up and placed in a camp for demobilized French soldiers, he escaped and made his way to the American Consulate in Marseilles, where he obtained an Emergency Intellectual Visa to the United States. After a brief delay in Spain in the summer of 1941, he reached New York via Cuba on a refugee ship. He arrived in wretched physical condition.

Rebel in Uniform

Ten months later, at Fort Dix, New Jersey, he was inducted into the United States Army. The Haller legend has it that some difficulty with the military psychologists ensued: asked by one of them if he could sing, he replied with a *fortissimo* rendering of *Die Wacht am Rhein*. This opening scene foreshadowed some later events. Assigned as a student to an army engineering school in Kentucky, he was placed in an elementary class. The instructor made frequent errors, and Haller's helpful corrections were appreciated neither by the teacher nor by the commanding officer. The latter had Haller on the carpet and informed him incisively that he was not the assistant instructor. Haller explained that he did not know anything about the army but did know mathematics, whereas the instructor's specialties were obviously the reverse. A compromise was effected: he was to remain silent in class in exchange for a nightly pass.

From September 1942 until April 1944 he was assigned to five different Army posts, usually instructing in the operation of a computer, while the OSS was frantically looking for men who knew Germany well. At last an IBM run turned up Stephan Haller; he knew the language, had detailed area knowledge, was a well-known SPD member, knew important personages. Almost all the holes in the card were in the right places.

The OSS brought him to Washington and gave him intelligence training. In June 1944 he was shipped to London and assigned to the labor division of the BACH section, an organization which supplied cover stories and documents for agents working behind enemy lines. In August he was transferred to a forward combat area in France. He served with one of the first OSS field detachments that accompanied the armies from the Normandy landings to the war's end. These detachments provided liaison from G–2 to OSS headquarters, ran border crossers, recruited spies from POW cages, briefed and debriefed agents, and performed many other intelligence tasks. Haller's exceptional capabilities led to his being recommended for a commission. The recommendation included the following job description:

> Haller is in charge of all BACH research work at Field Base C and acts as immediate assistant to the CO in all intelligence operations. . . . He (a) questions officials . . . interrogates prisoners of war, deserters, and escaped foreign workers . . . (b) collects and analyzes documents . . . (c) prepares written reports . . . covering such topics as: The German Rationing

System, Travelling in Germany, . . . Priorities in German War Production . . . (d) supervises the work of six other members of the detachment. . . .

When Haller's commanding officer was told to have him ready to appear before an ETOUSA commissioning board, he was advised to ensure that "Haller's actions in front of the board be strictly military," and to be sure that the candidate could salute and about-face correctly, that his uniform was neat, clean, and pressed, and that his buttons shone. Perhaps the candidate was aided less by the coaching than by his record. At any rate, on 20 April 1945, Stephan Haller was commissioned a second lieutenant in the Army of the United States.

For the next few months his principal task was to interview prospective agents and work out their cover stories. Supplementing his intimate knowledge of German, Germans, and Germany was his painstaking care in details, an incisively logical mind, and a quiet devotion to duty. He went from Verdun to Luxembourg to Belgium. In May his unit moved to Wiesbaden, where his pay and allowances were further increased by two free bottles of champagne each month.

In Wiesbaden, where the unit was known as "Field Base C" or "Triangle," Haller located old SPD friends and began to pick up the broken threads of German politics, while at the same time busy with counterintelligence work. During this period he established the unorthodox operational pattern which he usually followed afterwards. He installed himself in a house well away from the base, living alone and working with his agents there. This pattern of activity was threatened with abrupt termination by an order from Security that he be separated, but his commanding officer and others who knew him well obtained a reversal. During the argument over this order the acting chief of the area wrote, "We have no one in Europe today who has his scientific background," and forecast for him a brilliant career.

"Baron" Haller at Hochheim

The prediction proved right. In the years after the war Haller obtained extremely valuable political and scientific technical intelligence. Although promoted to first lieutenant in 1946, he asked to be given civilian status, and in July 1947 became an employee of CIG. He was graded at CAF-11 and paid $4,902 annually—a bargain if there ever was one. By this time he was established at Hochheim am Main, an imposing mansion—almost a castle—with marble halls and statuary, walls covered with damask and leather, and a cellar full of champagne. Thus ensconced in "Schloss Haller," which was listed in official records as a political research center, he began to exploit the intelligence potential of the SPD against East Germany and the USSR and to follow French activity in the French Zone of Germany and even in France itself. This second task, apparently carried out through friends made during the days of his exile, produced almost the only information available about Socialist activity in France and won him an official commendation.

The three years that Haller spent in Hochheim were probably the happiest of his life. The talents with which he was born, the scope and depth of his formal education, and the diversity of his international experience, both civil and military, now came into focus. He was working hard. At times he did not leave his apartment on the second floor of the "Schloss" for two or three weeks in a row. He held intense political discussions with visitors, many of whom were not agents but unwitting sources, friends and acquaintances who had known him as an SPD leader and who were more than willing to help him in the "political research" which he was now doing for the Americans. Among his visitors were Schumacher, Ollenhauer, Heine, and other German Socialist leaders. In fact, Haller even arranged formal meetings of the SPD Party Directorate in his quarters. The result of these meetings and discussions was unexcelled political reporting.

Hard as he worked, Haller also found time for fun and games. He was popular with both his colleagues and the townspeople, from the Mayor down. He always sat at the Mayor's table at civic festivities and was in demand as a dance partner among the wives of the local dignitaries. He drank and smoked with zeal, but few people claim to have seen him the worse for alcohol. His cellar was kept well stocked with champagne and the still wines of the Rhine and Moselle. He even had a false bottom installed in his car, so that whenever his driver was sent to the French Zone he could smuggle back

Stephan Haller

a few dozen bottles of Hoch. And his major domo, Kurt, was sometimes detailed to escort one or another fair young lady to the Schloss of an evening and drive her home again the next morning.

His pleasure in the present did not keep him from planning for the future. He suggested to his superiors that for operational purposes he renounce the U.S. citizenship acquired through military service and become a German again. He would then re-enter the SPD and thus give the newly established Central Intelligence Agency a high-level penetration of one of the two most important political parties in Germany. This position would make him an ideal agent, he felt, for both intelligence collection and political action. It would not be suspected that his renunciation of American citizenship and renewal of old ties were not genuine; the same thing had been done by others, including a former mayor of Hamburg. But Haller also made conditions. He wanted to keep his U.S. passport—he was quite proud of being an American—and he wanted assurances that when the time came he could return to the United States, his citizenship reactivated. This proposal was not accepted. He frequently referred to it in later days as a missed opportunity.

Haller was intuitive as well as logical. He had a remarkable ability to smell out Communist penetrations of the various civil governments set up in the German states. He felt sure, for example, that the Minister of the Interior for Land Hesse, Hans Venedey, was a Communist; and with his customary pertinacity he set out to prove it. His efforts led the Military Governor to complain to Haller's superior: he "had a good little government going there and Haller was upsetting it." It seems apparent that Haller then had a talk with the SPD leadership, for Venedey was expelled from the SPD for acts injurious to the party. He re-emerged as a functionary of the German Communist Party.

From Politics to Science

In March 1949 CIA headquarters for Haller's area moved from Heidelburg to Karlsruhe, and Haller set up shop in another castle, at Pforzheim. In part his work here was a continuation of the three years at Hochheim. His old SPD friends continued to visit him and furnish valuable political information. These visits also gave him a chance to explain his own views, which were of course those of the U.S. Government, and thus to combine intelligence collection with political action. But some of his duties were new. Because of his scientific background, he was placed in charge of a U.S. program for paying subsidies to German scientists, part of a much larger operation designed to deny German scientific talent to the Soviets. This assignment required him to establish and maintain a new cover, one suited to its purpose.

In 1951, his cover well established, he was shifted to Berlin, there to direct operations against scientific targets in the East Zone of Germany. As usual, he took a house which served as both living quarters and base of operations. He responded to the tighter operational environment by intensifying personal control. He rarely went to parties now. He refused to let anyone else handle his agents, even when he was ill. He did not like to put on paper the mass of information accumulated in his head.

He began work, with others, on an operation designed to hinder the Soviet atomic energy program by inducing large-scale defection among German specialist craftsmen in the East Zone. These workers made the fine nickel wire mesh used for the essential separation of uranium isotopes. The scheme worked; technicians and their families defected in droves and were flown to West Germany. But Haller was disappointed to learn later that the Soviets were only inconvenienced, not thwarted. The vanished craftsmen were replaced. His own part in the operation, however, was well done, and in April 1951 headquarters sent him a congratulatory wire. One of his chiefs at about this time took written note of his lone-wolf tendencies, but all were unanimous that his work, and particularly his reporting of scientific intelligence, was excellent.

The German and Austrian scientists who had served with Haller in the *Prestation Savante* in France soon after the beginning of World War II now constituted a pool of assets. For two more years he worked with some of them in acquiring scientific and technical intelligence. A love affair with a young German actress ended when she married his rival, but his disappointment did not impair his work. The quality and quantity of his output is evidenced in the repeated efforts of his superiors to get him paid more nearly what it was worth:

> His production is phenomenally high, and the many cases he runs are distinguished for the professionalism evident in their conduct. Although outstandingly qualified in background for conduct of positive intelligence operations covering technical and scientific subjects, he has demonstrated marked ability in conducting other kinds of positive intelligence and CE cases. . . . I should like to underline the fact that in the handling of agents and the production of intelligence, particularly in the scientific and technical field, in this area, Haller is, in my opinion, without a peer.

His scope expanded as scientific conferences in Switzerland and elsewhere enabled him to discuss the meetings with old friends who had attended, professors and other intellectuals. Both the briefings and the debriefings of this period are classics. In late 1955 he debriefed Leo Bauer, former leading functionary of the East German Communist Party, who because of his personal acquaintance with Haller had refused to talk to any other American official. He also debriefed Erica Glaser Wallach, who had gone to East Germany to locate her foster-father, Noel Field.

His friends remember only one interview that left him shaken. Dr. Gustave Hertz, one of the leading German scientists who worked on the Soviet atomic energy program, had returned to Germany with his secretary, Ellen Mueller, her husband, and their four children. The family was rushed to a safehouse, and Haller was called. As he began his careful questioning, little hands started tugging at his trouser-legs and clutching at his coat. Soon one and then another child, chomping hard candies, had struggled into his lap. While their mother beamed with a pride that was obviously a factor in her cooperativeness, the two continued the ascent, reaching Haller's sagging shoulders and making room for the other two members of the expedition. Haller has been called both a man's man and a lady's man, but no one ever called him a children's man. Somehow he struggled through the questioning. He emerged perspiring and a little stunned, as though he had been kicked in the stomach. Perhaps he had. All future dealings with Frau Mueller were handled by his assistant.

The Sheer Pinnacle

By now he was near the peak of his career. He was using fully his keen intellect, depth of recall, sensitivity, practical astuteness and imagination, his background in languages, science, and politics, and his feel for operations. His ability to deal with people amounted to genius. He was good at it because he was patient and, above all, because he was interested in people. Unlike most refugees, he had no political or personal axe to grind. He was an accurate observer and reporter. He could talk to all classes of Germans, from artists and professors to farmers and laborers, each in their own language—an indispensable skill in a country in which speech differences mirror both social levels and geography. His relations with his contacts were on two levels—of friendly personal participation and of impassive objectivity—without the latter being evident to them. Perhaps his membership in a race recently and bitterly persecuted by the Germans strengthened this faculty and sharpened his ability to use German agents for the purposes of his new homeland.

He did not grow careless or conceited with success. He remained a meticulous craftsman. Before he debriefed a source, he mastered the subject to be discussed. His agents were made comfortable not only by his cigars and beer but also by the easy flow of communication. And he did not end until he had every last scrap of useful information. He never failed, moreover, to remain alert for operational leads—potential agents, counterintelligence indicators, propaganda possibilities. When Haller was finished, there were no more questions to be asked. And though he groaned over the chore of putting it on paper, his reporting became thorough—and more than thorough, illuminating—for he rarely failed to make interpretive comments. Despite the bulk of his reporting he wrote everything in longhand.

His work remained consistently solid, even brilliant. Some of it was considered sufficiently important to be brought to the personal attention of the Director of Central Intelligence. The Director, impressed, thought that the promotions which his superiors had got for him were not enough. Stephan Haller thus became a rarity, a man promoted to the top of Civil Service ranks not because he was an exceptional executive—he had never occupied an executive position—but solely because he was an exceptional case officer. The Director sent him a personal letter of congratulation, and shortly thereafter, when he was called to headquarters, gave a luncheon in his honor. Haller was deeply moved. He often spoke later of the great honor conferred on him in Washington. His life and work reached on that day the top of a rocket-like trajectory. It was for him a moment of true glory.

After his return to Germany and a period of hard work in Berlin, he went in mid-1956 to Darmstadt to visit friends. Awakening in a strange room, in the middle of the night, he reached out for the light, but on the wrong side, and fell out of bed. The fall broke his hip. A German doctor placed a pin in the fracture, but the leg kept on giving him trouble. He went to a hospital in Munich, where leeches were used in an effort to reduce his blood pressure. The results were not good. He developed phlebitis.

These physical misfortunes would not have been the beginning of the end for most of us, who can learn to be satisfied with past achievements and past honors, financial comfort, and a familiar circle of family and friends. Stephan Haller was a man of different breed. With all the intensity of his character he had wound his life around one thing, his work. Work and the feeling that what he did was recognized were his entire psychological sustenance. Now that appeared to be gone.

Lying month upon month in bed in the Army Hospital in Frankfurt, he grew ever more depressed, thinking of how he could do nothing now to justify those honors heaped on him, and how little he would ever be likely to do again. Remembering that it had once been only his performance which had saved him from the Security axe, he even developed a growing fear that he would be released from the service, after thirteen years, because he had stopped producing. No amount of reassurance by friends and fellow-workers could dispel this irrational figment of his frustrated energy. His collapse was so alarming that he was returned to Washington in February 1957 and treated at the George Washington University Hospital. About a month later he was discharged.

He took an apartment on Sixteenth Street. Far from familiar Europe, out of touch with his world of operational activity, Haller fell victim of that sense of uselessness with which the jealous gods, perhaps, had visited him at the summit of his life. On 26 April 1957 he was stricken by a heart attack and died.

INTELLIGENCE OPERATIONS OF THE OSS DETACHMENT 101

Aspects of a classical scouting and resistance-leading unit behind Japanese lines in Burma, from the viewpoint of its commander.

INTELLIGENCE OPERATIONS OF OSS DETACHMENT 101

W. R. Peers

For Detachment 101 intelligence was an all-pervasive mission. The Detachment did plan and carry out espionage operations specifically to collect both strategic and tactical information, but intelligence was also a by-product of all its other operations, including guerrilla actions, sabotage, and psychological measures. Its intelligence activities were therefore augmented rather than decreased when large-scale guerrilla operations were initiated in the spring of 1944.

Early Operations

The history of Detachment 101 began in the spring of 1942, when a small group of officers and men was assembled in Washington under the Office of the Coordinator of Information. Captain (later Colonel) Carl Eifler was the first commander. After a short period of training and equipping, the unit shipped overseas to the China-Burma-India Theater. In the summer of 1942 it received its first directive from General Stilwell, short and to the point: "Establish a base camp in northeast India and from there plan and conduct operations against the roads and railroad leading into Myitkyina in order to deny the Japanese the use of the Myitkyina airfield. Establish liaison with the British authorities to effect coordination with their operations."

The remainder of the year was spent in locating and developing a base camp in Assam Province of northeast India and in recruiting and training agent personnel for subsequent operations. An office was established in Calcutta to receive supplies from headquarters in the United States and to procure

Detachment 101

bulk goods from the Army Service of Supply. At that time there was available no small, portable military or commercial radio capable of transmitting from northern Burma to Assam, a distance of 200 to 500 miles. Accordingly it was necessary for the unit to design and construct its own radio set. The result was crude, but it worked well. It became the model from which the SSTR series of sets was built by OSS, which by now had succeeded to the intelligence and paramilitary function of COI.

In 1943 exploratory field operations were carried out in Burma on a trial-and-error basis. Some of them were failures; but they taught us many lessons as to what could be done and, even more important, what should not be done. By the end of the year six base camps had been established behind the lines in northern Burma, three east of the Irrawaddy River and three to the west. Each of these had recruited and trained a small group of indigenous Kachin personnel for local protection and to perform limited operations, principally simple sabotage and small ambushes. Each also trained a few native personnel as low-level intelligence agents, who reported their information by means of runners or via the bamboo grapevine. From the field bases this information was forwarded to the base camp in India by radio. By the end of the year it was possible to assemble a fairly comprehensive picture of Japanese strengths and dispositions in northern Burma.

The field bases also selected native recruits for more intensive intelligence training. These were flown by light aircraft or infiltrated through the Japanese lines to the airfield at Fort Hertz in the northern tip of Burma and thence flown to the base camp in India. Their training, of three to five months duration, followed the normal curriculum for intelligence agents. The Kachins were particularly adept at CW radio communications; by the end of the course most of them were able to operate at 25 to 45 words per minute. When their training was completed, some of them were returned to their field bases to expand local information procurement and others were parachuted into Burma for independent operations.

The Myitkyina Campaign

With the initiation of orthodox military operations in the winter of 1943-44 by the Chinese ground forces, later augmented by Merrill's Marauders, General Stilwell directed the Detachment to expand its guerrilla force to a strength of approximately 3,000 in order to assist in the drive down the Hukawng Valley and the eventual attack on Myitkyina, and also to extend its intelligence operations south of Myitkyina at least to the area of Bhamo and Katha. He made available the arms, ammunition, personnel, and airlift necessary to fulfill this directive. He also stated that should the Detachment be successful in providing this clandestine support to the combat forces, approval would be forthcoming to expand its guerrilla forces to a strength of 10,000, with a commensurate increase in intelligence and other operations.

That the Detachment was indeed successful in this assignment can be illustrated by several incidents from the Hukawng-Myitkyina campaign. The final drive on Myitkyina was made in May 1944 by the Galahad Force (Merrill's Marauders and two Chinese regiments) across the Kumon Range and thence south through Arang to the Myitkyina airfield. Detachment 101 assisted this movement by providing two companies of Kachin guerrillas to reconnoiter and screen the front and flanks. When the Galahad forces reached Arang they picked up additional guides and scouts from a Detachment field base located there. One of the scouts, who had been bitten by a poisonous snake and was so weak that he had to ride horseback, nevertheless led the Galahad Force to the airfield over some old unused trails, completely surprising the Japanese. The airstrip was thus occupied with but little resistance. The part played by the Detachment in this operation points up the interrelationship between its intelligence and other activities.

A day or so before the Galahad Force seized the airfield, Detachment 101 had some of its agent personnel in and out of Myitkyina town. They estimated the Japanese strength there at that time to be only approximately 300, and this information was given to the Northern Combat Area Command and the Galahad Force. After the airstrip was seized, two Chinese

Detachment 101

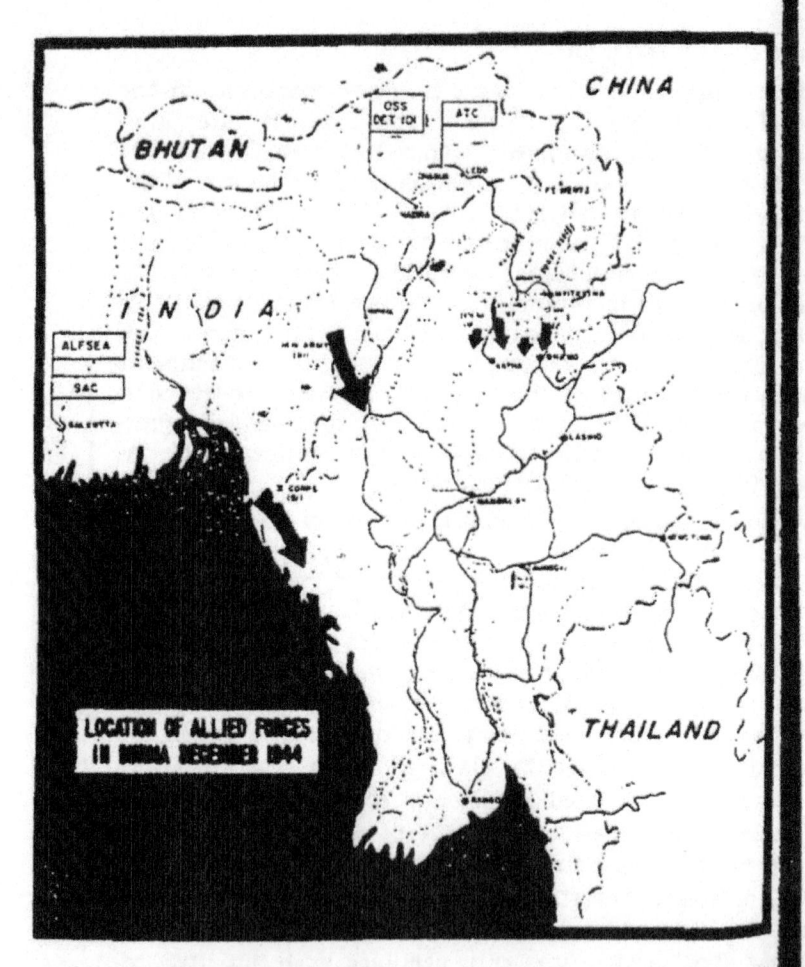

[Map: LOCATION OF ALLIED FORCES IN BURMA DECEMBER 1944]

units were therefore assigned to secure the town. It was to be a double envelopment, one Chinese unit moving north along the Irrawaddy River and the other attacking from the west. All went well until the two converged on the railway station in the center of town at about dusk. It has been reported that Japanese snipers between them started picking them off. Whatever the reason, they soon became heavily engaged with each other and inflicted such severe mutual casualties that they had to be withdrawn. The attempt at an early seizure of the town thus came to nought.

It was two days before the forces were reorganized and made another assault on the town, and when they did they encountered a hornets' nest. In the interim the Japanese had reinforced the town from every direction. They came by road and railroad from Mogaung to the west, from the supply installations to the north along the Irrawaddy, from Maingna and Seniku across the river from the town, and from elsewhere. Within two days, it was estimated, Japanese strength in the town had been augmented to over 1,500, by the end of a week it exceeded 3,000, and it still continued to grow.

This build-up was so rapid as to create for a while the feeling in some quarters that our original strength estimates must have been wrong. But Detachment intelligence agents and guerrilla patrols placed along all the access roads and trails leading into the city confirmed by observation the frantic effort of the Japanese to reinforce the garrison. And subsequently the interrogation of Japanese POW's by NCAC and Galahad intelligence staffs verified as proximately accurate the 300 figure which had been provided by the Detachment. The only discrepancy was in the other direction: an original strength figure of 275 for the Myitkyina garrison was obtained through the interrogations.

The battle for Myitkyina town continued beyond June and into the monsoon. Meanwhile Detachment 101 had expanded its activities to the south as directed by General Stilwell and was providing intelligence and operational support to the combat forces. By the time Myitkyina fell to the allied forces in August 1944, the Detachment had organized its guerrilla forces across an area generally 100 miles farther south and was well on its way toward its ultimate strength of 10,000. Intelligence operations were also increased, and espionage groups were deployed along Japanese lines of communication as far south as Toungoo, approximately 400 miles away.

Mandalay and Beyond

In the fall of 1944 the allied forces in northern Burma opened their drive from Myitkyina toward central Burma. Detachment 101 moved its guerrilla operating area to a line generally through Lashio to Mandalay and thence to the Chindwin River and the India border. At that time it reached its greatest strength and highest stage of development. In the area

Detachment 101

of Lashio there were seven separate battalions, each capable of independent operations. North of Mandalay there were approximately 2,500 guerrillas, organized into units of varying size, depending upon the local situation. To the west, between the railway corridor and the British 14th Army in the Imphal area near the India-Burma border, lay a stretch of over 250 miles in which no allied combat forces were operating. Through this gap ran a series of parallel corridors, excellent natural approaches for the enemy to the Ledo Road being constructed behind the allied combat forces. General Sultan, who had succeeded General Stilwell as Commanding General NCAC, directed Detachment 101 to utilize its guerrilla and intelligence resources to block these several approaches. Guerrilla forces were accordingly deployed in each of them, and with information supplied through intelligence activities were able—although not without some severe fighting—to fend off several Japanese probes through the area.

Intelligence operations during this phase of the campaign were widely developed and reached their greatest degree of reliability. There were over 100 operations involving in excess of 350 agent personnel. Through these and the collection of information by the guerrilla forces, Detachment 101 was able to stay abreast of the changing organization, deployments, and strengths of the Japanese forces. In fact, its intelligence officers probably knew at least as much about the Japanese tactical organization and capabilities as the Japanese themselves did.

When Lashio and Mandalay were captured by allied forces, the Detachment was directed to withdraw its forces from the field and inactivate. Soon, however, the combat situation in southern China became extremely critical, and it was necessary to withdraw all Chinese and American combat forces from northern and central Burma to try to stem the Japanese drive there. General Sultan therefore directed the Detachment to reconstitute whatever force was necessary to conduct a mopping-up operation in the southern Shan States and seize the Taunggyi-Kengtung road, the Japanese escape route to Thailand. Most of our intelligence operations had been retained, fortunately, so there was a sound basis for embarking on this assignment: with some of the Kachin guerrillas as a nucleus, a force approximately 3,000 strong was organized into four battalions. The Japanese, however, had evidently not been told that this was to be a mopping-up operation; it resulted in some of our bloodiest fighting of the war. In less than three months the Detachment's forces killed over 1,200 Japanese and suffered more than 300 killed in action themselves, far more than in any other period. When the escape route to Thailand had been secured, Detachment 101 was inactivated. This was 12 July 1945.

Requirements and Collection

Intelligence requirements on the Detachment stemmed from a variety of sources. Tactical information was required chiefly by Headquarters NCAC, its subordinate commands, and the 10th Air Force, but requests were also received from the British 14th Army and Headquarters Allied Land Forces Southeast Asia. Information of a strategic type would be requested by higher OSS headquarters, CBI Theater Headquarters, and the allied Strategic Air Command under General Stratemeyer in Calcutta. Detachment 101 itself required information of all varieties for planning and conducting its field operations.

With the NCAC, broad intelligence requirements were normally received from the Commanding General in conference. Specific requests came through the Detachment's liaison officer maintained on his G–2 staff. The same general procedures obtained with the 10th Air Force. On the basis of these requirements, along with all others, an intelligence plan would be drawn up, outlining the information to be obtained, the probable target areas, and the likely sources. If sources were already available in the target area, they could simply be asked for the information through normal communication channels. When sources were not available, it was necessary either to adjust operations to obtain the information or to plan new intelligence operations, for which indigenous personnel would have to be recruited, trained, and infiltrated.

The infiltration of agent personnel into proposed areas of operation was effected by parachute or light aircraft or along land routes. The infiltration procedures were in general similar to those used in other theaters of war; but there was one device we employed that involved a unique use of pigeons. Each agent parachuted behind the lines had attached to him a small bamboo cage just large enough to hold a pigeon by which he could report the condition of the radio that had been dropped along with him. After the agent had landed, cleared the drop zone, and had an opportunity to test his radio, he would release the pigeon, preferably near daylight, with a coded message either indicating that all was well or giving instructions when and where to drop another one. For ranges up to two or three hundred miles the pigeons were highly reliable; beyond 400 miles their dependability decreased rapidly.

The intelligence requirements levied on the Detachment were such that almost anything taking place behind the enemy lines was of interest. Primary emphasis was placed upon military information, such items as the strength, identity, and movement of Japanese units, details on supply installations, airfields, and equipment, and whatever else was required to provide a continuous, composite picture of the enemy situation. Much terrain information was also reported, principally on the condition of roads and railroads, the water level and fordability of streams, and the location of potential airfields and drop zones. Since most of the Detachment's personnel were indigenous to the area and intimately familiar with its physiography, this information was rather easy to assemble and report. Economic, sociological, and political intelligence was also in great demand in higher OSS headquarters in the theater, in such agencies as OWI for psychological warfare operations, and in air units for pilot briefing and survival training. It was also needed by the Detachment itself both for morale operations aimed at psychological subversion and for developing agent cover.

The main sources of information were the numerous intelligence agents trained at the Assam base or in the field. Each major field unit had an intelligence officer, usually an American but in some instances a foreign officer or an indigenous recruit trained for the position, whose principal duties were to interrogate captured enemy soldiers or agents, debrief guerrilla personnel, and direct the activities of the espionage agents assigned to the unit. Intelligence personnel at the forward operational headquarters and at the base camp were also engaged in collecting information, principally through interrogation of prisoners and debriefing of operational personnel returned from the field.

Weather and Air Targets

In conjunction with Air Weather Service of 10th Air Force, the Detachment developed a capability for collecting and reporting weather data. The Weather Service provided the equipment, instruction, and weather codes. These were given to selected agents who were then so dispersed, singly or with other groups, that in the aggregate they provided coverage of all of central and northern Burma. According to the A-2, 10th Air Force, this service was of considerable assistance in developing meteorological forecasts for cargo flights over the "hump" and for tactical air operations in northern Burma.

Of especial interest were some of the procedures used in reporting air targets for the 10th Air Force. In the lower reaches of the Hukawng Valley an intelligence agent worked out some simple but ingenious ways to pinpoint and report Japanese supply installations concealed by dense jungle foliage. One method was to select a landmark such as a trail junction, bridge, or prominent tree which could be identified readily on an air photo or by the pilot of the fighter-bomber aircraft. From the landmark the location of the target was given by polar coordinates (distance along a given azimuth). Another method was to lead the pilot from such a landmark to the target by a series of reference points.

Numerous Japanese installations located by these means were bombed or strafed without the pilot being able to see his target; huge explosions or fires erupting through the trees would indicate a successful attack. The Japanese knew that something was amiss. Since the targets were completely hidden from the air, they deduced that the attacks were being directed from the ground and suspected the Kachins. They accordingly restricted entry to their supply areas and would shoot a Kachin on sight. To protect the Kachins these operations had to be suspended for a time.

In the later phase of the Burma campaign procedures were worked out with the 10th Air Force for immediate air strikes against targets of opportunity. Pilots flying air alert and

Detachment 101

agents on the ground were given duplicate sets of air photos with a special grid superimposed. To obtain action against a target the agent would send a coded radio message specifying the type of target and its grid location to the Detachment's forward operations headquarters, located in the immediate vicinity of Headquarters NCAC and the 10th Air Force. 10th Air Force would relay this to the pilot in the aircraft, and after a normal elapsed time of 20 to 30 minutes from the origination of the message an air strike would be made on the target.

Transmission Channels

To expedite the flow of intelligence to user agencies the Detachment established comprehensive handling and transmission procedures. All messages from the field came in to the forward operations headquarters, where field operations were coordinated by an operations officer and a staff including members of the morale operations, intelligence, resistance, and other sections. The intelligence personnel on the operations staff screened all incoming information. If it was of an urgent nature, it was given a hasty evaluation and immediately dispatched to the using agency. Other intelligence messages were routed to the intelligence section for review and subsequent transmission to user agencies on a routine basis.

Detachment 101 had liaison groups with each of the major combat commands it supported—NCAC, 10th Air Force, British 14th Army, and ALFSEA. These officers represented the Detachment in all operational matters, an arrangement that served to enhance their stature and give them considerable prestige in their intelligence dealings within the headquarters. Intelligence-wise, they were responsible for accepting information requests from the headquarters and forwarding them to the Detachment, for passing information and intelligence received from the Detachment on to the intelligence staff, and for representing the Detachment in all other intelligence matters. Information was transmitted to NCAC and the 10th Air Force by teletype and could be moved most rapidly. The communication link with 14th Army and ALFSEA was radio, which required additional time for coding and transmission; the elapsed time, however, was sufficiently small that it could be measured in terms of minutes.

Field liaison groups were also maintained with the Chinese 1st and 6th Armies, the British 36th Division, and the Mars Task Force, which had succeeded Merrill's Marauders. These liaison groups were small, normally consisting of one officer (generally one with considerable field experience) and a radio operator. They performed intelligence functions comparable to those of the higher headquarters liaison groups.

The intelligence transmitted via radio and teletype was summarized and supplemented in the Detachment's weekly and monthly situation reports, distributed through ordinary military messenger service. These were given fairly wide distribution in the theater, going to approximately 100 agencies.

Reliability and Security

Detachment personnel concerned with the evaluation of information arrived at some unusual conclusions. They found, for example, that information reported by the Kachins was generally highly accurate, but that their reports of enemy strength were almost invariably about three times the actual figures. Strength reporting was then stressed in the training program to the extent that the pendulum swung the other way, and the strengths given in Kachin agent reports were so underestimated that they had to be increased by a factor of three. It was not until the winter of 1944-45 that it was possible to obtain reliable strength figures from Kachin personnel. Other ethnic groups were found to have comparable traits, more or less uniform within each group. The evaluators developed correction factors for the Shans, Chins, Burmese, Padaungs, and even the remnants which had remained behind in Burma from the original Chinese Expeditionary Force. All of these groups overestimated strengths, but the Chinese grossly exaggerated them. Their strength figures had to be reduced approximately ten times, and this practice remained constant to the end of the campaign.

The Detachment's counterintelligence operations were purely defensive, designed to protect it and its field operations from infiltration by enemy agents. The number of counterintelligence personnel assigned was consistently small, 3 to 5. They arranged for the physical security of base installations and for the indoctrination of U.S. and indigenous personnel.

Detachment 101

The indoctrination was concerned principally with the methods used by Japanese agents to penetrate and mislead allied clandestine operations and with means for isolating such agents. Counterintelligence functions in the field were the responsibility of the Area Commander or Group Leader in charge of a unit. As a general rule the commander relied mainly on his intelligence officer to ferret out enemy agents, uncover double agents, and of course determine what should be done with them. The Detachment attempted to make all personnel security- and counterintelligence-conscious for their own benefit and to avoid attracting undue attention to the clandestine activity. As a result, the security of the Detachment and its operations, despite some minor infractions, was very good. Not a single agent or operation was known to have been eliminated through enemy intelligence penetration.

Appraisal

Detachment 101's two principal intelligence consumers made attempts to weigh its intelligence contribution to the northern Burma campaign. G-2, NCAC, estimated that it provided between 80% and 90% of all of the combat intelligence utilized by that headquarters. The 10th Air Force reported that it furnished up to 70% of its usable information and designated between 90% and 95% of its air targets. In addition, the Detachment was one of the principal sources of bomb damage assessment information for the 10th Air Force and for SAC. No attempts were made to measure the intelligence contributed to other headquarters, but letters of appreciation showed that it was welcome and considerable. This intelligence was also an indispensable ingredient in the development of the Detachment's own resistance and other clandestine operations.

Units comparable to Detachment 101 collected information behind the lines in France, Italy, the Philippines, China, and other areas. In the aggregate they represented an immense intelligence capability of a type for which, if there should be another war, there would in all probability be a strong requirement. Each of these operations, however, experienced growing pains, and there was a lag time of from one to two years before they were able to produce tangible results. It would be highly desirable, therefore, that the personnel who may be used in such operations in the future should be so oriented, trained, and organized that this critical lag could be minimized. How this is to be accomplished appears as a pressing and continuous problem for the intelligence community.

PRESIDENT HARRY S. TRUMAN ON CIA COVERT OPERATIONS

Whether he would have been more effective if he hadn't gone public, is for others to address

HARRY S. TRUMAN ON CIA COVERT OPERATIONS

Hayden B. Peake

INTRODUCTION

"Parkinson's Law" applied to institutions could suggest that as organizations are handsomely housed, symptoms of decline appear. Applied to the Central Intelligence Agency in 1961, one observes that as the new headquarters building neared completion so did the planning for Operation Zapata—the Bay of Pigs invasion. By the time the first CIA employee began to occupy the new headquarters in late September 1961, the Bay of Pigs was a matter of public record. Whether one chooses to invoke Parkinson, henceforth covert operations came under increasing scrutiny and the reputation of the Agency suffered a blow from which it has recovered erratically.

An unexpected contribution to the early criticism of the Agency came from former President Harry S. Truman in a syndicated article published in the *Washington Post* on 22 December 1963.[*] That article addressed two subjects—Truman's rationale for establishing the CIA to provide integrated intelligence to the President and CIA "operations," a term which Truman did not define although the context in which he used it suggested covert political and paramilitary actions. Truman wrote that the CIA had been "diverted from its original assignment. It has become an operational and at times a policymaking arm of the government. This has led to trouble . . . in several explosive areas." He then went on to make a characteristically declarative statement which caused considerable consternation in and out of the government:

> I never had any thought that when I set up the CIA that it would be injected into peacetime cloak and dagger operations. Some of the complications and embarrassment that I think we have experienced are in part attributable to the fact that this quiet intelligence arm of the president has been so removed from its intended role that it is being interpreted as a symbol of sinister and mysterious foreign intrigue—and a subjecter of cold war enemy propaganda.

This article appeared at a time when the CIA was under attack for supporting the Diem government in South Vietnam and for engineering a coup in Laos, when the U-2 incident and the Bay of Pigs failure were still fresh in the public mind, when prominent journalists like Stewart Alsop (a former OSS man himself) were charging that the CIA at times had more power than the Department of State. There were calls for increased Congressional oversight. Truman's remarks stunned CIA officials all the more since it had been during his administration and with his explicit but secret approval that CIA covert action and clandestine collection operations were initiated to help contain the communist threat. Although attempts would be made to have Mr. Truman clarify his position, the 1963 article proved to be his final written comment on the issue.

---

[*] Reprinted on Page 40.

NON-GOVERNMENT LITERATURE AND THE "TRUMAN ARTICLE"

For reasons that remain unclear, many of the nation's major newspapers did not mention the story; those that did presumed that Truman was right. The now defunct *Washington Daily News*, on 5 January 1964, carried an article by Richard Starnes, "Harry S. Fires Telling Broadside at the CIA," which is typical, though more strident in tone, of the early press reaction:

> The Central Intelligence Agency, a cloudy organism of uncertain purpose and appalling power, promises to have an uncomfortable time of it in the year just begun. Former President Truman, who hatched the coiling, mysterious creature, spoiled the holidays for the busy apologists of the CIA by firing a telling broadside in a copyrighted newspaper article. Mr. Truman is no great shucks as a writer, but there is nothing wrong with his thinking or his facts. He echoed the charge (early made here) that the monstrous spook apparatus had metastasized into policymaking and operational functions, neither of which was intended by the founders of the CIA . . . in spite of the outraged howls of denial by the nominal head of the CIA, both charges are quite true.

Editorials in many local papers argued that having created the CIA, Truman possessed "impressive credentials" to criticize it, concurred in general terms with the view that the Agency should not conduct covert operations. The examples they cited were all covert operations undertaken by Truman's successors, implying in the process that the Agency indeed had been diverted from its original mission.

Surprisingly, the "Truman article" received much less foreign attention. On 15 January 1964, Moscow's TASS International Service quoted a short portion of the Starnes article (not the strongest rhetoric by any means) but did not stress the issue. Cuban radio broadcast a comment on the article on 29 December 1963, adding a few critical embellishments. The European media ignored the issue.

The "Truman article" was first cited in a book, *The Invisible Government*,[*] in the fall of 1964 by David Wise and Thomas B. Ross, the first of a number of works criticizing U.S. intelligence activities in general and the CIA in particular. Wise and Ross asserted, inter alia, that the CIA had exceeded the intent of Congress, as expressed in the National Security Act of 1947, by engaging in covert political operations "all over the world." They stated that even President Truman "maintained that he had no idea that this was going to happen." But Wise and Ross did recognize the dilemma: "It was under President Truman, however, that the CIA began conducting special operations." They concluded that Truman in his article was "lamenting damage to the national prestige caused by . . . the U-2 affair, the Bay of Pigs and the episodes in Indonesia, Burma, Laos, Vietnam and elsewhere." Thus they asked: "The real question is whether the operational activities of the CIA have grown to a size and shape Truman had not intended . . . has the dagger become more important than the cloak?"

In his 1970 study, *The Intelligence Establishment*,[**] Harry Howe Ransom, a professor at Vanderbilt University, twice quoted the "Truman article." The first time he noted Truman's "surprise" at CIA's having been injected into "peacetime cloak-and-dagger operations" in order to support his (Ransom's) assertion that the Agency was exceeding both Truman's and Congress' intent. This second quotation was Truman's sentence: "There is something about the way the CIA has been functioning that is casting a shadow over our historic position, and I feel that we need to correct it."

---

[*] Random House, New York, 1964.
[**] Harvard University Press, Cambridge, Mass., 1970.

Harry Truman

Paradoxically, unlike Wise and Ross, Professor Ransom did not remind the reader of the implicit contradictions between Truman's relationship with the Agency as Chief Executive and his later criticism of it. He left the impression that the CIA had not been authorized by either Congress or the President to undertake covert operations, thus justifying the ex-President's apparent dismay and his own conclusion: "Since Truman wrote in 1963, the CIA has remained the uncorrected problem child of American foreign policy."

The Truman article was quoted five times in L. Fletcher Prouty's *The Secret Team: The CIA and its Allies in Control of the United States and the World,** a bitter attack on the CIA and its covert action operations, published in 1973. Prouty used the "Truman article" with a twist.

> Although even in his time he (Truman) had seen the beginning of the move of the CIA into covert activities, there can be little doubt that the "diversion" to which he made reference was not one that he would have attributed to himself or to any other President. Rather, the fact that the CIA had gone into clandestine operations and had been "injected into peacetime cloak-and-dagger operations" and "has been so much removed from its intended role," was more properly attributable to the growing and secret pressures of some *other power source* (emphasis added). As he said the CIA had become "a symbol of sinister and mysterious foreign intrigue.

Prouty never identifies his "other power source." In an exhibition of questionable scholarship, Prouty cites a National Security Council directive, NSC-10/2 (which he claims to have read), as the source of the objectionable covert operations policy—but ignores that fact that it was Truman who approved that same directive in 1948. Almost in passing, Prouty points out that NSC-10/2 requires a covert operation to be conceived and executed so that the U.S. government can plausibly disclaim any role if necessary. He implies, without acknowledging the inconsistency, that Truman would have been less upset had this doctrine been followed. The reader is left with the inaccurate impression that the CIA conducted its clandestine operations in loose conformity with NSC guidance but contrary to the intent of the President and that Truman came to hold his view.

Two other books published in 1973 also appeared to reinforce some of the views that President Truman expressed in his *Washington Post* article. In *Plain Speaking,*** Merle Miller relates Truman's response to Miller's question, "How do you feel about the CIA now?"

> I think it was a mistake. And if I had known what was going to happen, I never would have done it . . . it got out of hand. The fella . . . the one that was in the White House after me never paid any attention to it, and it got out of hand. Why, they've got an organization . . . that is practically the equal of the Pentagon . . . one Pentagon is too many . . . those fellas in the CIA don't just report on wars . . . they go out and make their own and there's nobody to keep track of what they're up to.

While this might appear to mean that Truman opposed the CIA generally, an equally likely alternative is that he disapproved of the way the Agency was run by his succes-

---

* Prentice Hall, New Jersey, 1973.
** Berkley Publishing Corporation, New York, 1973.

Harry Truman

sors. In her affectionate book, *Harry S. Truman*,* Margaret Truman Daniels states that "one of his (Truman's) proudest accomplishments as President was the creation of the Central Intelligence Agency," and that through it he received the intelligence he wanted. She leaves the clear impression that the need for integrated analyzed intelligence was the primary reason Truman established the CIA.

Aside from a few references to and reprinting of the "Truman article" in the press after the December 1974 *New York Times* exposé by Seymour Hersh, the "Truman article" apparently has been quoted only infrequently—by Marchetti and Marks in *The CIA and the Cult of Intelligence*;** in *The CIA File*,*** edited by Marks and Borosage in 1975; and in *The CIA's Secret Operations*[†] by Harry Rositzke, a former CIA officer. In a summary of events leading to the creation of the CIA's initial covert action program, Rositzke wrote that ". . . Truman's role . . . has been obscured by his apparent denunciation of covert operations years later." Then Rositzke makes a startling assertion that Truman may not even have been the author of the article:

> The critical remarks (Truman) supposedly made in a syndicated article . . . have often been quoted. . . . In a conversation with President Truman the following April, the then CIA Director Allen Dulles brought up the President's published statement, and recalled to him some of Truman's own decisions authorizing covert operations in Italy, Greece, Turkey and the Philippines. After reading the article Truman expressed puzzlement and said, in effect, that the story was all wrong and gave a very unfortunate impression. Apparently, the article had been written by David Noyes, his former White House assistant and not read by the President himself who was then in his eighties.

The use of the "Truman article" is found in *American Shadow*[††] by Darrell Garwood, who, attempting to support his argument that the CIA exceeded its original purpose under Dulles, quotes Truman: "I never had any *idea* when I set up the CIA that it would be injected in the peacetime cloak-and-dagger *business*" (emphasis added). Garwood then suggests by way of explanation that "other than outright lying," Mr. Truman's comments can only be explained by an "uncharacteristic loss of memory or else—like his successors Presidents Eisenhower and Kennedy—he did not know what the CIA was planning and doing. He may have been told so little that in later years he was thinking of the earlier and admittedly innocuous group called the CIG." To accept Garwood's view one must believe Eisenhower and Kennedy knew nothing of the Bay of Pigs—let alone the other covert operations during their administrations. It is necessary, therefore, to determine the details of the actual covert action policy President Truman authorized.

THE RECORD ON COVERT OPERATIONS

The first National Security Council directive authorizing covert operations was approved at the initial meeting of the National Security Council on 19 December 1947 (NSC directive 4/A). It assigned to the CIA the mission of executing covert activities to prevent a Communist takeover in Italy. On 22 December 1947, the responsibility for

---

* William Morrow and Co., New York, 1973.
** Alfred A. Knopf, Inc., New York, 1974.
*** Grossman Publishers, New York, 1976.
[†] Reader's Digest Press, New York, 1977.
[††] Dan River Press, Stafford, Virginia, 1980.

Harry Truman

covert operations management was given to the CIA Office of Special Operations which, in turn, formed the Special Procedures Group to do the work. In May 1948, George F. Kennan, Director of the State Department, Policy Planning Staff, recommended creation of a permanent organization to continue covert political operations elsewhere. With the support of Secretary of State Marshall, Secretary of Defense Forrestal and President Truman, on June 18, 1948 NSC 4/A was superseded by NSC 10/2 which authorized the establishment of a new organization responsible for covert action within CIA—the Office of Special Projects (OSP). It was soon to be the Office of Policy Coordination (OPC).

NSC 10/2 states that the National Security Council:

> . . . has determined that, in the interests of world peace and U.S. national security, that overt foreign activities of the U.S. government must be supplemented by covert operations. . . . It therefore seems desirable, for operational reasons, not to create a new agency for covert operations, but in time of peace to place the responsibility for them within the structure of the CIA and correlate them with espionage and counterespionage operations under the overall supervision of the Director of Central Intelligence.

Citing the authority for such action (Section 102(d) (5) of the National Security Act of 1947), NSC 10/2 defines responsibilities and directs the planning, personnel, issues, reporting chain and the general conduct of covert operations.

Truman's actions regarding covert operations were not limited to the short-term policy embodied in NSC 10/2. In February 1948, he appointed Allen W. Dulles, William H. Jackson and Mathias F. Correa, to undertake a one-year study of CIA operations. Their report (NSC-50) included an extensive analysis of and support for "the Conduct of Secret Operations" which were defined as " . . . covert psychological warfare, clandestine political activity, sabotage and guerrilla activity" as well as the organization of OPC within the CIA, clearly laying the foundation for covert operations. The efforts of Frank G. Wisner, the first Director of OPC, were made easier by the demands on the CIA during the Korean War when covert action operations grew rapidly in both personnel and budget. In 1949, OPC had 302 total personnel with a budget of $4.7M. By 1952, there were 2,812 OPC staff employees and 3,142 overseas contract personnel—the budget was $82 million. Notwithstanding this increase, covert operations remained largely shielded from the public view and conformed in this respect to NSC guidance for wartime operations.

In sum, there is no doubt that President Truman was intimately involved with the creation and implementation of the CIA covert operations capability. Nor is there doubt that he approved written policy direction through the NSC as to their nature and purpose of such operations.

Further light on Truman's views is provided in an exchange of letters between Admiral Sidney Souers[*] and Truman. On 27 December 1963, Souers, then retired, wrote Truman to comment on the newspaper article which had been sent him by a friend:

> Dear Boss . . . This was a splendid statement and I am delighted you made it because it needed to be said. . . . Allen Dulles caused the CIA to wander too far from the original goal established by you and it is certainly a different animal than I tried to set up for you. . . . It would seem that its principal effort was to cause revolutions in smaller coun-

---
[*] Later Executive Secretary of the National Security Council.

tries around the globe. . . . As bad as that was, it was worse to try to conduct a 'war' invading Cuba with a handful of men and without air cover. . . . With so much emphasis on operations, it would not surprise me to find that the method of collecting and processing intelligence suffered some.

Truman replied on 17 January 1964:

Dear Sid . . . Thanks for yours of 27 December. I more than appreciated it and I am happy as I can be that my article on the Central Intelligence Agency rang a bell with you because you know why the organization was set up. It was set up so the President would know what was going on.

It would appear from this exchange that Rositzke's assertion that Truman may not have written or even read the article has been repudiated.

There are several points in the Souers-Truman exchange that require clarification. Souers' allusion to the "animal" he set up for Truman refers to the CIA's predecessor, the Central Intelligence Group (CIG) which was not charged with covert operations. Souers was never Director of the CIA; and the first NSC directives authorizing covert operations were promulgated after he had left the CIG. There was, however, a common element shared by the CIG and the CIA; i.e., Truman's requirement for integrated intelligence collection and analysis. In this context then Truman's response that Souers knew "exactly why the organization was set up," had to refer to those integrated intelligence functions. Likewise, when Souers criticizes Dulles for letting the CIA "wander too far from the original goal established by you" and for conducting revolutions and wars, he must have had the same idea in mind. Souers well knew that NSC-10/2 prohibited paramilitary action by regular military forces because he was the Executive Secretary of the NSC when it was approved. In short, the Souers-Truman exchange criticizes Dulles et al., for exceeding the intent of NSC-10/2 at the expense of the CIA's primary mission as they saw it.

It is not surprising, then, that Dulles[*] was deeply upset by the "Truman article" as he wrote the former President to say so. At first, Dulles cited those portions of the article with which he agreed; i.e., that the primary function of the CIA was indeed that of providing intelligence to the President:

I thoroughly agree with your basic premise that the primary mission of the CIA is to provide the President with the intelligence he requires. . . . This should be done faithfully and fearlessly. Nothing should be allowed to divide the Agency from fulfilling this function which you had primarily in mind when you sought and obtained the CIA legislation in the 1947 National Security Act. . . .

Dulles then was equally frank in making clear where his judgment differed from Mr. Truman's:

I respectfully differ, however, from what you have written . . . particularly what you say about the CIA being injected into peacetime cloak-and-dagger operations and your admonition that CIA should terminate its operational duties which you suggest are 'sometimes akin to a subverting influence in the affairs of other people'; also, I differ with your comment that CIA has become 'at times a policymaking arm of the government.'

---

[*] Then in retirement.

Harry Truman

After hailing the "Truman Doctrine," as "the first official and public recognition of the great dangers of communist subversive action against free government," Dulles then chided the former President:

> You will recall that about a year after the Truman Doctrine declaration of April 1947 you also were *first* to take stock of the fact that the communist subversive threat could not be met solely by the overt type of assistance which you were able to render to the beleagured countries of Greece and Turkey.

This recognition, Dulles recalls, resulted in an NSC directive on covert activities (presumably 10/2) and the reorganization of "covert functions" in which Truman himself assigned the responsibility to the CIA.

For reasons of security, Mr. Dulles did not discuss operations undertaken since the Truman administration, but he did suggest that if informed of their purpose, Mr. Truman would look favorably on their continuation within the CIA:

> "Over the years since 1948 when this program was initiated by you, there have been a whole series of quiet successes and a certain number of publicized failures. I feel sure that if I had an opportunity of describing to you, point by point, what has been accomplished since your approval of this program, you would have reason to be proud of your initiative in this field. To destroy the expertise which has been developed over the last decade and a half . . . —would, I fear, seriously prejudice our national security."

As to the allegation that the CIA was a policymaking organization, something he publicly was on record as opposing, Dulles offered to respond privately. In closing, he suggests that Mr. Truman's *Washington Post* article might be used to damage a policy for which Mr. Truman should receive great credit:

> I can say—frankly—that I feel there are parts of your article of 21 December 1963 which might be interpreted as a repudiation of a policy which you had the great courage and wisdom to initiate 15 years ago.

It is likely that this comment caught Mr. Truman's attention, especially if he had not intended such an interpretation in the first place.

Mr. Truman accepted Dulles' offer of a private meeting at the Truman Library on 21 April 1964. After the visit, Dulles wrote a memorandum to Lawrence Houston, CIA General Counsel, reporting the substance of the exchange:

> I then reviewed with Mr. Truman the part he had had in supplementing the overt Truman Doctrine affecting Greece and Turkey with the procedures largely implemented by CIA to meet the creeping subversion of Communism, which could not be met by open intervention, military aid, under the Truman plan. I reviewed the various covert steps which had been taken under his authority in suppressing the Huk rebellion in the Philippines, of the problems we had faced during the Italian election in 1948. . . .
>
> Mr. Truman followed all this with keen interest, interjected reminiscences of his own, recalled vividly the whole Italian election problem, as well as the Huk situation. I then showed him the article in the *Washington Post* of December 22, 1963, which I suggested seemed to me to be a misrepresentation of his position. He studied attentively the Post story and seemed quite astounded at it. In fact, he said this was

all wrong. He then said that he felt it had made a very *unfortunate impression*. (emphasis added)

At no time did Mr. Truman express other than complete agreement with the viewpoint I expressed, and several times he said he would see what he could do about it, to leave it in his hands.

I cannot predict what will come of all this. It is even possible, maybe probable, that he will do nothing when he thinks it over. He may, of course, consult with those, whoever they are, who induced him to make the original statement.

The final sentence indicates Dulles did not doubt Truman's authorship of the original statement. Both Dulles' memorandum to Houston and letter to Truman suggest that the reason for Truman's "astonishment" was that his article had created an "unfortunate impression" about CIA covert operations *during his administration*—an interpretation Truman would have considered "all wrong" if he was concerned mainly with the change in covert operations since he left office. The Souers-Truman exchange of letters supports this view. While Dulles had offered to review with Mr. Truman covert operations undertaken after the former President left office, the operations mentioned in his memorandum indicate he did not do so. Instead, Dulles apparently reviewed only those operations undertaken during Truman's administration, arguing that those initiated during the Eisenhower administration were only "slightly modified."

This was not the case—and Dulles certainly knew it. There was far more than a "slight modification" of covert action policies under the Dulles brothers and Eisenhower. The first step in that direction, published in March 1954 as NSC-5412,* was a revision of Truman administration policy. Whereas 10/2 and its successor 10/5 devoted one paragraph to covert operations guidance, 5412 used more than a page which included the single operations paragraph from 10/2 cited above. Where 10/2 cited only the Soviet Union and its satellites and spoke in general terms about covert action against "hostile foreign states," 5412/2 *directed* covert operations designed to combat the international communist threat from the "USSR and Communist China and the governments, parties and groups dominated by them." Like NSC 10/2, 5412 also required plausible denial and prohibited armed conflict, but its direction to the CIA to conduct covert operations was considerably expanded.

a. Create and exploit troublesome problems for International Communism. . . .

b. Discredit the prestige and ideology of International Communism. . . .

c. Counter any threat . . . directly or indirectly response to Communist control to achieve dominant power in a free world country.

d. Reduce International Communist control over any areas of the world.

e. Strengthen the orientation toward the United States of the peoples and nations of the free world. . . .

f. To the extent practicable in areas dominated or threatened by International Communism, develop underground resistance and facilitate covert

---

* National Archives, Modern Library Branch, *National Security Council Directive on Covert Operations* NSC-5412 (superseding NSC-10/5), dated 15 March 1954, declassified by NSC, EO11652, 20 Dec 1977 (only 12 copies made), Box No. 3. Revised on 12 March 1955 and NSC 5412/1, and 28 December 1955 to NSC 5412/2.

Harry Truman

and guerrilla operations and ensure availability of those forces in the event of war, including . . . provision for stay-behind assets and escape and evasion facilities.

It was under these expanded marching orders that the CIA undertook its more extensive and sometimes controversial covert action operations. For reasons which the records do not reveal, Dulles apparently chose to minimize the difference in his exchange with Mr. Truman. As a result, Mr. Dulles probably misled the ex-President by avoiding discussion of the post-1950 covert actions which very likely provoked the "Truman article." In turn, this caused Mr. Truman to focus during their meeting on the potential damage his article could do to the reputation of his administration. In this way, Mr. Dulles may have sought to get some public retraction from Mr. Truman. He failed in this attempt, however, and the confusion described above was the result.

There was one final attempt by the CIA to clarify Truman's remarks. During one of the periodic intelligence briefings provided him on orders from President Johnson, CIA Deputy Director Lt. Gen. Marshall Carter and his Executive Assistant, Enno H. Knoche, met with Truman at the Truman Library in June 1964. Prior to the briefing, The Washington Post article was raised by Carter and Knoche with David Noyes, an assistant to Mr. Truman. In a memorandum, based on Knoche's notes of the meeting, it is recorded that:

> Noyes evidently drafts Mr. Truman's statements and articles, and admitted quite freely the authorship of the "Truman article" on the CIA. . . . Carter did get into this subject. . . . He referred in general to recent criticism of the Agency and its operations and reminded Truman that it was he himself who authorized most of the early clandestine operations in response to such challenges as Italy and Greece. Truman broke in on the General's statement to say yes he knew all that, it was important work, and he would order it to be done again under the same circumstances. He went on to add that he had set up the CIA to pull together basic information required by the President but which had been denied to him by State and Pentagon handling procedures. He said that was his main purpose.[*]

Mr. Knoche's memo becomes the best evidence that while Truman may not have written the article personally, he very likely initiated or at least supported the action. Moreover, Mr. Knoche told this author in a telephone conversation on 30 August 1980 that it was clear that President Truman was very concerned about the CIA creating policy under the Eisenhower administration and that it was to the CIA covert actions during that administration Truman objected most.

THE DENOUEMENT

What Harry S. Truman wrote in the Washington Post he had said before (though not in public) in much the same language. The question, then, is what did he mean? Non-government commentators nearly all concluded that he was concerned about "recent" (post-Truman era) covert operations which had failed and/or become public knowledge to the embarrassment of the U.S. Truman's characterization of the CIA as "the quiet intelligence arm of the President" is a reasonable description of the situation during his term of office. He had kept covert operations secret and relatively free from public charges of being "a subverting influence in the affairs of other

---

[*] Onate, Benjamin F., "What Did Truman Say about the CIA?" *Studies in Intelligence* CIA, V. 17, No. 3, 1973, p 10-11.

people" even during the Korean War. NSC directive 10/2 sets forth his policy stressing secrecy and plausible denial, while prohibiting the use of conventional military forces except during time of war. His successors did not adhere to this policy and the Souers-Truman exchange of letters clearly indicates Truman's dissatisfaction with covert operations under Eisenhower and Kennedy.

Mr. Truman's article was critical of Eisenhower-Kennedy era covert operations—not covert operations *per se*. He was saying if you can't keep them secret and protect the U.S. Government's good name, get out of the business—give it to the Pentagon—you're doing more harm than good.

Whether Mr. Truman could have been more effective had he discussed the matter quietly with Allen Dulles, or even Presidents Johnson or Kennedy rather than going public, is for others to address.

The "Truman Article" as it appeared in: *The Washington Post*, 22 December 1963

Independence, Mo. December 21—

I think it has become necessary to take another look at the purpose and operations of our Central Intelligence Agency—CIA. At least, I would like to submit here the original reason why I thought it necessary to organize this Agency during my Administration, what I expected it to do and how it was to operate as an arm of the President.

I think it is fairly obvious that by and large a President's performance in office is as effective as the information he has and the information he gets. That is to say, that assuming the President himself possesses a knowledge of our history, a sensitive understanding of our institutions, and an insight into the needs and aspirations of the people, he needs to have available to him the most accurate and up-to-the-minute information on what is going on everywhere in the world, and particularly of the trends and developments in all the danger spots in the contest between East and West. This is an immense task and requires a special kind of an intelligence facility.

Of course, every President has available to him all the information gathered by the many intelligence agencies already in existence. The Department of State, Defense, Commerce, Interior and others are constantly engaged in extensive information gathering and have done excellent work.

But their collective information reached the President all too frequently in conflicting conclusions. At times, the intelligence reports tended to be slanted to conform to established positions of a given department. This becomes confusing and what's worse, such intelligence is of little use to a President in reaching the right decisions.

Therefore, I decided to set up a special organization charged with the collection of all intelligence reports from every available source, and to have those reports reach me as President without department "treatment" or interpretations.

I wanted and needed the information in its "natural raw" state and in as comprehensive a volume as it was practical for me to make full use of it. But the most important thing about this move was to guard against the chance of intelligence being used to influence or to lead the President into unwise decisions—and I thought it was necessary that the President do his own thinking and evaluating.

Since the responsibility for decision making was his—then he had to be sure that no information is kept from him for whatever reason at the discretion of any one

Harry Truman

department or agency, or that unpleasant facts be kept from him. There are always those who would want to shield a President from bad news or misjudgments to spare him from being "upset."

For some time I have been disturbed by the way CIA has been diverted from its original assignment. It has become an operational and at times a policymaking arm of the Government. This has led to trouble and may have compounded our difficulties in several explosive areas.

I never had any thought that when I set up the CIA that it would be injected into peacetime cloak-and-dagger operations. Some of the complications and embarrassment that I think we have experienced are in part attributable to the fact that this quiet intelligence arm of the President has been so removed from its intended role that it is being interpreted as a symbol of sinister and mysterious foreign intrigue—and a subject for cold war enemy propaganda.

With all the nonsense put out by Communist propaganda about "Yankee imperialism," "exploitive capitalism," "war mongering," "monopolists," in their name-calling assault on the West, the last thing we needed was for the CIA to be seized upon as something akin to a subverting influence in the affairs of other people.

I well knew the first temporary director of the CIA, Admiral Souers, and the later permanent directors of the CIA, Gen. Hoyt Vandenberg and Allen Dulles. These were men of the highest character, patriotism and integrity—and I assume this is true of all those who continue in charge.

But there are now some searching questions that need to be answered. I, therefore, would like to see the CIA be restored to its original assignment as the intelligence arm of the President, and that whatever else it can properly perform in that special field—and that its operational duties be terminated or properly used elsewhere.

We have grown up as a nation, respected for our free institutions and for our ability to maintain a free and open society. There is something about the way the CIA has been functioning that is casting a shadow over our historic position and I feel that we need to correct it.

COVER IN UNCONVENTIONAL OPERATIONS

Broad reflections on the role of concealment in unconventional warfare and other clandestine operations.

COVER IN UNCONVENTIONAL OPERATIONS
Harvey B. McCadden

Mr. James Thurber, reviewing a book about caterpillars, complained that "the author has told me more about the caterpillar than I wished to know." Prospective readers of this paper are promised no such exhaustive or exhausting treatment, but some remarks on cover and concealment seem appropriate at a time when studies are in progress looking toward a more effective and better polished conduct of unconventional warfare operations.

Unconventional operations, bellicose or otherwise, if they are to retain the conspiratorial and secret attributes they have had in the past, bespeak cover and concealment, at least in their organizational stages and sometimes through their entire life cycle. Cover is almost always necessary for the protection of conspiracy and conspirators as they organize for action. If surprise is to play any part in the fruition of the conspiracy, cover is a useful and sometimes a necessary ingredient in mounting the action. And if for political reasons abroad the government sponsorship or perpetration of the action is not to be revealed, then cover is a *sine qua non* throughout. Cover affords protection against counteraction either of a direct sort or through mobilization of adverse public opinion.

Cover is therefore a consideration to be weighed in connection with any examination or re-examination of the modus of unconventional operations. It is not, of course, the only pertinent consideration; for one thing, it is never quite separable from other pervasive protective elements of the operational plan, particularly security and counterintelligence. But cover and concealment are worth singling out here as one aspect of unconventional operation sometimes obscured by the complexity of the whole.

Cover as Integral to Planning

A major point to be emphasized is that cover, the assumption of some ostensible legitimate status to conceal the hand of intelligence or operations personnel and protect their activities, must be treated as an integral part of the plan for the conduct of any clandestine operation. It does not fall into the category of a support factor on the peripheral framework of the plan nor is it an element solely of its executional phase. Such views are intrinsic hazards to the basic philosophy of clandestine operation. Cover is a determining element in the plan itself, and a sound concept of its application must be worked out in advance. All persons responsible for the execution of the plan must know the "legend" beforehand, and during the execution they must accept the discipline it requires and adhere to the regimen it imposes.

Because of this burden of maintaining cover and the hazards of exposure,[1] if for no other reason, clandestine procedure should not be adopted for an action unless the national interest clearly demands it. For once it is decided that an operation is to be clandestine, there is no recourse in its execution from this burden and these hazards.

An example of operational cover consistently maintained is the Soviet deployment of a trawler fleet into international waters, including the sea lanes of the Western powers. Whatever the plan of clandestine operations for this fleet may be, the cover of commercial fishing is an integral part of it. When suspicions have been voiced that the "fishing" is of a peculiar surreptitious kind, the Russians have steadfastly maintained a position of international legality and rectitude. The fishing legend is always vigorously reasserted, and it is accepted by those who are inclined to believe the best of the Bulwark of Socialist Society. In adopting this cover the Russians apparently considered protection against adverse public opinion worth the cost—in men, money, materials, and planning effort—of creating for their clandestine activity this elaborate equipment identified with peacetime pursuits.

---

[1] The usual agents of exposure are not only enemy counterintelligence services, but also friendly counterintelligence services, newsmen with exaggerated zeal, and fellow citizens competing in the cover capacity or just infected with one-upmanship.

As corollary to the proposition that cover is integral to the concept of an operation, it follows that the conduct of the operation must be shaped to fit its cover legend. For one thing, personnel overtly connected with the operating agency, or with other government agencies and departments, can play only a limited role in the execution of a clandestine operation, one that permits them to remain in the background unidentifield with the plan or its execution.[2] And the drive to "get things done" must frequently give way to measured, often cumbersome, sometimes inefficient, methods necessary to preserve the cover legend.

Extemporization of cover in the conduct of a clandestine operation must be closely controlled and in each instance carefully evaluated in relation to the totality of the coverture. Cover contrived empirically for an act ancillary to a planned operation may conveniently cover the act but at the same time be inimical to or inconsistent with the cover legend; coverture of the part may tend to expose the whole. For example, the purchase of expensive equipment by a "private citizen" for cash may hide the identity of the buyer but may create a whirlwind of conjecture in the business community, leading to a consensus, particularly if the purchase is one of a series of suspicious incidents, that the cover legend is an official contrivance. Even in an agency composed of civilians trained in the use of cover, it is a formidable task to enforce unremitting application of a cover legend in the face of more expeditious ways of "getting on with the job." Within a military structure, the accommodation to such an inhibiting factor poses an even graver problem to personnel trained in traditional methods of direct action.

Magnitude and Concealment

Since requirements for concealment may vary according to circumstance, cover may be considered a variable both qualitatively and quantitatively. It may vary qualitatively accord-

---

[2] Although it is almost a truism, it is perhaps worth repeating that once an individual, however well qualified for a particular assignment, is publicly identified with a government department or agency, there are no mechanics of disassociation that can assure him protection from identification by hostile intelligence services and propagandists, or for that matter by *friendly* enemies.

ing to the depth of concealment required by political considerations, and also quantitatively with the size of the operation or the nature of the support available for it. Operations undertaken in a favorable political climate and with the tacit consent of the local government may require only a thin veil to conform to political niceties, whereas those mounted under a hostile regime may require the ultimate in concealment.

With respect to size and complexity, it may be said that in general the smaller the operation in terms of men, money, and materials, the better the chance for its complete coverture. Some large operations are of such a nature that they may be covered up to a given point in their unfoldment but then inevitably become apparent. For these a judgment must be made as to whether the advantages of a temporary cover legend are worth the effort entailed and any ill effects of the subsequent exposure. The sheer magnitude of a given operation sometimes limits the reliance that can be placed on cover and concealment, but even here particular aspects of the whole may be cloaked by the controlled use of physical security, surprise, and operational deception, as well as cover. When all tricks of the trade are skillfully applied, much can be accomplished, probably more than is realized by the current crop of expostulators who seek the public ear and eye. In this broad sense remarkably good coverture was attained for many aspects of the largest operation in which this nation ever participated, Overlord.

There are of course other limiting influences on cover and concealment besides the magnitude of the operation—geography, for example, if we speak of an infiltration operation. It goes without saying that a cross-border operation from a contiguous wooded area can be concealed much more easily than a penetration from across a large intervening stretch of water, sand, or exposed flatland. In addition, ethnological and ecological limitations play their part. These latter have been well debated and categorized in the past and this information is available for future guidance.

It is, however, the limitations imposed by magnitude and complexity that undoubtedly need re-examination and debate at this point. We came out of World War II with some fairly firm ideas on the limitations inherent in clandestine operations by their very nature, particularly those of the kind undertaken by the early Resistance, based largely on hope with little assurance of ultimate deliverance from the Nazis. The dogma of small, compartmented units and closely held knowledge, so painfully achieved at that time, seems of late to have lost its currency. We have fallen into habits of thought which permit covert operations to take on any degree of magnitude from the deployment of a solitary agent to actions involving hundreds of people.

But it is not our purpose here to prejudge the problem of scope and magnitude; it should be the subject of a careful and well-paced examination, which should at the same time consider the inhibitions imposed on unconventional operations by the necessity of maintaining a benignant world opinion. In the process of any such evaluation, however, we must especially guard against any tendency to derogate the very concept of the use of covert operations in the nation's interest.

Having begun these reflections with a quotation from a prophet of joy, we might end with comment on one from a prophet of gloom. A columnist in the *Washington Post* of 9 May 1961 was moved to say, "It is not possible for a free and open society to organize successfully a spectacular conspiracy. The United States, like every other government, must employ secret agents. But the United States cannot successfully conduct large secret conspiracies. It is impossible to keep them secret."

A free society may not be able to organize a "spectacular conspiracy," for that is an outright contradiction in terms. But as a nation we can do just about all we need to do in the way of conspiracy—if it is carefully planned with due regard to the integrity of its elements, if the plan is continuously weighed against the consequences of failure, and if it is executed with the required care and deliberation. Our freedom was gained in substantial part by conspiratorial action; in the same fashion much can be done to keep it.

REMINISCENES OF A COMMUNICATIONS AGENT

A technician's personal story of his work in radio and photographic transmission of intelligence to the British service affords a glimpse of wartime espionage through foreign agent eyes.

REMINISCENCES OF A COMMUNICATIONS AGENT
Expatriate

During World War II, I was employed by the British intelligence service in one of the European countries which was at first neutral, then a German ally, and finally under German occupation. I had two concurrent jobs. One was to maintain radio communications with a base on the Mediterranean some 750 miles away. The other was to photograph intelligence reports, maps, and sketches and to conceal the films in inconspicuous objects which could be smuggled across the border.

Some of the techniques used in these operations were supplied by my superior and some were of my own devising. Although these procedures have now undoubtedly been antiquated by technical progress since the war, they should still hold some historical interest. Certainly some general principles of conduct which were important to me have continuing validity as precepts for the clandestine agent of today.

After the Germans had overrun my homeland and imprisoned me along with many others, I escaped and made my way to this country which was still neutral and where the people were traditionally well disposed toward my people. I wanted to avenge the ravaging of my homeland, within my small individual power, and to continue the struggle against its brutal occupier. Therefore, although I am not British nor a great admirer of the British, I entered their intelligence employ as the occupation most promising for fulfillment of this my purpose.

The work was dangerous, very dangerous after the Germans came in. Every person living in the city where I worked had to be registered. Block managers and the superintendents of apartment houses were charged with seeing to this registration; they enforced it scrupulously, so that it was virtually impossible to live there without having a card in the file at police headquarters. A separate file was kept on foreigners. When the Germans came, one of their first acts was to take over this file, and they began arresting suspects on the very first day.

That I was not arrested I attribute to the virtue of my simple and partly genuine cover. I was actually a student at the polytechnic institute, and I remained by choice a very needy one. I found quarters in a servants' boarding house, a small room not opening on the hallway but directly off the kitchen, which fortunately had an outside entrance. Foreign students who lived in better quarters or could afford luxuries the Germans became curious about.

With respect to my radio work it is not the techniques I used but my lack of techniques and procedures for security that is noteworthy. I made the transmitter myself, and it was a good one for those days; but there was no way its frequency could be changed to throw anyone who might be suspicious of my traffic off the scent. I therefore limited my transmissions to two hours each.[1] I changed the location from which I made radio contact as often as I could, but I had to work in the city or its inner suburbs. Most of my transmitting, in fact, was done from a house only about 30 yards from one of the Gestapo offices.

Moreover, there was no securely established schedule for these radio contacts, and at the end of each transmission a time for making the next one had to be arranged. If the Germans had deciphered these arrangements they would have known when to look for me next. There was no kind of guard or even lookout during the transmission; I was always alone, with two pistols for protection.

Once when I was called upon to lend my transmitter to a friendly intelligence service in an emergency, I had an opportunity to observe the security precautions they took for their operators. They had the use of isolated buildings in the coun-

---

[1] Under the circumstances described a limitation to fifteen minutes would have been the proper precaution. — Editor

Reminiscences of an Agent

try for their radio contacts, and they kept five to eight armed guards around the house, lying in the grass at a distance of fifty yards or so, all during the transmission. On one occasion, they recalled, the Germans had come raiding, but the guards held them off while the operator escaped with his equipment.

Unfortunately, my superiors were not willing to furnish this kind of protection, and the work of transmitting was consequently quite enervating. I was compensated and heartened, however, whenever the American bombers would come over and destroy some enemy airfield and I knew that my efforts had helped make the raid possible.

In my photographic work I felt less exposed, if scarcely at ease. The Germans usually made their house raids and arrests either between six and eight in the morning or between ten in the evening and midnight, so the hours between one and six a.m. were comparatively safe. Once every two weeks or so there would be an accumulation of material for photographic forwarding and a courier, witting or unwitting, to take it out of the country. My superior would bring me this material after midnight. I would get to work on it by one o'clock and finish by about five. Then I could get an hour's sleep before meeting my superior at six to deliver the product.

The material consisted of typewritten intelligence reports, maps locating bombing targets, sketches of military installations, layout plans of airfields and refineries, etc. The language was usually French, sometimes German, never English to point to the identity of the service. Some of the reports were enciphered. Usually there would be 30 to 40 pages of typing and three to five maps or plans; but once there were 80 typed pages and 40 sketches, a substantial quantity of incriminating paper in my little room. The sketches required quite a bit of preliminary work before photographing. They had been made by agents employed at the installations they pictured, and they needed some cleaning up and a calculation of the proper enlargement ratio to keep their scale true. An accompanying report would usually refer to the sketch and give further data on the plant or airfield, such as precise location, whether surface or underground, number of planes, troops, fuel tanks, etc.

I used a Leica camera with a 24x36 mm (1"x1½") frame, usually without the close-up attachment. I laid the original materials out on the floor and fixed the camera perpendicular to them. It could accommodate six typed sheets in one frame, but usually only one of the large sketches at a time. I shot each frame three times, to get two negative copies to keep in reserve. This part of the work was done under the greatest tension, with the material spread out all over the room. Whenever the gate opened, I stopped and listened to the footsteps on the stairs which told me what floor the late comer was heading for. If he stopped climbing at my floor, I frantically tried to get things out of sight. The Gestapo did make arrests in this boarding house, but never came to my room.

The next job was developing the film. (I had often considered lightening my work by sending out undeveloped film, which would also have been less dangerous for the courier; but I wanted to check the developed negatives to be sure they were good, and I was reluctant to risk the damage in transit to which undeveloped film is liable. I therefore never tried it.) After washing off the fixer solution I rinsed the film in alcohol to hasten its drying, and then immediately checked the legibility of the photographed texts with a special magnifying glass. When I was satisfied that the negatives were all good I could start burning the originals in the kitchen stove next to my room.

By the time I had disposed of the original papers, the film would be dry. Taking a strip of a dozen frames at a time, I placed it emulsion side down on a sheet of plate glass and wiped the back with a piece of cotton dipped in acetone until the heavy celluloid was dissolved and only the thin emulsion remained. I now cut the emulsion strips into individual frames and separated the negatives which were to be sent out from the two copies to be kept in reserve against the possibility of loss in transit. The reserve copies I put in a match box or wrapped in a paper. I tied this tiny package on the end of a string and suspended it through a hole in the wall under the kitchen sink, sealing the hole afterward so the end of the string was not visible. It would be only through the unluckiest of coincidences that this cache would be discovered.

Reminiscences of an Agent ~~CONFIDENTIAL~~

I then returned to the negatives to be dispatched. You recall that there were six pages of typing on each frame. These I cut apart, so that each page of the original report was now represented by a wafer of emulsion less than a quarter-inch square, and very thin. Stacked together in page sequence, 40 pages would be less than an eighth of an inch thick. When packaged for the courier the stack was usually rolled into a pellet the size of a small pea.

How the film was packaged depended on whether the courier was witting or unwitting and how he would cross the border. One of the unwitting couriers was a German — and a Nazi Party member — who traveled on business to Switzerland and Turkey. For him I once concealed the film in the lining of a lady's compact which my superior asked him to carry as a gift to a friend in Ankara. A sentimental letter accompanying the compact secretly instructed her what to do with it.

For witting couriers who were not likely to be suspected a good place of concealment was the heel of a shoe. Safer, however, was a pack of cigarettes. I would open a new pack, being careful not to leave any evidence of tampering, take a cigarette from the middle of it, remove half the tobacco, insert the film pellet, repack the tobacco, and reseal the pack so that it looked fresh from the factory. The report might possibly be lost, but there was little chance that it would be discovered.

But it was best not to use the same method repeatedly. One variation I used was the flashlight battery. I took apart the middle cell of a three-cell battery, replaced part of the contents with my film pellet, and resealed the cell. This cell would be dead, so I substituted a lamp rated at two volts for the original rated at three and a half in order to avoid any suspicion arising from a weak light.

When word was received by radio that the report had arrived, I would recover the two reserve copies from under the kitchen sink and burn them, so as to be left briefly without any compromising material on hand. The reports, as a matter of fact, always got through, and I was praised for my packaging. There were never even any complaints that passages were illegible.

I should like to emphasize again, in conclusion, that my success was due in large measure to the fact that I always lived in very humble circumstances. None of my friends and acquaintances could have imagined that I was doing intelligence work. The landlady thought me a poor and simple student. I stipulated to my employers that I should be paid only enough to subsist on from month to month, for an agent who spends freely, shows that he has money, or frequents expensive places is not a secure agent.

PHOTO INTELLIGENCE AND PUBLIC PERSUASION

The Nicaraguan military buildup

Photo Intelligence and Public Persuasion

Peter S. Usowski

In late 1981, President Reagan and his senior policymakers assigned a high-level national priority to Nigaragua because they feared the spread of the Sandinista revolution throughout Central America and because they were disturbed by the growth of Soviet and Cuban security ties to Nicaragua. The common denominator underlying these concerns was the Soviet-sponsored military buildup of the Sandinistas. In trying to form a nationwide consensus on US policy toward the Sandinistas, the President, during his first six years in office, conducted a public relations offensive that included the release of the contents of defector reports and press conferences given by Salvadoran and Nicaraguan defectors. Most often, however, the administration used photo intelligence to portray the situation in Nicaragua. From March 1982 through May 1988, the Reagan administration released a series of aerial reconnaissance photographs depicting military developments in Nicaragua.

Using Declassified Photos

The first and perhaps most dramatic use of declassified material took place at the State Department on 9 March 1982, when CIA Deputy Director Bobby Inman and DIA Deputy Director John Hughes presented a photographic briefing on the Sandinista military buildup.[1] A year later, on 23 March 1983, the President took his case to the public using declassified reconnaissance photographs. Before a national television audience, he talked about the Soviet Union's military threat and its efforts to project power in the Caribbean. To illustrate the growing Soviet influence in the region, the President showed four declassified intelligence photographs, one of which was of Managua's Sandino Airfield.[2] Throughout the remainder of the administration's term of office, the release of additional classified photos was presented through a series of unclassified State and Defense Department publications. These background papers were produced at least once a year from 1983 through 1987.[3] Together, they covered various aspects of the political and military developments in Central America and the Caribbean. They included over 60 declassified aerial reconnaissance photographs of military-related areas in Nicaragua and neighboring El Salvador. In May 1988, four additional reconnaissance photographs of recent military developments in Nicaragua were declassified and made available to *The New York Times*.[4]

---

[1] Adm. Bobby Inman and John Hughes, "Evidence of Military Buildup in Nicaragua," statement at the State Department, Washington, D.C., 9 March 1982; "U.S. Offers Photos of Bases to Prove Nicaragua Threat," *The New York Times*, 10 March 1982, p. A18; "Taking Aim at Nicaragua," *Newsweek*, 22 March 1982, pp. 22-29.

[2] "President's Speech on Military Spending and a New Defense," *The New York Times*, 24 March 1983, p. A20.

[3] These publications included: *Background Paper: Central America* (May 1983); *Background Paper: Nicaragua's Military Buildup and Support for Central American Subversion* (July 1984); *The Soviet-Cuba Connection in Central America and the Caribbean* (March 1985); *The Sandinista Military Buildup (May 1985); The Challenge to Democracy in Central America* (June 1986); and *The Sandinista Military Buildup: An Update* (October 1987).

[4] Robert Pear, "Sandinistas Said to Prepare an Attack," *The New York Times*, 25 May 1988, p. A3.

Assessing the Results

If success in using declassified photographic intelligence as a tool of public persuasion is measured by the subsequent achievement of a consensus on a policy initiative, then the Reagan administration's efforts regarding its policy on Nicaragua would be seen as a failure. In most cases, however, the equation is not that simple. In policymaking circles, where intelligence is routinely received and digested, intelligence information rarely is the sole determining factor in shaping a policy line. This also holds true among members of Congress and the American people. But intelligence information does have a bearing on the formation of the policy ideas and opinions held by those outside the policymaking circles. In some instances, declassified information will have a major impact in consensus building. In most cases, it will at least raise the public's awareness on the substance of the policy and create a foundation for an enlightened debate. Furthermore, within the context of a serious national debate, hard data, such as photographic intelligence, can add credibility to an argument as doubts and questions emerge during the course of the debate.

The conclusiveness and persuasiveness of the data contained in the collection of reconnaissance photographs released by the Reagan administration varied according to the intelligence topics. The photographs directly related to the military buildup in Nicaragua provided solid evidence. While the interpretation of overhead photography can be a somewhat esoteric discipline, the selection of the photographs released and the manner in which they were presented made them understandable to the untrained eye. Annotations were added to point out significant items, and ground-level prints of military equipment were frequently used to provide a better visual perspective of the same equipment seen in the overhead view. The photographs not directly related to the military buildup—Salvadoran rebel training and logistic bases, and Nicaraguan prisons—were less persuasive. In these cases, the interpretation and complete understanding of the significant points contained in the graphics required additional information from other sources. This data was either not provided or was subject to question because of the undetermined reliability of the sources. When the photography was directed at hard military targets in Nicaragua, it did prove to be fairly persuasive.

Seeking Smoking Guns

To justify its concerns about the situation in Nicaragua, the administration had to prove that the nature of the military buildup there threatened the hemispheric interests of the US and its Central American allies. This could be done by clearly illustrating that the buildup was exceeding any legitimate defensive needs and that, as part of the newly established Soviet-Nicaraguan military relationship, the USSR had begun to use or, at least had plans to use, Nicaragua as a base of military operations in the hemispere. In this context, the relevance of the photographic intelligence to the administration's fundamental policy concerns varied. The images of such areas as radar sites and air defense sites could hardly be viewed as threatening to Nicaragua's neighbors. On the other hand, the construction of new army garrisons and military depots, the improvement of airfields, and the acquisition of new military equipment could be seen as tipping the regional balance of power in Nicaragua's favor. The one element of the buildup that would have clearly demonstrated the threatening nature of the Sandinistas' program would have been an air force equipped with jet fighter-bombers. Despite the many references to the Sandinista acquisition of Soviet MiG fighters, the administration could only show improved airfields capable of handling fighter-bomber aircraft.

The administration faced a similar situation in addressing the Soviet threat. The photographic evidence clearly revealed that the airfield under construction at Punte Huete near Managua was going to be a military airbase. Although the facilities at Punte Huete did indicate that it could handle any aircraft in the Soviet arsenal, the administration could not graphically support its warnings regarding potential Soviet air operations out of Nicaragua.

There was no smoking gun in the photographic evidence released by the Reagan administration. The various graphics accurately created a visual story of what was actually happening in Nicaragua, a slow, methodical military buildup supported and influenced by Cuba and the Soviet Union. In that respect, the photo intelligence was relevant and supported the administration's basic assertions and its fundamental concerns regarding a widespread military buildup in Nicaragua. This evidence, however, could not back up some of the worst-case scenarios that had frequently been part of the Reagan administration's foreign policy rhetoric.

Protecting Security

The declassified photographs contained a wealth of information on military activity in Nicaragua. In releasing this intelligence, however, the administration neither revealed specific sources and methods nor compromised collection operations. Many public accounts asserted that the sources of the reconnaissance photographs were the U-2 and the SR-71 "spy planes."[5] The administration, however, never specifically identified the platform from which the photographs were taken. On at least one occasion, administration officials had debated the release of satellite photographs of developments in Nicaragua. According to *The New York Times*, the intelligence agencies argued that the publication of satellite photographs would provide the Soviet Union with data on US surveillance technology.[6] The President, accordingly, chose to limit the disclosure of intelligence photos to those taken by manned reconnaissance aircraft.

A Measured Reaction

The Sandinista government had been aware of reconnaissance flights over its territory, and it filed protests against US violations of Nicaraguan airspace. According to the data released by the Reagan administration, however, the Sandinistas took no action to prevent such overflights by acquiring and deploying high-altitude surface-to-air missiles. Furthermore, the Nicaraguan military, at least as far as the declassified reconnaissance revealed, instituted no camouflage or concealment and deception measures to cover its actions. Years after the first photographs were declassified, the administration was still able to release new evidence that confirmed the ongoing construction of military facilities and the acquisition of new military equipment. The extent to which the US, through its aerial collection efforts against Nicaragua, was able to obtain a picture of the miltary buildup had apparently not been affected by the intelligence disclosures.

An Important Contribution

The release of aerial reconnaissance photographs on developments in Nicaragua did have an impact on the overall foreign policy debate. Identifying that impact is essential in understanding what can realistically be expected when intelligence is used as a tool in public persuasion. In the case of US policy on Nicaragua, the debate revolved around the way in which the US should address the changes taking place in Central America. The reconnaissance photography could confirm the military buildup and, to a lesser degree, could reveal the threat. It could not, however, persuade those who advocated a diplomatic approach to approve the use of force either directly by the US or indirectly by the Contras. The crux of the administration's difficulty was its inability to form a consensus that military pressure was the only effective option in confronting the Sandinista revolution. This was part of the policy debate where declassified intelligence had limited persuasiveness.

The photography supported many of the administration's charges and, when combined with data obtained from other sources, provided a detailed picture of ongoing events in Nicaragua. The release of this intelligence fostered an environment where the national debate was not limited to emotional pleas or ideological pronouncements but was broadened to include a discussion of the evidence. In that regard, the role of photo intelligence in the policy process was significant.

---

[5] For example, see "High-Tech Spycraft," *Newsweek*, 22 March 1982, p. 29; and "Peeking in on Managua," *Newsweek*, 19 November 1984, p. 46.

[6] Philip Taubman, "Intelligence Aides Debated Reagan's Show of Satellite Photos," *The New York Times*, 24 March 1983, p. A22.

THE CIA AND ACADEME

Symbiosis

THE CIA AND ACADEME

Close ties between the Central Intelligence Agency and American colleges and universities have existed since the birth of the Agency in 1947. The bonds between national intelligence and the academic world actually predate the Agency, for William J. Donovan, President Roosevelt's Coordinator of Information, established a research team of distinguished academicians to assist him in 1941. Donovan proposed a novel idea: have the information that he was collecting, mostly from the military services and the Department of State, analyzed not only by the intelligence components within the War and Navy Departments but by his team of "scholars, economists, psychologists, technicians, and students of finance." To head his research group, Donovan chose James Phinney Baxter, president of Williams College and a noted specialist in American diplomatic history.

Following the attack on Pearl Harbor, the Research and Analysis Branch of what became the Office of Strategic Services (OSS) rapidly expanded. After Baxter's departure in 1942, William L. Langer, the distinguished historian from Harvard, took over direction of the branch and remained in that post until disestablishment of OSS in late 1945.

While many of the scholars who had participated in the analytic part of OSS returned to their campuses after the war, some remained with the government. Those who had been in the Research and Analysis Branch were transferred to the State Department. Then, as the Central Intelligence Group and, after 1947, the Central Intelligence Agency grew in size and responsibility, a number of academicians who had served with OSS returned as analysts in the new Office of Research and Evaluation.

During the great expansion of CIA following the outbreak of the Korean War in 1950, Agency recruiters appeared in significant numbers on academic campuses across the nation. Also in 1950, the Director of Central Intelligence, General Walter Bedell Smith, called upon William Langer to return to Washington to organize the new Office of National Estimates (ONE). This office had seven board members, including four historians and an economist drawn from the ranks of academe,* a combat commander, and a lawyer. One of the historians, Sherman Kent, succeeded Langer as Director of ONE in 1952 when Langer again returned to Harvard. At roughly the same time, the noted economist at the Massachusetts Institute of Technology, Max Millikan, was brought to Washington to organize the economic intelligence effort in the newly created Office of Research and Reports.

---

* The four historians were Sherman Kent, Ludwell Montague, De Forrest Van Slyck, and Raymond Sontag; the economist was Calvin Hoover.

DECLASSIFIED

Meanwhile, as the Agency expanded, its recruiters turned to established figures in the academic world for leads and referrals to the best among their students.* Many of the personnel already on board similarly informed their colleagues still on the university campuses of the need for and opportunities awaiting those who had the requisite background for work in the Agency.

As a large number of the members of OSS and the early recruits to CIA came from prestigious private schools in the Northeast and the Far West, with some representation from the large Midwestern universities, it is not surprising that a disproportiate number of the new recruits came from the same schools. Similarly, professors who had joined the Agency often turned to their former colleagues still on the campuses for consultation and assistance. This "old boy" system was quite productive in providing new employees in the professional ranks. Thus, there was an early linkage between the Agency and the Ivy League, or similar schools.

A Souring in the Sixties

Relations between academe and the CIA were cordial throughout the 1950s. During much of that period the Cold War was at its height and the nation's need for the Agency and its activities were seldom questioned by faculty or students. There was no criticism worthy of note following the Agency's alleged involvement in Iran in 1953 or Guatemala the following year. The 1960s were to be different.

There was some criticism on campuses over CIA involvement in the Bay of Pigs expedition in 1961 and the barrage of denunciation increased as the Agency, along with the rest of the government and the "establishment," found itself under intensified attack as the war in Vietnam continued. In part to mitigate this opposition, the Office of Personnel in 1962 established the Hundred Universities Program in which recruiters and senior officials of CIA made presentations before selected faculty members and placement officers in an effort to publicize CIA's role in national security and to emphasize the Agency's recurrent personnel needs.

Meanwhile, the Deputy Director of Central Intelligence, aware that the close ties that had bound Agency officials and analysts with their colleagues on the campuses were loosening, and concerned about developments in China (explosion of an atomic device in 1964 and the subsequent beginning of the Cultural Revolution), asked the Deputy Director for Intelligence in 1966 to take action to improve the Agency's expertise on China. The DDI created the office of Coordinator for Academic Relations (CAR), a part-time job for John Kerry King, a former professor at the University of Virginia who had been with the analytic part of the Agency for several years.

---

* Beginning in 1951 and continuing for several years thereafter, the Agency tried, without much success, to establish a "University Associates Program"—a program of using professors at a selected list of 50 colleges and universities as consultant-contacts who would receive a nominal fee for spotting promising students, steering them into studies and activities of interest to the Agency, and eventually nominating them for recruitment.

Academe

The DDI specifically charged the CAR with, *inter alia*, responsibility for exploiting the capabilities of the various China studies centers in the universities, devising means for attracting China specialists to work for the Agency, and developing and managing relations with academic consultants on China.

One of the nation's best China centers was at Harvard. It was logical that the Agency would seek help from that institution. Subsequently, several DDI analysts were enrolled in the graduate program at the Harvard East Asian Research Center. Unfortunately, by 1967 the local chapter of Students for a Democratic Society was aware of the participation of these analysts and a campaign against their presence on campus was launched. Attempts by Professor John K. Fairbank, director of the Center, to explain the difference between operations officers and analysts at CIA fell on deaf ears.

King also set about organizing a number of "China seminars" in Boston, New York, Chicago, and San Francisco, in which a few noted China scholars engaged Agency experts in low-profile and informal discussions. King, during his four-year tenure as CAR, also initiated a program of passing unclassified reports prepared by the Agency to a select group of academicians in an attempt to gain comment on the reports and good will for the CIA.

Despite individual examples of continuing cooperation with the Agency, relations with academia as a whole continued to sour. The deterioration was given impetus in February 1967 by the disclosure in *Ramparts* magazine that the CIA had been funding the National Student Association for a number of years. Additional disclosures of Agency involvement with private voluntary organizations and foundations resulted in President Johnson's appointment of a three-person committee, chaired by Undersecretary of State Nicholas Katzenbach, to review government activities that might "endanger the integrity and independence of the educational community."* Following its investigations, the Katzenbach Committee recommended that federal agencies halt covert financial relationships with "any of the nation's educational or private voluntary organizations." While the recommendation was never issued as an executive order or enacted as a statute, it was accepted by the President and led to major adjustments within the Agency.

Recruiters for the Agency, meanwhile, were experiencing increasing problems on college campuses. Many of the schools that had provided superior candidates in the past were now home for the most militant of students. Picketing of recruiters began in 1966, rapidly spread across the nation, and peaked in 1968 when 77 incidents or demonstrations occurred. Procedures were changed with interviews held off campus and, whenever it appeared that a visit might precipitate incidents, the visit was canceled. The Hundred Universities Program was suspended in 1968.

The Academic Coordinator, working on behalf of the analytic offices, continued to expand contacts with academicians wherever possible. By 1970, seminars on Soviet matters were added to those on China. By 1974, scholars on

---

* The other two members were Secretary of Health, Education, and Welfare John Gardiner and DCI Richard Helms.

Cuba and most of the rest of the world had been added to the list of academicians with whom the CAR kept in touch. The CAR was promoting visits by academicians to CIA Headquarters to confer with those in the DDI having similar interests and he was assisting analysts and administrators in securing the participation of outside experts in Agency-sponsored conferences and seminars.*

Sensational allegations of wrong doing by CIA and other components of the intelligence community, which erupted in the media in the early 1970s, led to congressional demands for investigations and the creation in 1974 of select committees in the House, under Representative Pike, and in the Senate, under Senator Church. (Two other groups also were formed to investigate intelligence activities—a Commission on the Organization of the Government for the Conduct of Foreign Policy, known as the Murphy Commission, and a commission appointed by President Ford and led by the Vice President, the Rockefeller Commission.) The various investigating bodies focused much of their attention on CIA's covert action, most of which had little to do with the Agency's relations with academia. There was some discussion, particularly in the Church Committee final report, which tended to lump relations with schools along with Agency relations with the media and religious organizations.

The final report of the Church Committee (the Pike Committee report was never formally released) interpreted "academic community" far more broadly than had the Katzenbach Committee. In particular, the former focused more heavily on individuals whereas the latter had concentrated on institutions. The Church Committee found that hundreds of academicians in over 100 colleges, universities, and related institutions had a covert relationship with the Agency providing leads and "making introductions for intelligence purposes." Others engaged in intelligence collection abroad, assisted in the writing of books and other propaganda materials, or collaborated in research and analysis.

While the Church Committee recognized that the CIA "must have unfettered access to the best advice and judgment our universities can produce," it recommended that that advice and judgment be openly sought. The committee concluded by placing the principal responsibility for altering the existing relationship between CIA and academe on the backs of the college administrators and other academic officials. "The Committee believes that it is the responsibility of . . . the American academic community to set the professional and ethical standards of its members. This report on the nature and extent of covert individual relationships with the CIA is intended to alert (the academic community) that there is a problem."

---

* Harold Ford succeeded John Kerry King as CAR in 1970 and was followed in 1974 by Gary Foster. In late 1976, with the reorganization of the DDI as the National Foreign Assessment Center (NFAC), relations with academics were coordinated by two professional staff employees working full time. ▓▓▓▓▓▓▓▓ were the original incumbents and were followed by James King and ▓▓▓▓▓▓▓ In January 1981, the author became CAR as the post reverted to one-person status. In 1982, the CAR was transferred from the Office of the DDI to the Office of External Affairs under the DCI and in mid-1983 to the newly created Public Affairs Office.

Academe

The report set off a flurry of activity within academic ranks and led to numerous articles in newspapers and periodicals. Among several letters addressed to DCI George Bush was one from William Van Alstyne, president of the American Association of University Professors, demanding that Bush give the same assurance against covert use of academics that he had earlier given to missionaries and journalists. The DCI replied that the Agency sought only "the voluntary and witting cooperation of individuals who can help the foreign policy processes of the United States." Where relationships are confidential, noted Bush, they are usually so at the request of the scholars rather than of the Agency. He refused to isolate the Agency from the "good counsel of the best scholars in our country."

Bush's argument was to be adopted and enlarged upon by his successor, Stansfield Turner, who engaged in a long and eventually unsuccessful effort to reach agreement with Derek Bok, president of Harvard University, on relations between that university and the Agency. Bok, acting on the Church Committee suggestion, appointed a committee to prepare guidelines to assist members of the Harvard community in dealing with the CIA. The guidelines were accepted by Bok and published in May 1977. It was immediately apparent that some of Harvard's concerns (unwitting employment of academics and use of scholars in preparing propaganda materials) were no longer at issue due to changes in Agency policy and issuance of Executive Order 11905 by President Ford. There were still two issues on which no meeting of the minds was possible. One of these had to do with what the guidelines termed "operational use" of faculty and staff by the CIA. The other concerned covert Agency recruitment of foreign students for intelligence purposes. Additionally, the guidelines specified that all faculty and staff "should" report any and all relations with the Agency to their deans, who should report them in turn to President Bok.

Attempts by the DCI to point out that these were exceptional cases of academics who might be employed by the Agency on a strictly confidential mission abroad because of their unique access to foreign individuals or information failed to change Bok's mind as did Turner's contention that the confidentiality of a relationship with an academic was frequently at the professor's, rather than the Agency's, request. Finally, Turner pointed out that the CIA's responsibility to provide secret foreign intelligence left the Agency with no alternative to engaging in the activities which Bok deplored, but Bok was assured that "the rein" would remain tight in such cases.

Publicity regarding the dispute over the Harvard guidelines allowed Morton Halperin and John Marks of the Center for National Security Studies to launch a campaign to have other colleges and universities adopt similar or more stringent restrictions on intelligence activities on campuses. While some ten academic institutions took action toward adoption of similar guidelines, in most cases modifications were included which limited the impact of any restriction on Agency operations. For the great majority of schools where the issue arose, the faculty and the administration rejected any guidelines, usually on the ground that existing regulations and practices were adequate to protect both the institution and the individual from corruption.

Academe

Scope of Current Cooperation

Relations between the Agency and the academic world have slowly improved since 1977, more or less in inverse correlation to the state of East-West relations.* The Soviet Union's invasion of Afghanistan in 1979, in particular, opened new doors to cooperation with CIA on many campuses. The depressed state of the economy in recent years has also been cited as a catalyst for greater interest in Agency employment on the part of recent graduates as well as the cause of increased willingness to cooperate with CIA by those who sell their services as consultants or external research contractors.

A number of recognized authorities who could be of value to the Agency's research effort decline all attempts to gain their assistance. Most are political scientists, or in an allied social science, and many have expertise in the Third World. Many scholars on the developing nations of the world, aware that reports that they have collaborated with American intelligence could prejudice their research activities (including their sources), are reluctant even to come to Langley. Interestingly, some of these scholars are prepared to discuss substantive issues if an Agency analyst is willing to visit them in their homes or at their offices.

Specialists on the Soviet Union or other communist countries have traditionally been less reluctant to work with the intelligence community, presumably because they are believed to be in touch with the Agency anyway. Experts on Western Europe and other developed nations, in their willingness to cooperate with the Agency, fall somewhere between the general cooperativeness of the Sino-Soviet specialists and the reluctance of the Third World experts.

At present the Agency enjoys reasonably good relations with academe and gains much from its contacts with faculty and students. The Office of Training and Education uses a large number of academics in its courses. Other offices within the Directorate of Administration, specifically Logistics and Medical Services, have contracts with educational institutions or with individual academicians. This fall, 27 professors spent two and one-half days at Headquarters in the Conference on US Intelligence: the Organization and the Profession, conducted by the Center for the Study of Intelligence.

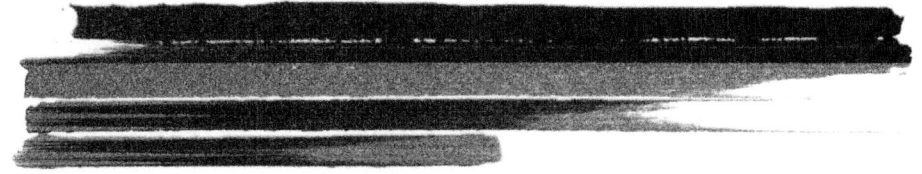

The Foreign Resources Division has relationships with scores of individuals in US academic institutions. In all cases these links are voluntary and

---

* Harry Howe Ransom of Vanderbilt University has written extensively on the CIA. He maintains that congressional attempts to restrict Agency activities are strongest and most likely to be implemented during periods of detente in East-West relations; conversely they are most unlikely to succeed in periods of increased tension. The charting of relations between the CIA and academe would appear likely to show a similar pattern of close ties during periods of heightened tension between the US and USSR and strained relations during periods of detente.

witting. Many of the individuals also are contacts of the DCD. These American scholars do not "recruit" foreign students or researchers for the Agency, but assist by providing background information and occasionally by brokering introductions.

Many academicians are willing to provide expert assistance to Agency analysts and the research components ▬▬▬▬▬▬▬▬▬▬▬▬▬▬▬▬▬. Additionally, scores of other academicians were willing to consult on an ad hoc basis, some without reimbursement. Components within the National Intelligence Council and the Directorates of Intelligence and of Science and Technology sponsored nearly 50 conferences during 1982 at which specialists from colleges, universities, or "think tanks" were present.

The DDI, the DDS&T, and the NIC also sought help from the academic world through contracts for external research, with the results usually presented as written reports. ▬▬▬▬▬▬▬▬▬▬▬▬▬▬▬▬▬▬▬▬▬▬▬▬▬▬▬▬▬

Since 1977, the Intelligence Directorate has also brought in eleven scholars, usually on sabbatical, to the Agency as contract employees to assist analysts through an exchange of ideas, a review of written reports, and the production of finished intelligence for dissemination to policy makers. In exchange, these "Scholars-in-Residence" are, for one or two years, privy to information that would never be available to them on campus.

The Supreme Court decision in the Snepp case in early 1980 had some dampening effect on the willingness of professors to work with the Agency. Some of them feared that if they signed the requisite secrecy agreement, their future independence to publish would be severely restricted. Another potential Scholar-in-Residence declined to take the polygraph test, describing it as "demeaning."

The Agency also provides numerous services for the academic community. Since 1972, unclassified CIA reports have been available to the public and have been widely sought by colleges, universities, and individual scholars. The FBIS —Daily Reports have long been standard items on the shelves of many university libraries.

Requests for unclassified briefings of students or faculty members at CIA Headquarters or on campuses normally receive a positive response. During 1982, 31 groups containing over 1,100 individuals were given briefings on intelligence or on some substantive topic at Headquarters. In the same year, at least 60 Agency officials spoke at various schools throughout the nation.

Fourteen college presidents were brought to Langley in 1982 to meet the Director and other senior officials and to be briefed on Agency activities. This program, which has generated considerable good will and understanding for the Agency, was begun in 1977 and has involved a total of 58 presidents from large and small schools throughout the nation, all of the schools important to the Agency as sources for recruitment of staff employees or consultants, or for other operational requirements.

The Office of Personnel presently is active at approximately 300 schools. Several offices in the DDI and DDS&T also recruit directly from colleges and universities. Recently there has been a program, originating in the Directorate of Operations, sending special representatives onto campuses in an attempt to attract high-caliber career trainees.

The Graduate Studies Program, which began in 1967, provides summer internships for students who will be attending graduate school in the fall. Most of the 57 graduate students from 42 schools accepted in 1983 were attached to the Intelligence Directorate. A number of "alumni" of earlier Graduate Studies programs subsequently became staff employees.

For undergraduates, the Agency maintains a cooperative Student Trainee Program. The goal of this program today, as it was when it began in 1961, is to provide a long-range method of recruiting occupational skills which are in short supply. The program allows the student, who must be registered in a college with an established coop program, to gain practical work experience by alternating periods of study at school and work at the Agency. Originally, the program sought engineers exclusively but in recent years has added those who major in computer science, mathematics, physics, chemistry, and accounting.

The Office of Equal Employment Opportunity since 1969 has been recruiting at, and negotiating contracts with, minority schools. Faculty members and placement officers from traditionally black schools have been brought to Headquarters for briefing sessions.

Finally, the Agency has long sought to gain recognition for itself as a center for intellectual activity comparable to the best institutions in the academic world. The claim has often been made that CIA could staff a major university because of the diversity of disciplines represented among its employees. Graduate degrees earned by staff employees give some indication of the training acquired—over 600 Ph.Ds and more than 2,300 Masters' degrees.

To gain recognition for the Agency's employees among their counterparts in academe, overt employees have been encouraged to participate in meetings of academic and professional societies. Of the over 700 attendees in 1982, a significant number joined in panel discussions or presented unclassified research papers.

Work for the Future

The wide ranging program described above puts the Agency on generally good terms with the academic community. There is, however, considerable work for the future if CIA is to continue to count on securing the best possible recruits for its staff employees and the participation of faculty members in improving its analytic product. One of the problems, a long-term trend in academic institutions toward ever decreasing numbers of students in area studies programs, is currently being examined by a joint committee made up of representatives from the universities, business, and the federal government, including CIA.

Academe

There is also a continuing need to improve the Agency's image at many colleges and universities. While the number of demonstrations against CIA has drastically diminished over the past decade, there are still occasional minor incidents, as happened when CIA and NSA recruitment was protested at Middlebury College last winter.

Some recent Agency activities, including expanded recruitment efforts by substantive intelligence officers on the campuses, increased numbers of CIA participants at academic conventions and conferences, and a growing use of external research contracts with non-annuitants, are all valuable tools in breaking down barriers and increasing confidence betweeen the Agency and the academics.

One promising recent activity involves visits to selected college campuses by intelligence officers who are seeking to locate, or create, a body of faculty members favorably disposed toward the Agency. This is accomplished principally through conversations with faculty members and by briefings, when requested, to classes or to faculty groups. These friendly contacts in the ranks of academe can be of inestimable value. The goals are to have professors remind their best students that CIA is a potential employer, to correct erroneous accusations on campus against the Agency, and, perhaps, to identify other faculty members who might be willing to attend conferences or participate in substantive consultations at Langley.

There is some danger from an uncoordinated rapid expansion of recruitment trips by the many Agency components now engaged in the effort. Unless oversight of the campaign is centralized, it could result in several Agency representatives appearing on a campus in rapid succession or even concurrently. This "overexposure" could have negative repercussions; specifically, irritation on the part of Agency friends and consternation among others—both faculty and students. All recruitment visits to academic institutions should be cleared in advance at some point within the Agency—possibly within the Office of Personnel, possibly at the Academic Coordinator's office.

The opportunity exists, of course, for any overt employee attending an academic convention or symposium to assist in furthering good relations for the Agency. Understandably, many academicians are most impressed by the participation of Agency employees on panels. Beyond that, any Agency officer attending a professional meeting can gain good will for CIA by being friendly and, within the limitations of security, informative about the Agency. Most academicians are curious about CIA and grateful for any clarification of its mission and its activities.

The occasional vigorous criticism of the Agency from faculty members or students tends to focus on covert action. While some critics will not be satisfied by any argument, others can be reconciled to the need for covert action through a dispassionate explanation of its synergistic role with other more conventional means of conducting international relations and a reminder of the oversight function of the Congress.

Academe

From the author's own experience with a number of college groups briefed at Headquarters over the last few years, it is obvious that there is a vital need to correct misconceptions held by a large percentage of students and also by some faculty members. Illustrative of this point were the comments on a short written quiz given by an Agency briefing officer *prior* to her presentation before a student group. To the question, what is your reaction and that of your classmates on campus to the words "Central Intelligence Agency?" the recurring response was "fear."

Yet, when the briefings are over there are often voluntary expressions of support for the Agency, inquiries regarding careers, and, from the faculty, offers to meet with DCD or to serve as Agency consultants. If the students and their teachers are made aware of the truly symbiotic relationship between the academic and intelligence worlds, there is little question but that the great majority will support the continuing efforts of what Ray Cline terms this "peculiarly American combination of spies and scholars, working in tandem."

This article is classified CONFIDENTIAL.

CRANKS, NUTS AND SCREWBALLS

Volunteers for intelligence—the fringe and farther-out.

CRANKS, NUTS, AND SCREWBALLS
David R. McLean

"I have always had adequate sex that no one appreciated. I need a better grade of iron to eat, and so do the astronauts." (Excerpt from a July 1964 letter to the Director of Central Intelligence.)

"A defenseless woman having husband trouble sincerely requests your help." (June 1964 letter to the DCI, enclosing picture of a convertible and address of a suburban motel.)

"O.K.! Keep me off the payroll. I'll try and sell my abilities to the Soviet Union." (1965 postcard peevishly addressed to the U.S. Lower Intelligence Agency.)

"Please be informed, old pal, I have entered my name with the 87th Congress as a candidate for the Presidency of the United States in the next elections. If I make it, I am going to reinstate you in CIA." (1962 letter to Allen W. Dulles.)

"You can tell John A. McCone to go to hell if you think I'm going to be treated this way after all I've done for you people." (Early morning telephone call from "Agent 44" on his release from the drunk cell of a Washington police precinct.)

"ORNISCOPYTHEOBI BLIOPSYCHOCRYSI ARROSCI-OAEROGEN ETHLIOMETEOR OAU STRAHIEROAN-THRO VICHTHYOPYROSI DEROCH PNOMYOALE ..." (Excerpt from a 1963 telegram to CIA.)

Something about a secret intelligence agency attracts an endless stream of letters, cards, telegrams, phone calls, and personal visits from deranged, possibly dangerous, or merely daffy citizens who want to horn in on the cloak-and-dagger act. Mixed into the CIA morning mail, these unsolicited testimonials to the Agency's drawing power create some delicate screening problems, waste a lot of time, and justify elaborate security precautions to protect its top officials.

The Agency's Office of Security keeps a watch list of nearly four thousand persons or organizations who have tried to visit, write, or phone its officials and who have been, at a minimum, a source of annoyance. Every suspected crank contact is checked against this list. The signatures include "The Green Russian" in Charlotte, N.C., and "Your Aunt Minnie" in San Francisco. Nearly all crank letters are domestic, but alongside addresses in Pewee Valley, Ky., and Big Bear City, Cal., are foreign listings from Quito to Warsaw and from Edinburgh to Australia.

Steadies and One-Timers

The flow of oddball letters and phone calls increases perceptibly when CIA is in the news. Less than 48 hours after President Johnson announced he would nominate Admiral Raborn to be the DCI, a Detroit man had sent the Director-designate 8,000 words of complaint about the high cost of prescription medicines and a New Yorker had asked his help in controlling a whistling brain. The file of letters to him was mounting even before his appointment had been confirmed. On 17 April a Massachusetts man sent him some well-intentioned advice. "Dear Admiral," he wrote, "as you may be aware, L.B.J. ain't got much Brains or he wouldn't be President. I dealt with his type for 37 years. The best way to get along with him is humor him."

But a faithful nucleus of loyal intelligence fans always contributes about 25 percent of the total. Probably most of the cranks are as harmless as the childish codes they sometimes use. The trouble is, they're unpredictable. A few might have complaints worth hearing; others might pose a real threat to an unsuspecting officer who received them.

Nut-and-dolt visits to headquarters offices have practically disappeared since CIA moved out to Langley; an occasional walk-in still calls at its personnel office downtown. Its overt or semi-overt domestic offices, which are more approachable, have now compiled an impressive record of coping with off-beat visitors.

Clairvoyance and Contrivances

A fairly common complaint of the walk-ins is getting messages from the Communists by thought-transference or through the fillings in their teeth. One disturbed gentleman from Buffalo claimed the Communists had kidnapped him, cut open his head, removed his brains, and substituted a radio. After warning his interviewer to say nothing the opposition should not hear, he asked CIA to remove the radio and replace the brains. For sheer imagination in fielding such a complaint, the prize probably goes to the CIA man who assured a woman she might indeed be getting radio messages by static electricity. Reminding her of the chains that drag under gasoline trucks, he linked a series of paper clips, hooked one end in her skirt, let the other end trail on the floor, and sent her happily on her way with the static safely grounded.

Then there was the man who came in to volunteer as a spy in the Czechoslovakian uranium mines. He confided that he had been stalling because he feared the radiation might make him sterile. Now, however, he had solved this problem: he planned to carry along a carton of Chesterfields and wrap the tinfoil around his private parts. The Agency secretary who transcribed a memorandum on his visit never could understand why he insisted on Chesterfields.

Some fairly far-out ideas have been seriously proposed by sensible citizens. One responsible businessman developed a mechanical chess-playing machine which countered any move according to prepunched IBM cards. He proposed to take his machine to Moscow, consolidate his position there, and then suggest that the machine could be used as a training aid for any move-and-countermove situation, such as military tactics. Instead of chessmen he would use symbols for tanks, infantry, hills, forests, planes, and fields of fire. Since he knew nothing about military tactics, the Soviet general staff would have to tell him the prescribed response to every move. As soon as he had all the responses punched on IBM cards he would deliver duplicates to the American Embassy. Then if we ever faced the USSR in battle we could always run the IBM cards and tell what the Soviets would do next.

The most intriguing case investigated by a domestic office involved a school superintendent of unassailable reliability who dabbled in hypnotism as a hobby and reported that he could induce clairvoyance in his subject, an engineering student. In 1957, while in a hypnotic trance, the subject described in minute technical detail a Soviet ballistic missile of a type unknown in the United States but consistent with expert private assessments of Soviet capabilities. The research chief of a respected American aircraft plant was present at the demonstration, framed many questions, and made a tape recording of the answers. The subject used technical and scientific terminology which neither he nor the hypnotist could be expected to know. Washington experts who studied the tape found "just enough substantive data to stimulate the imagination" but decided that clairvoyance would be "a very risky approach to the collection of Soviet guided missile data." The mystery remains unsolved.

Other Field Office Walk-ins

Some unlikely sources have produced usable information. In 1959 a soldier of fortune fresh from Cuba wearing yellow canvas shoes, red denim slacks, and a gaudy sport shirt contacted a domestic office. His debriefing was worth while but abbreviated by his arrest for having a bag of dynamite in his hotel room. In October 1964 a Miami man brought to CIA a box which he had bought sight-unseen at an auction of shipments abandoned in U.S. customs. The box contained more than 2,000 negatives of Cuban propaganda. And on 8 July 1960 an admitted swindler and diamond smuggler volunteered the information that five Soviet missile experts had just travelled to Cuba by way of Mexico. This report was taken with a grain of salt at the time.

One probable James Bond fan seems obsessed with finding unusual ways of eliminating the opposition. Besides the usual poisons and trick guns, he has suggested a lethally exploding cigar disguised with a band reading "It's a boy!" He has also offered to dispose of bodies for us in his home meat grinder. An attractive divorcee leads a sober life in this country as an airline secretary but regularly flies to another country and cuts loose there among the political leaders. For all her Mata Hari complex she has brought useful information.

Ever since 1948 a Slovak economist has been trying to peddle information he claims to obtain through a private underground net. He is presentable and persuasive and has impressed countless high officials, including a senator who brought him to lunch with the upper echelons of CIA. Fortunately these official contacts quickly lead back to a burn notice identifying him as a fabricator. As late as 1963, however, he was still trying with some success to interest leading American industries in technical data from anti-Communist researchers behind the iron curtain. Having abandoned the atomic cannon he offered the government, he was tempting industry with everything from synthetic fibers to jet engine designs, high-temperature ceramics, and flexible concrete. Meanwhile he had hired a lawyer

Screwballs

and sued a Washington shoe store for $25,000 because his shoes were too tight; in the brief he filed with the court he claimed that as a spy he needed to run fast.

Letters to Langley

By far the greatest number of crank contacts are by mail. In the first eight months of Fiscal Year 1965, 1,143 letters addressed simply to CIA were identified as from cranks. This does not count those addressed otherwise—to the DCI by name or to specific field offices.

Neither does it include some unsolicited letters which may be helpful, pathetic, or merely misguided but are not from cranks. The following examples are all from March 1965: An ex-Marine sent a possibly practical suggestion for guerrilla warfare. A 17-year-old Thai girl asked how to get training in police investigation. A German student asked for help in locating his father, who had been captured by the Soviets in World War II. A 14-year-old boy asked if there were really such organizations as SMERSH and U.N.C.L.E. All such writers receive courteous replies.

But in the same month there arrived elaborate greetings to the DCI from a Maryland woman who thinks she is Catherine III, Empress of all the Russias, and who had previously sent a 5,000-word report on how she insured the successful invasion of Europe by entertaining Hitler privately for 12 hours on D-Day. Also in March 1965 came the advice that "now is the time—at last—to train 100 of the top CIA men to penetrate every possible beauty parlor and Chinese restaurant . . . the results will amaze and constantly astound your organization." On 13 March a New York correspondent informed us that Rudolph Hess, from his cell in Spandau, was controlling ten leading Southern segregationists by long-distance hypnotism. And on 25 March a woman wrote to the Director from Massachusetts: "As near as I can make out there normally is a grey cloud at the base of the psyche. When the cloud backs up you go out of focus. But after taking Alka Seltzer and sodium bicarbonate I can sing Hokus Pokus you're in focus."

A 1964 letter was addressed to "Snuffy McDuffy, Top Floor, Closed Door, CIA, Washington, D.C." Perceptive mail clerks sent it to the Director's office, where it was found to contain a fairly reasonable suggestion for propaganda. The letter ended: "P.S. If you don't take appropriate action I'll write to the President and tell him you're chicken."

The Fox

Probably the most imaginative and persistent correspondent is a gaunt long-faced man with sunken eyes and prominent ears who first wrote to CIA on 27 January 1952 asking for a high-powered rifle with telescopic sights and terrain maps of Siberia, Manchuria, and Korea. Since then he has sent thousands of letters, postcards, and telegrams and used more than 50 aliases ranging from "Alexis Alexandrovich" to "Old Woody, The Fox." Usually he signs his true name followed by "U.S. Code 143," CIA's government tie-line code. Here we shall call him Old Woody.

Even though his handwriting and literary style are well known around the DCI's office, age cannot wither nor custom stale Old Woody's infinite variety. One letter told the Director: "I have allotted you a maximum life span of 94 years, not to exceed the year 1987." Another complained that "someone has wired my head for sight and sound." A third urged the Director to "tell Hoffa to require seat belts in all trucks." A fourth began: "Allen, I regret to inform you Kennedy won the election fair and square." Then came a telegram (collect) from Florida: "REQUEST FEDERAL TROOPS, MARTIAL LAW. MIAMI SITUATION OUT OF CONTROL."

Old Woody travels widely, usually first class. He has written from Cuba, Puerto Rico, Nassau, Honolulu, and Hong Kong, as well as from most major cities in the United States. On domestic airlines and in American hotels he has often registered as "A.W. Dulles, Jr." and mailed cancelled tickets and receipted bills to CIA. He likes luxury hotels; his suite at a Washington hotel in 1960 was billed at $52 a day. On many of his trips he listed CIA's street address as his residence and the DCI as his next-of-kin, often reinforcing the latter claim by taking out $62,500 in flight insurance with the Director as beneficiary.

In October 1964 Old Woody was arrested for vagrancy in Richmond. Allowed only one phone call, he used it to notify CIA of his plight. A couple of weeks later he phoned to report his new motorcycle license, and still later he wrote that he was working on a boat in Miami. Back in the money early in 1965, he wrote from Bermuda that he had been appointed King of the British Empire.

The risk of arrest does not dampen Old Woody's enthusiasm for the service. In August 1960 he made a telephone appointment with the commanding officer of an Air Force base in Nevada, conducted a "CIA security inspection," used the base commander's telephone

Screwballs

to call CIA headquarters in Washington, and on departure warned the commander that some officers were out of uniform at Harold's Club. After sending MP's on a wild goose chase to the gambling club, the base commander somewhat grumpily reported the incident in an official letter to CIA. A few months later Old Woody was not so lucky. In Ponce, Puerto Rico, he represented himself as an FBI agent, borrowed a jeep from the National Guard, and drove it across the island to San Juan, where he was arrested. "Dear Allen," he wrote from jail, "I am in trouble again." A few days later he grew petulant. "You are wasting your time and the Armed Forces' time," he wrote, "I do not intend a reconciliation."

Generous to a fault, Old Woody rented a Cadillac limousine and chauffeur at $100 a day just before Christmas 1960 and drove to the Soviet embassy, where he left $100 for Francis Gary Powers. Then he drove to the Cuban embassy with $100 for prisoners on the Isle of Pines, and then to the American Red Cross, where he contributed $70 to help unmarried mothers. Finally he came to CIA headquarters and handed the receptionist an envelope addressed to Mr. Dulles containing $50 as a Christmas present. These activities landed him in St. Elizabeth's Hospital, from which he escaped a few days later after getting back the $50 from CIA. But he was pleased with the episode; nearly two years later he wrote Mr. Dulles that "some day I'll give you another $50 bill as a token of my affection."

In November 1961 he wrote from El Paso: "When the new Director takes over, I guess I'll wash my hands of CIA." But Old Woody didn't, and the flow of letters continues. In December 1961 he put down CIA as his home address when he opened a bank account in Wilmington, Delaware. In October 1962 he telegraphed from Chicago: "FIDEL CASTRO MINUS HIS BEARD ARRIVED CHICAGO THIS P.M. HAVE DETAIL COVERING HIM." In September 1963 a Washington-Miami airliner turned back and off-loaded him; he had alarmed fellow-passengers by claiming to be a personal friend of Fidel Castro and trying to communicate with CIA by radio.

Is Old Woody just a harmless screwball? In 1960 he wrote: "Allen, I am going to start carrying a regulation FBI revolver and if someone forces me into a situation I intend on using it." In 1961 he warned Mr. Dulles: "The bomb attached to my radio in Room 313 has not availed you anything so far." Who knows what Old Woody will interpret as "a situation"? At a minimum, he has cost the Government a great many dollars in wasted time, filing space, analyses, and precautions. As he himself put it in a 1960 letter from West Palm Beach: "Allen, you should deduct me from your income tax."

Fish and a Record

Some crank correspondents are remarkably well educated and successful in business or the arts. Take the 50-year-old daughter of a high-ranking Army officer who now owns a prosperous small-town shop. Educated in Europe and widely travelled, she served abroad with the Red Cross in World War II and has written many successful books—including one which was made into a major motion picture. She writes beautifully and, at first glance, convincingly.

It was the fish that gave her away. Her early letters just asked for information about an inner circle of Government officials who used a drawing of a fish as the symbol of "a confidentially shared community of patriotic attitude." Then she started sending CIA officials postcards with crude drawings of fish. Later she adopted the fish as a signature to her own letters.

In 1962 the fish-woman asked the vice president of a Washington bank to help finance a small private counterespionage organization working to expose "the mammoth traitorous operation at present flourishing within our Government." Meanwhile she wrote threatening anonymous letters, mailed them to herself, and then forwarded them to CIA to prove the existence of a conspiracy. Ignored for years, she continues writing long and quite articulate letters. The most recent one, mailed in March 1965, contains roughly 11,000 words.

One might think that if no one answered their letters the crank correspondents would eventually get discouraged and quit writing. This is not always true. CIA's most faithful correspondent has been plugging a single theme steadily since 1951, when he decided a "CIA agent" had welshed on a job offer. Almost every day he mails a postcard with the same message: "Take Action on CIA Agent Joe Blank!" He has been arrested and released on his promise to stop writing; within a few days the postcards arrive again. He has written from Miami, Las Vegas, San Francisco, Phoenix, Denver, Rochester, Colorado Springs, and Hampton, Va.—hitting his peak in 1962 with a total of 332 postcards to CIA. He has also carried his complaint

Screwballs ~~CONFIDENTIAL~~

to the Secretary of Defense, but a special assistant at the Pentagon politely suggested in reply that he deal directly with CIA.

Violence

Are such cranks actually dangerous? Read on.

On 13 March 1963 a "consulting nuclear engineer" called at CIA's downtown personnel office and tried to see the DCI. File checks showed that four years earlier he had sent the Director a letter marked "DEATH" and signed "Lord God, God of Israel." On 28 October 1958 he had hired a taxi in Richmond, picked up two hitchhikers and a 9-year-old boy, and tried to invade the Quantico Marine Corps School brandishing the boy's toy pistols.

The night of 21 February 1962 a man who thought he was a CIA agent telephoned four times trying to report to the Director. On 11 November 1962 the same man was arrested in Rapid City, S.D., after terrorizing residential areas of that city, firing dozens of shots through windows, and wounding one resident. When arrested he was carrying a high-powered rifle, a .22-caliber rifle, and a large quantity of ammunition.

One crank has been bombarding more than 50 top Government officials with details of alleged Communist electronic thought-control by "a coherent light process of inducing a state of controlled hypnosis by radiation of radio frequency energy on a wavelength of approximately 4×10^{-5} centimeters." The writer is officially diagnosed as a paranoiac schizophrenic, potentially dangerous.

On 12 December 1964 a 53-year-old Florida real estate salesman mailed the DCI a crude threat note ending "Your card is the ACE OF SPADES." This man had tried to see the Director in the past—once to discuss a proposed trip to Russia, again to report his invention of the hardest metal in the world. He is diagnosed as a chronic schizophrenic paranoiac with "delusions of grandeur, seclusiveness, and hostility" who should be kept in a "structured and supervised setting." He was arrested three times in 1964, once for carrying a concealed weapon. Earlier he had been arrested for armed robbery and in 1960 in Arlington, Va., for attempted murder.

In 1962, with the arrival of a new DCI, CIA informally reviewed protective measures with Secret Service and Metropolitan Police Department officers. It was reaffirmed that, while the threat of an attack on top Agency officials was unpredictable and might never

~~CONFIDENTIAL~~   Screwballs

Dec 12, 1964

To: McCone
 Were you ever a marine?
 ~~You~~ bled ~~my~~ **MY** country of
 Forty Four Million Dollars —
 In War Time.

 You ARE A TRAITOR.

 Remember the Famous words —

 I am a Berliner.

 WHAT ARE YOU ???

The Marine Corps Builds Men - Body - Mind - Spirit

 My name is Joe - not Oswald.
 Your card is the ACE of SPADES.

materialize, it was nevertheless real enough to require professional protection. Events since then have underlined this view, although there has been no (knock on wood) actual injury. Probably the closest call was when a woman wrestler traced one top official to the home of relatives and lunged at him with a bouquet of roses which was afterwards found to hide a jagged broken beer bottle.

In any intelligence agency it is important to keep track of crank contacts, not only to improve protection but also to assure continuity of control and analysis. Centralization of records in CIA's Office of Security permits quick identification of phonies and time-wasters. Professional security officers know how to handle the off-beat approach, and others would do well to rely on the professionals when they receive an irrational letter or find themselves face to face with an apparently unbalanced stranger.

TRUTH DRUGS IN INTERROGATION

Effects of narcosis and considerations relevant to its possible counterintelligence use.

"TRUTH" DRUGS IN INTERROGATION
George Bimmerle

The search for effective aids to interrogation is probably as old as man's need to obtain information from an uncooperative source and as persistent as his impatience to short-cut any tortuous path. In the annals of police investigation, physical coercion has at times been substituted for painstaking and time-consuming inquiry in the belief that direct methods produce quick results. Sir James Stephens, writing in 1883, rationalizes a grisly example of "third degree" practices by the police of India: "It is far pleasanter to sit comfortably in the shade rubbing red pepper in a poor devil's eyes than to go about in the sun hunting up evidence."

More recently, police officials in some countries have turned to drugs for assistance in extracting confessions from accused persons, drugs which are presumed to relax the individual's defenses to the point that he unknowingly reveals truths he has been trying to conceal. This investigative technique, however humanitarian as an alternative to physical torture, still raises serious questions of individual rights and liberties. In this country, where drugs have gained only marginal acceptance in police work, their use has provoked cries of "psychological third degree" and has precipitated medico-legal controversies that after a quarter of a century still occasionally flare into the open.

The use of so-called "truth" drugs in police work is similar to the accepted psychiatric practice of narco-analysis; the difference in the two procedures lies in their different objectives. The police investigator is concerned with empirical truth that may be used against the suspect, and therefore almost solely with *probative* truth: the usefulness of the suspect's revelations depends ultimately on their acceptance in evidence by a court of law. The psychiatrist, on the other hand, using the same "truth" drugs in diagnosis and treatment of the mentally ill, is primarily concerned with *psychological* truth or psychological reality rather than empirical

"Truth" Drugs

fact. A patient's aberrations are reality for him at the time they occur, and an accurate account of these fantasies and delusions, rather than reliable recollection of past events, can be the key to recovery.

The notion of drugs capable of illuminating hidden recesses of the mind, helping to heal the mentally ill and preventing or reversing the miscarriage of justice, has provided an exceedingly durable theme for the press and popular literature. While acknowledging that "truth serum" is a misnomer twice over—the drugs are not sera and they do not necessarily bring forth probative truth—journalistic accounts continue to exploit the appeal of the term. The formula is to play up a few spectacular "truth" drug successes and to imply that the drugs are more maligned than need be and more widely employed in criminal investigation than can officially be admitted.

Any technique that promises an increment of success in extracting information from an uncompliant source is *ipso facto* of interest in intelligence operations. If the ethical considerations which in Western countries inhibit the use of narco-interrogation in police work are felt also in intelligence, the Western services must at least be prepared against its possible employment by the adversary. An understanding of "truth" drugs, their characteristic actions, and their potentialities, positive and negative, for eliciting useful information is fundamental to an adequate defense against them.

This discussion, meant to help toward such an understanding, draws primarily upon openly published materials. It has the limitations of projecting from criminal investigative practices and from the permissive atmosphere of drug psychotherapy.

Scopolamine as "Truth Serum"

Early in this century physicians began to employ scopolamine, along with morphine and chloroform, to induce a state of "twilight sleep" during childbirth. A constituent of henbane, scopolamine was known to produce sedation and drowsiness, confusion and disorientation, incoordination, and amnesia for events experienced during intoxication. Yet physicians noted that women in twilight sleep answered questions accurately and often volunteered exceedingly candid remarks.

"Truth" Drugs

In 1922 it occurred to Robert House, a Dallas, Texas, obstetrician, that a similar technique might be employed in the interrogation of suspected criminals, and he arranged to interview under scopolamine two prisoners in the Dallas county jail whose guilt seemed clearly confirmed. Under the drug, both men denied the charges on which they were held; and both, upon trial, were found not guilty. Enthusiastic at this success, House concluded that a patient under the influence of scopolamine "cannot create a lie . . . and there is no power to think or reason." [14] His experiment and this conclusion attracted wide attention, and the idea of a "truth" drug was thus launched upon the public consciousness.

The phrase "truth serum" is believed to have appeared first in a news report of House's experiment in the *Los Angeles Record*, sometime in 1922. House resisted the term for a while but eventually came to employ it regularly himself. He published some eleven articles on scopolamine in the years 1921-1929, with a noticeable increase in polemical zeal as time went on. What had begun as something of a scientific statement turned finally into a dedicated crusade by the "father of truth serum" on behalf of his offspring, wherein he was "grossly indulgent of its wayward behavior and stubbornly proud of its minor achievements." [11]

Only a handful of cases in which scopolamine was used for police interrogation came to public notice, though there is evidence suggesting that some police forces may have used it extensively.[2,16] One police writer claims that the *threat* of scopolamine interrogation has been effective in extracting confessions from criminal suspects, who are told they will first be rendered unconscious by chloral hydrate placed covertly in their coffee or drinking water.[16]

Because of a number of undesirable side effects, scopolamine was shortly disqualified as a "truth" drug. Among the most disabling of the side effects are hallucinations, disturbed perception, somnolence, and physiological phenomena such as headache, rapid heart, and blurred vision, which distract the subject from the central purpose of the interview. Furthermore, the physical action is long, far outlasting the psychological effects. Scopolomine continues, in some cases, to make anesthesia and surgery safer by drying the mouth and throat and reducing secretions that might obstruct the air passages. But the fantastically, almost painfully, dry "desert" mouth brought on by the drug is hardly conducive to free talking, even in a tractable subject.

The Barbiturates

The first suggestion that drugs might facilitate communication with emotionally disturbed patients came quite by accident in 1916. Arthur S. Lovenhart and his associates at the University of Wisconsin, experimenting with respiratory stimulants, were surprised when, after an injection of sodium cyanide, a catatonic patient who had long been mute and rigid suddenly relaxed, opened his eyes, and even answered a few questions. By the early 1930's a number of psychiatrists were experimenting with drugs as an adjunct to established methods of therapy.

At about this time police officials, still attracted by the possibility that drugs might help in the interrogation of suspects and witnesses, turned to a class of depressant drugs known as the barbiturates. By 1935 Clarence W. Muehlberger, head of the Michigan Crime Detection Laboratory at East Lansing, was using barbiturates on reluctant suspects, though police work continued to be hampered by the courts' rejection of drug-induced confessions except in a few carefully circumscribed instances.

The barbiturates, first synthesized in 1903, are among the oldest of modern drugs and the most versatile of all depressants. In this half-century some 2,500 have been prepared, and about two dozen of these have won an important place in medicine. An estimated three to four billion doses of barbiturates are prescribed by physicians in the United States each year, and they have come to be known by a variety of commercial names and colorful slang expressions: "goofballs," Luminal, Nembutal, "red devils," "yellow jackets," "pink ladies," etc. Three of them which are used in narcoanalysis and have seen service as "truth" drugs are sodium amytal (amobarbital), pentothal sodium (thiopental), and to a lesser extent seconal (secobarbital).

As with most drugs, little is known about the way barbiturates work or exactly how their action is related to their chemistry. But a great deal is known about the action itself. They can produce the entire range of depressant effects from mild sedation to deep anesthesia—and death. In small doses they are sedatives acting to reduce anxiety and responsiveness to stressful situations; in these low doses, the drugs have been used in the treatment of many diseases, including peptic ulcer, high blood pressure, and various psychogenic disorders. At three to five times the sedative dose the same barbiturates are hypnotics and induce sleep or unconsciousness from which the subject can be aroused. In larger doses a barbiturate acts as an anesthetic, depressing the central nervous system as completely as a gaseous anesthetic does. In even larger doses barbiturates cause death by stopping respiration.

The barbiturates affect higher brain centers generally. The cerebral cortex—that region of the cerebrum commonly thought to be of the most recent evolutionary development and the center of the most complex mental activities—seems to yield first to the disturbance of nerve-tissue function brought about by the drugs. Actually, there is reason to believe that the drugs depress cell function without discrimination and that their selective action on the higher brain centers is due to the intricate functional relationship of cells in the central nervous system. Where there are chains of interdependent cells, the drugs appear to have their most pronounced effects on the most complex chains, those controlling the most "human" functions.

The lowest doses of barbiturates impair the functioning of the cerebral cortex by disabling the ascending (sensory) circuits of the nervous system. This occurs early in the sedation stage and has a calming effect not unlike a drink or two after dinner. The subject is less responsive to stimuli. At higher dosages, the cortex no longer actively integrates information, and the cerebellum, the "lesser brain" sometimes called the great modulator of nervous function, ceases to perform as a control box. It no longer compares cerebral output with input, no longer informs the cerebrum command centers of necessary corrections, and fails to generate correcting command signals itself. The subject may become hyperactive, may thrash about. At this stage consciousness is lost and coma follows. The subject no longer responds even to noxious stimuli, and cannot be roused. Finally, in the last stage, respiration ceases.[10, 23]

As one pharmacologist explains it, a subject coming under the influence of a barbiturate injected intravenously goes through all the stages of progressive drunkenness, but the time scale is on the order of minutes instead of hours. Outwardly the sedation effect is dramatic, especially if the subject is a psychiatric patient in tension. His features slacken, his body relaxes. Some people are momentarily excited; a few become silly and giggly. This usually passes, and most subjects fall asleep, emerging later in disoriented semi-wakefulness.

The descent into narcosis and beyond with progressively larger doses can be divided as follows:

I. Sedative stage.
II. Unconsciousness, with exaggerated reflexes (hyperactive stage).
III. Unconsciousness, without reflex even to painful stimuli.
IV. Death.

Whether all these stages can be distinguished in any given subject depends largely on the dose and the rapidity with which the drug is induced. In anesthesia, stages I and II may last only two or three seconds.

The first or sedative stage can be further divided:

Plane 1. No evident effect, or slight sedative effect.
Plane 2. Cloudiness, calmness, amnesia. (Upon recovery, the subject will not remember what happened at this or "lower" planes or stages.)
Plane 3. Slurred speech, old thought patterns disrupted, inability to integrate or learn new patterns. Poor coordination. Subject becomes unaware of painful stimuli.

Plane 3 is the psychiatric "work" stage. It may last only a few minutes, but it can be extended by further slow injection of the drug. The usual practice is to bring the subject quickly to Stage II and to conduct the interview as he passes back into the sedative stage on the way to full consciousness.

Clinical and Experimental Studies

The general abhorrence in Western countries for the use of chemical agents "to make people do things against their will" has precluded serious systematic study (at least as published openly) of the potentialities of drugs for interrogation. Louis A. Gottschalk, surveying their use in information-seeking interviews,[13] cites 136 references; but only two touch upon the extraction of intelligence information, and one of these concludes merely that Russian techniques in interrogation and indoctrination are derived from age-old police methods and do *not* depend on the use of drugs. On the validity of confessions obtained with drugs, Gottschalk found only three published experimental studies that he deemed worth reporting.

One of these reported experiments by D. P. Morris in which intravenous sodium amytal was helpful in detecting malingerers.[22] The subjects, soldiers, were at first sullen, negativistic, and non-productive under amytal, but as the interview proceeded they revealed the fact of and causes for their malingering. Usually the interviews turned up a neurotic or psychotic basis for the deception.

The other two confession studies, being more relevant to the highly specialized, untouched area of drugs in intelligence interrogation, deserve more detailed review.

Gerson and Victoroff [12] conducted amytal interviews with 17 neuropsychiatric patients, soldiers who had charges against them, at Tilton General Hospital, Fort Dix. First they were interviewed without amytal by a psychiatrist, who, neither ignoring nor stressing their situation as prisoners or suspects under scrutiny, urged each of them to discuss his social and family background, his army career, and his version of the charges pending against him.

The patients were told only a few minutes in advance that narcoanalysis would be performed. The doctor was considerate, but positive and forthright. He indicated that they had no choice but to submit to the procedure. Their attitudes varied from unquestioning compliance to downright refusal.

Each patient was brought to complete narcosis and permitted to sleep. As he became semiconscious and could be stimulated to speak, he was held in this stage with additional amytal while the questioning proceeded. He was questioned

"Truth" Drugs

first about innocuous matters from his background that he had discussed before receiving the drug. Whenever possible, he was manipulated into bringing up himself the charges pending against him before being questioned about them. If he did this in a too fully conscious state, it proved more effective to ask him to "talk about that later" and to interpose a topic that would diminish suspicion, delaying the interrogation on his criminal activity until he was back in the proper stage of narcosis.

The procedure differed from therapeutic narcoanalysis in several ways: the setting, the type of patients, and the kind of "truth" sought. Also, the subjects were kept in twilight consciousness longer than usual. This state proved richest in yield of admissions prejudicial to the subject. In it his speech was thick, mumbling, and disconnected, but his discretion was markedly reduced. This valuable interrogation period, lasting only five to ten minutes at a time, could be reinduced by injecting more amytal and putting the patient back to sleep.

The interrogation technique varied from case to case according to background information about the patient, the seriousness of the charges, the patient's attitude under narcosis, and his rapport with the doctor. Sometimes it was useful to pretend, as the patient grew more fully conscious, that he had already confessed during the amnestic period of the interrogation, and to urge him, while his memory and sense of self-protection were still limited, to continue to elaborate the details of what he had "already described." When it was obvious that a subject was withholding the truth, his denials were quickly passed over and ignored, and the key questions would be reworded in a new approach.

Several patients revealed fantasies, fears, and delusions approaching delirium, much of which could readily be distinguished from reality. But sometimes there was no way for the examiner to distinguish truth from fantasy except by reference to other sources. One subject claimed to have a child that did not exist, another threatened to kill on sight a stepfather who had been dead a year, and yet another confessed to participating in a robbery when in fact he had only purchased goods from the participants. Testimony concerning dates and specific places was untrustworthy and often contradictory because of the patient's loss of time-sense. His veracity in citing names and events proved questionable. Because of his confusion about actual events and what he thought or feared had happened, the patient at times managed to conceal the truth unintentionally.

As the subject revived, he would become aware that he was being questioned about his secrets and, depending upon his personality, his fear of discovery, or the degree of his disillusionment with the doctor, grow negativistic, hostile, or physically aggressive. Occasionally patients had to be forcibly restrained during this period to prevent injury to themselves or others as the doctor continued to interrogate. Some patients, moved by fierce and diffuse anger, the assumption that they had already been tricked into confessing, and a still limited sense of discretion, defiantly acknowledged their guilt and challenged the observer to "do something about it." As the excitement passed, some fell back on their original stories and others verified the confessed material. During the follow-up interview nine of the 17 admitted the validity of their confessions; eight repudiated their confessions and reaffirmed their earlier accounts.

With respect to the reliability of the results of such interrogation, Gerson and Victoroff conclude that persistent, careful questioning can reduce ambiguities in drug interrogation, but cannot eliminate them altogether.

At least one experiment has shown that subjects are capable of maintaining a lie while under the influence of a barbiturate. Redlich and his associates at Yale [25] administered sodium amytal to nine volunteers, students and professionals, who had previously, for purposes of the experiment, revealed shameful and guilt-producing episodes of their past and then invented false self-protective stories to cover them. In nearly every case the cover story retained some elements of the guilt inherent in the true story.

Under the influence of the drug, the subjects were cross-examined on their cover stories by a second investigator. The results, though not definitive, showed that normal individuals who had good defenses and no overt pathological traits could stick to their invented stories and refuse confession. Neurotic individuals with strong unconscious self-punitive tendencies, on the other hand, both confessed more easily and were inclined to substitute fantasy for the truth, confessing to offenses never actually committed.

In recent years drug therapy has made some use of stimulants, most notably amphetamine (Benzedrine) and its relative methamphetamine (Methedrine). These drugs, used either alone or following intravenous barbiturates, produce an outpouring of ideas, emotions, and memories which has been of help in diagnosing mental disorders. The potential of stimulants in interrogation has received little attention, unless in unpublished work. In one study of their psychiatric use Brussel et al.[7] maintain that methedrine gives the liar no time to think or to organize his deceptions. Once the drug takes hold, they say, an insurmountable urge to pour out speech traps the malingerer. Gottschalk, on the other hand, says that this claim is extravagant, asserting without elaboration that the study lacked proper controls.[13] It is evident that the combined use of barbiturates and stimulants, perhaps along with ataraxics (tranquillizers), should be further explored.

Observations from Practice

J. M. MacDonald, who as a psychiatrist for the District Courts of Denver has had extensive experience with narco-analysis, says that drug interrogation is of doubtful value in obtaining confessions to crimes. Criminal suspects under the influence of barbiturates may deliberately withhold information, persist in giving untruthful answers, or falsely confess to crimes they did not commit. The psychopathic personality, in particular, appears to resist successfully the influence of drugs.

MacDonald tells of a criminal psychopath who, having agreed to narco-interrogation, received 1.5 grams of sodium amytal over a period of five hours. This man feigned amnesia and gave a false account of a murder. "He displayed little or no remorse as he (falsely) described the crime, including burial of the body. Indeed he was very self-possessed and he appeared almost to enjoy the examination. From time to time he would request that more amytal be injected."[21]

MacDonald concludes that a person who gives false information prior to receiving drugs is likely to give false information also under narcosis, that the drugs are of little value for revealing deceptions, and that they are more effective in releasing unconsciously repressed material than in evoking consciously suppressed information.

Another psychiatrist known for his work with criminals, L. Z. Freedman, gave sodium amytal to men accused of various civil and military antisocial acts. The subjects were mentally unstable, their conditions ranging from character disorders to neuroses and psychoses. The drug interviews proved psychiatrically beneficial to the patients, but Freedman found that his view of objective reality was seldom improved by their revelations. He was unable to say on the basis of the narco-interrogation whether a given act had or had not occurred. Like MacDonald, he found that psychopathic individuals can deny to the point of unconsciousness crimes that every objective sign indicates they have committed.[10]

F. G. Inbau, Professor of Law at Northwestern University, who has had considerable experience observing and participating in "truth" drug tests, claims that they are occasionally effective on persons who would have disclosed the truth anyway had they been properly interrogated, but that a person determined to lie will usually be able to continue the deception under drugs.

The two military psychiatrists who made the most extensive use of narcoanalysis during the war years, Roy R. Grinker and John C. Spiegel, concluded that in almost all cases they could obtain from their patients essentially the same material and give them the same emotional release by therapy without the use of drugs, provided they had sufficient time.

The essence of these comments from professionals of long experience is that drugs provide rapid access to information that is psychiatrically useful but of doubtful validity as empirical truth. The same psychological information and a less adulterated empirical truth can be obtained from fully conscious subjects through non-drug psychotherapy and skillful police interrogation.

Application to CI Interrogation

The almost total absence of controlled experimental studies of "truth" drugs and the spotty and anecdotal nature of psychiatric and police evidence require that extrapolations to intelligence operations be made with care. Still, enough is known about the drugs' action to suggest certain considerations affecting the possibilities for their use in interrogations.

It should be clear from the foregoing that at best a drug can only serve as an aid to an interrogator who has a sure understanding of the psychology and techniques of normal interrogation. In some respects, indeed, the demands on his skill will be increased by the baffling mixture of truth and fantasy in drug-induced output. And the tendency against which he must guard in the interrogatee to give the responses that seem to be wanted without regard for facts will be heightened by drugs: the literature abounds with warnings that a subject in narcosis is extremely suggestible.

It seems possible that this suggestibility and the lowered guard of the narcotic state might be put to advantage in the case of a subject feigning ignorance of a language or some other skill that had become automatic with him. Lipton [20] found sodium amytal helpful in determining whether a foreign subject was merely pretending not to understand English. By extension, one can guess that a drugged interrogatee might have difficulty maintaining the pretense that he did not comprehend the idiom of a profession he was trying to hide.

There is the further problem of hostility in the interrogator's relationship to a resistance source. The accumulated knowledge about "truth" drug reaction has come largely from patient-physician relationships of trust and confidence. The subject in narcoanalysis is usually motivated *a priori* to cooperate with the psychiatrist, either to obtain relief from mental suffering or to contribute to a scientific study. Even in police work, where an atmosphere of anxiety and threat may be dominant, a relationship of trust frequently asserts itself: the drug is administered by a medical man bound by a strict code of ethics; the suspect agreeing to undergo narcoanalysis in a desperate bid for corroboration of his testimony trusts both drug and psychiatrist, however apprehensively;

and finally, as Freedman and MacDonald have indicated, the police psychiatrist frequently deals with a "sick" criminal, and some order of patient-physician relationship necessarily evolves.

Rarely has a drug interrogation involved "normal" individuals in a hostile or genuinely threatening milieu. It was from a non-threatening experimental setting that Eric Lindemann could say that his "normal" subjects "reported a general sense of euphoria, ease and confidence, and they exhibited a marked increase in talkativeness and communicability." [19] Gerson and Victoroff list poor doctor-patient rapport as one factor interfering with the completeness and authenticity of confessions by the Fort Dix soldiers, caught as they were in a command performance and told they had no choice but to submit to narco-interrogation.

From all indications, subject-interrogator rapport is usually crucial to obtaining the psychological release which may lead to unguarded disclosures. Role-playing on the part of the interrogator might be a possible solution to the problem of establishing rapport with a drugged subject. In therapy, the British narcoanalyst William Sargant recommends that the therapist deliberately distort the facts of the patient's life-experience to achieve heightened emotional response and abreaction.[27] In the drunken state of narcoanalysis patients are prone to accept the therapist's false constructions. There is reason to expect that a drugged subject would communicate freely with an interrogator playing the role of relative, colleague, physician, immediate superior, or any other person to whom his background indicated he would be responsive.

Even when rapport is poor, however, there remains one facet of drug action eminently exploitable in interrogation—the fact that subjects emerge from narcosis feeling they have revealed a great deal, even when they have not. As Gerson and Victoroff demonstrated at Fort Dix, this psychological set provides a major opening for obtaining genuine confessions.

Technical Considerations

It would presumably be sometimes desirable that a resistant interrogatee be given the drug without his knowledge. For narcoanalysis the only method of administration used is intravenous injection. The possibilities for covert or "silent" administration by this means would be severely limited except in a hospital setting, where any pretext for intravenous injection, from glucose feeding to anesthetic procedure, could be used to cover it. Sodium amytal can be given orally, and the taste can be hidden in chocolate syrup, for example, but there is no good information on what dosages can be masked. Moreover, although the drug might be introduced thus without detection, it would be difficult to achieve and maintain the proper dose using the oral route.

Administering a sterile injection is a procedure shortly mastered, and in fact the technical skills of intravenous injection are taught to nurses and hospital corpsmen as a matter of routine. But it should be apparent that there is more to narcotizing than the injection of the correct amount of sodium amytal or pentothal sodium. Administering drugs and knowing when a subject is "under" require clinical judgment. Knowing what to expect and how to react appropriately to the unexpected takes both technical and clinical skill. The process calls for qualified medical personnel, and sober reflection on the depths of barbituric anesthesia will confirm that it would not be enough merely to have access to a local physician.

Possible Variations

In studies by Beecher and his associates,[3-6] one-third to one-half the individuals tested proved to be placebo reactors, subjects who respond with symptomatic relief to the administration of any syringe, pill, or capsule, regardless of what it contains. Although no studies are known to have been made of the placebo phenomenon as applied to narco-interrogation, it seems reasonable that when a subject's sense of guilt interferes with productive interrogation, a placebo for pseudo-narcosis could have the effect of absolving him of the responsibility for his acts and thus clear the way for free communication. It is notable that placebos are most likely to be effective in situations of stress. The individuals most likely to react to placebos are the more anxious, more self-centered, more dependent on outside stimulation, those who express their needs more freely socially, talkers who drain off anxiety by conversing with others. The non-reactors are those clinically more rigid and with better than average emotional control. No sex or I.Q. differences between reactors and non-reactors have been found.

Another possibility might be the combined use of drugs with hypnotic trance and post-hypnotic suggestion: hypnosis could presumably prevent any recollection of the drug experience. Whether a subject can be brought to trance against his will or unaware, however, is a matter of some disagreement. Orne, in a survey of the potential uses of hypnosis in interrogation,[23] asserts that it is doubtful, despite many apparent indications to the contrary, that trance can be induced in resistant subjects. It may be possible, he adds, to hypnotize a subject unaware, but this would require a positive relationship with the hypnotist not likely to be found in the interrogation setting.

In medical hypnosis, pentothal sodium is sometimes employed when only light trance has been induced and deeper narcosis is desired. This procedure is a possibility for interrogation, but if a satisfactory level of narcosis could be achieved through hypnotic trance there would appear to be no need for drugs.

Defensive Measures

There is no known way of building tolerance for a "truth" drug without creating a disabling addiction, or of arresting the action of a barbiturate once induced. The only full safeguard against narco-interrogation is to prevent the administration of the drug. Short of this, the best defense is to make use of the same knowledge that suggests drugs for offensive operations: if a subject knows that on emerging from narcosis he will have an exaggerated notion of how much he has revealed he can better resolve to deny he has said anything.

The disadvantages and shortcomings of drugs in offensive operations become positive features of the defense posture. A subject in narco-interrogation is intoxicated, wavering between deep sleep and semi-wakefulness. His speech is garbled and irrational, the amount of output drastically diminished. Drugs disrupt established thought patterns, including the will to resist, but they do so indiscriminately and thus also interfere with the patterns of substantive information the interrogator seeks. Even under the conditions most favorable for the interrogator, output will be contaminated by fantasy, distortion, and untruth.

Possibly the most effective way to arm oneself against narco-interrogation would be to undergo a "dry run." A trial drug interrogation with output taped for playback would familiarize an individual with his own reactions to "truth" drugs, and this familiarity would help to reduce the effects of harassment by the interrogator before and after the drug has been administered. From the viewpoint of the intelligence service, the trial exposure of a particular operative to drugs might provide a rough benchmark for assessing the kind and amount of information he would divulge in narcosis.

There may be concern over the possibility of drug addiction intentionally or accidentally induced by an adversary service. Most drugs will cause addiction with prolonged use, and the barbiturates are no exception. In recent studies at the U.S. Public Health Service Hospital for addicts in Lexington, Ky., subjects received large doses of barbiturates over a period of months. Upon removal of the drug, they experienced acute withdrawal symptoms and behaved in every respect like chronic alcoholics.

Because their action is extremely short, however, and because there is little likelihood that they would be administered regularly over a prolonged period, barbiturate "truth" drugs present slight risk of operational addiction. If the adversary service were intent on creating addiction in order to exploit withdrawal, it would have other, more rapid means of producing states as unpleasant as withdrawal symptoms.

The hallucinatory and psychotomimetic drugs such as mescaline, marihuana, LSD-25, and microtine are sometimes mistakenly associated with narcoanalytic interrogation. These drugs distort the perception and interpretation of the sensory input to the central nervous system and affect vision, audition, smell, the sensation of the size of body parts and their position in space, etc. Mescaline and LSD-25 have been used to create experimental "psychotic states," and in a minor way as aids in psychotherapy.

Since information obtained from a person in a psychotic drug state would be unrealistic, bizarre, and extremely difficult to assess, the self-administration of LSD-25, which is effective in minute dosages, might in special circumstances offer an operative temporary protection against interrogation. Conceivably, on the other hand, an adversary service could use such drugs to produce anxiety or terror in medically unsophisticated subjects unable to distinguish drug-induced psychosis from actual insanity. An enlightened operative could not be thus frightened, however, knowing that the effect of these hallucinogenic agents is transient in normal individuals.

Most broadly, there is evidence that drugs have least effect on well-adjusted individuals with good defenses and good emotional control, and that anyone who can withstand the stress of competent interrogation in the waking state can do so in narcosis. The essential resources for resistance thus appear to lie within the individual.

Conclusions

The salient points that emerge from this discussion are the following. No such magic brew as the popular notion of truth serum exists. The barbiturates, by disrupting defensive patterns, may sometimes be helpful in interrogation, but even under the best conditions they will elicit an output contaminated by deception, fantasy, garbled speech, etc. A major vulnerability they produce in the subject is a tendency to believe he has revealed more than he has. It is possible, however, for both normal individuals and psychopaths to resist drug interrogation; it seems likely that any individual who can withstand ordinary intensive interrogation can hold out in narcosis. The best aid to a defense against narco-interrogation is foreknowledge of the process and its limitations. There is an acute need for controlled experimental studies of drug reaction, not only to depressants but also to stimulants and to combinations of depressants, stimulants, and ataraxics.

REFERENCES

1. Adams, E. Barbiturates. *Sci. Am.*, Jan. 1958, *198*(1), 60–64.
2. Barkham, J. Truth Drugs: The new crime solver. *Coronet*, Jan. 1951, *29*, 72–76.
3. Beecher, H. K. Anesthesia. *Sci. Am.*, Jan. 1957, *198*, p. 70.
4. Beecher, H. K. Appraisal of drugs intended to alter subjective responses, symptoms. *J. Amer. Med. Assn.*, 1955, *158*, 399–401.

5. Beecher, H. K. Evidence for increased effectiveness of placebos with increased stress. *Amer. J. Physiol.*, 1956, *187*, 163–169.
6. Beecher, H. K. Experimental pharmacology and measurement of the subjective response. *Science*, 1953, *116*, 157–162.
7. Brussel, J. A., Wilson, D. C., Jr., & Shankel, L. W. The use of methedrine in psychiatric practice. *Psychiat. Quart.*, 1954, *28*, 381–394.
8. Delay, J. Pharmacologic explorations of the personality: narcoanalysis and "methedrine" shock. *Proc. Roy. Soc. Med.*, 1949, *42*, 492–496.
9. deRopp, R. S. *Drugs and the Mind.* New York: Grove Press, Inc., 1960.
10. Freedman, L. Z. "Truth" drugs. *Sci. Am.*, March 1960, 145–154.
11. Geis, G. In scopolamine veritas. The early history of drug-induced statements. *J. of Crim. Law, Criminol. & Pol. Sci.*, Nov.–Dec. 1959, *50*(4), 347–356.
12. Gerson, M. J., & Victoroff, V. Experimental investigation into the validity of confessions obtained under sodium amytal narcosis. *J. Clin. and Exp. Psychopath.*, 1948, *9*, 359–375.
13. Gottschalk, L. A. The use of drugs in information-seeking interviews. *Technical report #2, ARDC Study SR 177-D Contract AF 18(600) 1797.* Dec. 1958. Bureau of Social Science Research, Inc.
14. House, R. E. The use of scopolamine in criminology. *Texas St. J. of Med.*, 1922, *18*, 259.
15. Houston, F. A preliminary investigation into abreaction comparing methedrine and sodium amytal with other methods. *J. ment. Sci.*, 1952, *98*, 707–710.
16. Inbau, F. G. *Self-incrimination.* Springfield: C. C. Thomas, 1950.
17. Kidd, W. R. *Police interrogation.* 1940.
18. Legal dose of truth. *Newsweek*, Feb. 23, 1959, 28.
19. Lindemann, E. Psychological changes in normal and abnormal individuals under the influence of sodium amytal. *Amer. J. Psychiat.*, 1932, *11*, 1083–1091.
20. Lipton, E. L. The amytal interview. A review. *Amer. Practit. Digest Treat.*, 1950, *1*, 148–163.
21. MacDonald, J. M. Narcoanalysis and criminal law. *Amer. J. Psychiat.*, 1954, *111*, 283–288.
22. Morris, D. P. Intravenous barbiturates: an aid in the diagnosis and treatment of conversion hysteria and malingering. *Mil. Surg.*, 1945, *96*, 509–513.
23. Orne, M. T. The potential uses of hypnosis in interrogation. An evaluation. *ARDC Study SR 177-D Contract AF 18(600) 1797*, Dec. 1958. Bureau of Social Science Research, Inc.
24. Pelikan, E. W., & Kensler, C. J. Sedatives: Their pharmacology and uses. Reprint from *The Medical Clinics of North America.* W. B. Saunders Company, Sept. 1958.
25. Redlich, F. C., Ravitz, L. J., & Dession, G. H. Narcoanalysis and truth. *Amer. J. Psychiat.*, 1951, *107*, 586–593.

26. Rolin, J. *Police Drugs.* Translated by L. J. Bendit. New York: Philosophical Library, 1956.
27. Sargant, W., & Slater, E. *Physical methods of treatment in psychiatry.* (3rd ed.) Baltimore: Williams and Wilkins, 1954.
28. Snider, R. S. Cerebellum. *Sci. Am.,* Aug. 1958, 84.
29. Uhr, L., & Miller, L. G. (eds.). *Drugs and Behavior.* New York-London: John Wiley & Sons, Inc., 1960.

THE COVERT COLLECTION OF SCIENTIFIC INFORMATION

The purloiner of scientific secrets pleads for patience, partnership, and better guidance.

THE COVERT COLLECTION OF SCIENTIFIC INFORMATION
Louise D. Omandere

This country, which has for over a hundred years led the world in technical development, is confronted by the very real possibility — some say probability — of falling behind in the scientific and technical race, and most dramatically in the contest for supremacy in space — in rockets and missiles, in earth satellite vehicles and manned space platforms, the emergent key elements of the power position of great nations. At this critical juncture it behooves this community to look to its performance in the field of scientific intelligence, to ask whether we are giving it sufficient emphasis, to review its processes and address ourselves to its problems.

This article is addressed to one aspect of scientific intelligence, perhaps its least prominent one, the clandestine collection of scientific and technical information. But covert collection cannot be considered in isolation from collection as a whole, nor collection in isolation from reporting, analysis and production; and we shall touch on all of these.

Pin-pointing the Covert Requirement

Let us begin with the first question the collector asks: "What shall I collect?" (Not *how*, but *what*. *How* is the second step.) Whence comes the answer to this question? Essentially from the analyst; the collector cannot determine which data among those available are critical and must be collected at no matter what risk unless he is informed by the man who day after day analyzes all available material in his particular field. The collector must rely on the analyst to direct him, and to a certain degree his success depends upon the aptness and precision of the requirements he is called upon to fill.

Particularly is this true in the field of scientific intelligence where frequently minute scientific data are crucial. A requirement which asks, "Tell us all you know about such-and-such a target or about research in such-and-such a field," is not calculated to develop the kind of intelligence information the analyst really needs. The intelligence officer running a scientific collection operation is no better equipped with this requirement than he was without it. Yet this is the type of requirement he most commonly receives.

Suppose, for example, that a field intelligence officer is running an operation against a target which comprises institutes in all the major basic sciences and in their military applications — a technical institute. (Lest it be assumed that such a target be purely hypothetical, it should be stated that there are several of this kind presently confronting the collector. One of them has, in addition to its general administrative set-up, the following military Divisions: Engineering, Artillery, Signal, Anti-Aircraft Artillery, Planning, and Experimental. It also has technical units as follows: War Technical Institute, Biology Department, Bacteriological Technical Unit, Meteorology Technical Unit, Security, Chemical Department, Textile and Material Laboratories, Radar and Radio Laboratories, Signal Corps Research and Storage, Explosives and Pyrotechnic Laboratory, and one unit the function of which is not known.) Faced with the necessity to collect information on such a target, where does the covert collector begin if he is armed only with a requirement for "all information available on the Target"?

Because such an institute would be vital to the scientific potential of the country in which it was located, its activities would be shrouded in secrecy. Even so, it would be next to impossible for some information on it not to get into semi-overt and overt channels. For example, if the institute were located in a city where service attachés are posted — and most of these institutes are so located — the attachés could undoubtedly report in some detail on the location, physical description, and physical security of the target. Except in highly classified military fields, there would probably also be local press releases concerning scientific developments at the institute.

More important is the wealth of information overtly derivable from the publications of any institute's staff. The amount of intelligence information on classified subjects obtainable by analysis of overt literature was recently put to the test by a highly sensitive U.S. installation which maintains rigid security precautions. As an experiment, a scientist well qualified in one of the specialties of the installation but without knowledge of its work or that of its subcontractors was engaged to study the overt publications of personnel at the installation. Although classified research cannot be published and all publications of the installation's staff must be cleared by the appropriate scientific and military authorities, this expert was able after studying the overt material which he found on his own in the Library of Congress to determine the entire program of that installation, including its most highly classified aspects. With one minor exception, he reconstructed its total research, development and production program.

It is true that Americans in defense work are allowed to publish more freely than their Soviet Bloc counterparts. But even in Iron Curtain countries the complete muzzling of scientists has been found impossible. Restrictions on the publication of scientific information have been considerably relaxed in the Soviet Bloc since 1955, and particularly within the last two years, in recognition of the fact that science flourishes or dies to the degree that the exchange of ideas among scientists is encouraged or constricted, and in deference to scientists' need to publish in order to establish nationally and internationally their professional reputation.

Information on much of the work of our secret target's scientific staff would thus be readily available to the U.S. intelligence community through the Library of Congress, the Department of Commerce, and the community's own program for exploitation of foreign documents. Moreover, scientists from this target would inevitably be allowed to attend international congresses in their fields of specialty, and would probably be permitted to present scientific papers at such congresses. The exploitation of these congresses through the multiple machinery of overt collection would furnish additional information on scientific developments at the institute.

Asking the covert collector for "all available information" on this target, then, is asking him to collect information which can be gathered by the analyst from overt and semi-overt sources to which he has ready access. A thorough analysis of these overt data would limit the areas which required covert coverage and enable the clandestine collector to concentrate his efforts on the really covert aspects of the target. Only the consumer can thus collate and analyze the overtly available information and levy a resultant meaningful requirement upon the collector.

We see, then, that the first step of collection — the What — rests in the hands of the analyst, and that only a sound, detailed and exclusively covert requirement will yield maximum results in the clandestine collection of information. Analysis of all the information at hand — overt, semi-overt and covert — and the levying of well-founded requirements to fill in its gaps constitute the first and basic step in the process of collection. Let us turn now to the next step in the process — the How.

The Man and His Methods

The covert collection of scientific information is fraught with many difficulties, more than any other field of intelligence. Special knowledge is required to understand the meaning of data in this field. The information most desperately needed by the scientific intelligence community is hidden deep within the folds of Soviet security in areas almost totally inaccessible to ordinary covert operations. In addition, certain highly critical scientific work can be carried on under the nose of the collector without the slightest risk of detection; biological warfare research is an example of such work. (BW is in fact the best form of do-it-yourself warfare. Enough pathogenic material can be manufactured in a camp kitchen in forty-eight hours to incapacitate a tremendous military installation. Dissemination of the material can be easily handled by one person who can drive through or even around the installation.)

The key individual in covert collection is the field intelligence officer, the "case officer" responsible for handling the agent — for contacting him, for maintaining the critically important rapport with him, for giving him instructions on what to do and how to do it, and for eliciting information from him according to prescribed requirements. The case officer is dependent upon his headquarters components, both in the field and in Washington, for support in maintaining the necessary relationships with his agent, for the formulation of information requirements tailored to the specific capability and location of the agent.

Covert Scientific Collection

In some fields of intelligence — the political, economic and even military — the case officer with operational experience and an informed knowledge of current events can, if necessary, formulate his own requirements when he is unable to obtain them from the consumer. If, for example, he is suddenly faced with an opportunity to debrief an important source of information on military plans and does not have time to cable for requirements, he can do a creditable job on his own and develop most of the required information. In the scientific field, however, this is not possible. Unless he is a highly qualified scientist in precisely the same field as his agent-scientist, he cannot debrief him without appropriate requirements received from the consumer. A case officer trained in physics, for example, would be ignorant of the field of microbiology. Without appropriate requirements, tailored specifically for the microbiologist, he would be as helpless as the case officer who specialized in political or counterespionage operations. And even if he is a scientist in the proper field, he still needs statements of requirements in order to keep abreast of the changing gaps in substantive intelligence while conducting operations in the field.

The case officer is a species of its own, possessing generalist abilities and specialist skills. It is a rare scientist who has all the qualifications of a good case officer, and an even rarer one who has them and is also willing to forsake his scientific career for an anonymous one in intelligence. The ideal scientific and technical case officer is this rare individual. It is therefore usually necessary, in selecting a scientific case officer, to make a foregone choice between these two sets of qualifications, those of the case officer and those of the scientist: the former are indispensable to a successful operation in any field, including the scientific. A good case officer, with appropriate training and good requirements, can conduct a very successful operation in the scientific and technical field. A good scientist who is not adaptable to operations cannot.

Faced with the shortage of the ideal scientific case officer and the resultant necessity of using a layman, the collector must first overcome the difficulty caused by the layman's reluctance to deal with scientific material. An excellent case officer may shrink from a scientific operation simply because the language is totally foreign to him. In the political or even economic field he is on familiar ground and is confident that if necessary he can fend for himself, but in the scientific field he feels lost. He cannot evaluate what he hears, and without guidance he does not know whether he has new and critical information, old and unwanted data, or mere fabrication. He also frequently feels at a great disadvantage in talking to his agent, who is highly learned in subjects of which he is himself totally ignorant and the basic principles of which he cannot understand. This reluctance to undertake scientific operations can be overcome by giving the case officer basic training in scientific principles and terminology and by interesting him in the importance of scientific and technical information.

We have said that the really critical scientific information needed by the United States is almost completely hidden in impregnable installations deep within the Soviet Union. Yet the collection of much-needed scientific intelligence information is not completely impossible. If we work at the primary targets from the periphery, we have a reasonable chance of success, of obtaining enough critical information to enable us at least to make educated guesses which may come satisfyingly close to an accurate estimate.

One of the potentially most fruitful sources of scientific intelligence information is the scientific congress. An international scientific congress or conference is the mecca of every scientist, and Soviet and Satellite scientists are attending these conferences in increasing numbers. Over one thousand such conferences, congresses, symposia and colloquia are held every year, providing for a substantial amount of intercourse among scientists of all nationalities. Many of the same scientists attend meetings of the same group held yearly or biennially.

In considering the scientific congress from the intelligence viewpoint, a clear distinction must be made between the congress as a source of positive information and as an operational arena. The positive information the congress yields is almost invariably overt. The scientific papers, the open floor discussions and the small seminar sessions are all easily covered through overt sources. Thus there is little need to expend the efforts of the clandestine collector at a scientific congress merely to collect positive intelligence information.

As an operational arena, however, the congress can hardly be surpassed. For one thing, scientists of all nationalities, Bloc and non-Bloc, can meet on common ground, in an atmosphere as free of political tension as can be found in present-day circumstances. For another, it is possible for the same scientist to reestablish, time after time, contact with his counterpart from behind the Curtain without being conspicuous in so doing. He can meet his counterparts not only on the conference floor and in closed sessions, but on social occasions as well. Particularly for Western scientists who have appropriate language qualifications, social intercourse with their Satellite colleagues is common and easily arranged. Through attendance at periodically recurring conferences, it is possible for Western scientists to meet their Satellite counterparts year after year, and it has become standard practice to correspond between meetings and to exchange reprints.

Over a period of time, sufficient rapport can often be established between Eastern and Western participants at these congresses to provide the basis for a clandestine operation, beginning, for example, with the introduction of a case officer to the target scientist for the purpose of recruitment. Once a Soviet Bloc scientist has agreed to work for the West, there will be little difficulty in maintaining subsequent communications. For, if the operation has been handled professionally and securely, the recruited scientist will within six months to a year be attending another conference, where he can be securely debriefed and rebriefed. Thus there is no necessity to attempt to lay on an elaborate secret writing method or code, which at best can yield only fragments of information and which is fraught with operational and security hazards. In short, what can be achieved through operations at international conferences is in fact penetrations of target installations within Bloc areas.

The greatest success so far achieved through this means has been the recruitment of Satellite scientists who travel to the USSR, sometimes for periodic short visits and occasionally for extended study or work, who can report on their observations and work within the Soviet Union when next they attend a conference in the West.

Inept or non-professional elicitation of Bloc scientists, however, has resulted in the discovery of these efforts by the opposition and the resultant loss of potentially valuable assets. Within recent months, the East German Government has announced in the press that GDR scientists would not be allowed to attend scientific congresses in West Germany because such congresses were so widely exploited by American intelligence. Thus, in order for the United States to derive maximum benefit from conference exploitation, our efforts in this field, both overt and covert, must be handled professionally and securely. These efforts and their security can be fortified by thorough coordination among the intelligence elements concerned. If the intelligence activity at scientific conferences were disclosed to Soviet intelligence, Soviet attendance at such conferences in the future would undoubtedly be curtailed and perhaps altogether prohibited. In that event a profitable long-range potential for covert collection of scientific information would disappear.

But if the program outlined above can be prosecuted in a well-planned manner for a period of time, the eventual penetration of the more important targets within the Soviet Union through scientists who have agreed to report on their activities becomes a realistic possibility.

Legal travelers are another source of scientific intelligence information. Western scientists have been allowed to tour wide areas of the Soviet Union and with the trained eye of the scientist can observe and report in accurate detail on the installations visited. While no really critical target can be adequately covered in this manner, still information of value which will contribute to the overall picture of Soviet scientific potential can be gathered. On a limited scale, Western scientists have been permitted to visit Soviet scientists in their homes. This enables the Westerner to collect information on the habits and attitudes of the Soviet scientist in his home atmosphere, his family attachments, hobbies and other characteristics, information which helps headquarters assess the scientist's potential with a view to future operations.

Even non-scientific legal travelers can be of considerable assistance when furnished simple collection techniques which can be applied with complete security, are non-compromising if discovered, but at the same time yield valuable and even critical scientific data. Such collection techniques can also be given to resident agents, legal or illegal travelers, and even couriers. While elaborate gadgetry and large black boxes are limited in their application to field operations, other more

Covert Scientific Collection

simple techniques with a wide variety of applications can be used without considerable risk to the agent. Great caution should be exercised in the employment of any such techniques in order to avoid an exposure which would render them useless in the future, but properly handled they have a real potential for developing answers to presently unanswerable questions.

SOME FAR-OUT THOUGHTS ON COMPUTERS

A Jules Verne look at intelligence processes in a coming generation.

SOME FAR-OUT THOUGHTS ON COMPUTERS
Orrin Clotworthy

Question: What does the size of the next coffee crop, bullfight attendance figures, local newspaper coverage of UN matters, the birth rate, the mean daily temperatures or refrigerator sales across the country have to do with who will next be elected president of Guatemala?

Answer: Perhaps nothing. But the question is not a frivolous one. There must be a cause behind each vote cast in an election. It may be a rational, emotional, superstitious, or accidental cause. The choice may derive from months of conscious effort to weigh the pros and cons of the aspirants to office. It may be an automatic, tradition-bound action that requires not even a cursory exercise of the thought process. Or the voter himself may not recognize why he decides as he does. But something will motivate him, and it may be closely correlative with one or more of the quantitative factors suggested in the opening question.

To learn just what the factors are, how to measure them, how to weight them, and how to keep them flowing into a computing center for continual analysis will some day become a matter of great concern to all of us in the intelligence community. I say "will" rather than "may" because it seems to me that this type of election analysis will be only the first faltering step by an infant quantified behavioral science that is going to be forced on us for its upbringing like a doorstep baby—and soon.

Instant Estimates

For elections offer a fairly simple starting point. They deal in tangible, discrete, measurable data—ballots. Ideally they reflect the attitudes of a populace, not just toward a handful of candidates but toward a host of related issues. Although in practice we have to compensate for incomplete voter participation, ballot-box stuffing, and other imperfections, means will be found to make such compensations and we will still wind up with good readings on popular attitudes at a given moment in history. Elections are in a sense history's benchmarks to which we can, and do, refer back when preparing estimates of public opinion in the long periods between them. They are also buoys to keep the analyst on course, a regular means of validating his estimates. When his prediction of an election outcome turns out to be way off target, he can find solace in that old Cape Canaveral philosophy, "We learn more from our failures than we do from our successes."

Note that what is proposed is to bypass the voter himself in this analytic process, looking beyond him for the reasons underlying his decisions. As the pollsters have discovered, even in an enlightened, democratic society it is not a simple matter to develop accurate election predictions from a sampling of the electorate. In an underdeveloped or overpoliced state of the type that we in intelligence are so often concerned with, the additional problems of obtaining a valid sample of opinion through direct interviews are so immense as to force us to more subtle methods. Isolating the factors that influence popular attitudes in a given area at election time would be one approach.

Once we had succeeded in isolating these factors, could we not then begin to watch the key phenomena continuously, gathering them in and collating them so that at any instant we could read from them the temper of the populace under study? Ten years ago, the answer would have been negative. Today, because of the tremendous strides that our technologists have made in electronic data processing, it is decidedly affirmative. The required mathematical computations and sophisticated statistical analysis are well within the present state of the computer art.

Molecules and People

Where we lag is not in processing technology, but in the behavioral science "laboratories," where only the faintest of beginnings have been made in the application of physical science techniques to the study of societies. We are doubt-

Thoughts on Computers

less years away from the knowledge of causes and effects that will permit us to predict mass human behavior with real confidence. Yet there is rising optimism among scholars that we will some day be able to foretell the behavior of large groups of people within reasonable limits, given accurate and timely measurements of certain telltale factors. A single person, they submit, follows an erratic course, just as a single gas molecule does. But when you put enough people together many of the individual erratic actions will cancel each other out and there will emerge a collective behavior that can be formulized. To be sure, what comes out is not likely to be so simple and aesthetically satisfying as Boyle's law for the isothermal pressure-volume relation of an ideal body of gas. Mass cause-and-effect relationships are more elusive for people than for molecules. But they must be there, somewhere, and scholars are looking for them.

The impact of new breakthroughs in this area upon the intelligence business is interesting to contemplate. Possibly some American discoveries in mass human behavior patterns could be kept secret for long periods to permit our unilateral exploitation of them. Let's imagine, for example, that we discover an extremely high correlation between Tito's popularity among the Yugoslavs and the consumption of slivovitz in that country: when per capita absorption goes up, his stock goes down. As long as we are aware of this and he is not, we will find it profitable to collect precise data on boozing among the Yugoslavs. To keep our interest undetected, we resort to clandestine collection techniques, because once he learns of it and knows the reason why, he can adopt countermeasures, for instance doctored consumption figures. The variations in this game are endless.

What Makes Sukarno Run?

While one group of researchers, largely sociologists and political scientists, pursues the gas molecule analogy, a more visionary one will be exploring possibilities with certain individual molecules. Can scientists ever simulate the behavior pattern of a Mao Tse-tung or a Sekou Touré? Theoretically, if a man's importance warrants it, they should be able to reduce to mathematical terms and store in an electronic memory most of his salient experiences and observed reactions to varying situations. Subjecting this stand-in brain to a hypothetical set of circumstances, they could then read out his probable reaction to the event hypothesized. Here the storage problem alone would be tremendous. Even greater would be the task of teaching the computer to ignore certain stimuli while responding to others. As you read this article, you are able to disregard the noise of the air conditioner nearby. It will be some time before a machine can be taught to distinguish between the relevant and the irrelevant in even this elementary fashion. Still, by say the year 2000, I wouldn't bet against it.

On another level, at any rate, much can be learned through comparisons of what national leaders say in their public pronouncements and what they subsequently do. The more sophisticated our techniques for content analysis become, the more we will be obliged to turn to electronic data processing for help in correlating statements with actions. This could be made an operationally practical method pending the hoped-for development of a stand-in brain: virtually *all* of the research data for content analysis can be obtained with relative ease, and the fact that content analysis deals with objective observations obviates the monumental task of synthesizing someone's subjective thought processes.

Your Move

Another application of computers to the intelligence business lies in the field of gaming. The Air Force has been experimenting for years with a mock-up of the strategic air battle, using a computer to simulate the clash between a surprise intercontinental air and space assault force and the defensive and counter-strike resources of this country. Not only are the planned aspects of both contending operations simulated; so are the unexpected or accidental factors such as weather, faulty intelligence, weapons and guidance imperfections. While these games are of great value as instructional aids, they are far more than that. With the computer alternate strategies are subjected to realistic tests, and aerospace doctrine emerges. And the time is not too remote when fresh intelligence on a potential enemy's capabilities and or-

Thoughts on Computers

der of battle, fed into a computer as it is received, will turn out constantly changing designs for an optimum counter-strategy.

Still pretty much in the concept stage are similar gaming ideas for students and formulators of foreign policy. Whereas military games involve factors readily susceptible of quantitative measurement, international political games by and large do not. Thus a great deal of quantifying needs to be done to instill sufficient realism into foreign policy games. Among those who have suggested an approach to the problem are the husband-and-wife team of George and Charlotte Dyer, who proposed a foreign policy game in which batteries of colored lights would represent the actual and potential strengths of the nations under study and foreign policy measures taken would be scored, by changes in the light pattern, according to whether judges ruled them beneficial or harmful. Photo-electric cells measuring light intensities would provide constant readings on the progress of the game.

Two aspects of the Dyers' game are especially interesting. First, it makes a beginning toward quantification by breaking down the factors affecting foreign policy; and the diversity of these factors immediately suggests that nothing less than a high-speed computer could keep simultaneous track of all of them and their interrelationships. For example, each nation's resources, in order to be rated on a numerical scale, are broken into ten broad areas—geography, sociology, politics, foreign affairs, economy, industry, transportation, science, armed forces, and history. Then each one of these ten is resolved into its components, with sociology, for example, embracing race, population, language, temperament of people, education, health and welfare, recreation and amusements, institutions and national culture, religion and philosophy. Then each of these is sub-divided, population, for instance, into eighteen groups and sub-groups.

Second, it would score moves in the ten major areas separately rather than keep a single comprehensive score. Thus if the United States and Communist China were the combatants, no effort would be made to compare a Chinese gain in industry with a U.S. gain in science, but ten different running scores would be kept, so that comparisons could be made at any moment of the relative positions of the contending powers in any of the ten areas. To assign meaningful numerical quantities to the starting positions of the competitors and to each of their subsequent moves, the Dyers suggest that an operational research team be employed. (This and other gainful intelligence employment for operations research might be a good subject for a future issue of this journal.)

From air battle and foreign policy games to intelligence games with computers does not appear to be a very broad jump. Intelligence operations certainly have diplomatic and military parallels. With the beginnings made in these fields we could take it from there. Intelligence games, like the others, might vastly assist not only in training but in testing operational proposals and in developing doctrine.

All A is Not B and So Forth

There will arise problems, or parts of problems, that cannot be solved by arithmetic operations, no matter how ingenious the quantifiers and their systems or how swift the computers. There will be points at which a "yes" or "no" is what the user needs from the machine. But here again, the people who construct computers have made a good start on the task of attacking non-mathematical—i.e., logical—problems. Logic machines date back, in fact, to the thirteenth century, when a Spanish theologian and visionary named Ramon Lull was the first to embark on such gadgetry. Others after him invented improved devices to prove whether a certain major premise and a certain minor premise led to a certain conclusion and to solve other more complex problems. It was not until the advent of electronic computers in the twentieth century, however, that a really spectacular advance in logic machine principles could be made. If life is a lot more complicated these days than it was in Lull's, at least we have some pretty sophisticated hardware to help in simplifying it.

The principles involved in translating into machine language such ideas as "A is either B or not B" are, after all, much like those of translating numbers from the decimal system to the computer's binary system, wherein all numbers are expressed as a series of ones and zeros. Computers can therefore tackle either arithmetic or logic problems by making use of the basic fact of electronic life that any part of a circuit has to be in one of two states—on or off. This characteristic permits comparisons and tests which essentially guide the computer through the logical decision-making process.

What the limitations on computer capabilities really are is anybody's guess. The late John Von Neumann speculated on this question from a novel angle a few years back. He set out, in preparation for a lecture series at Yale, to draw comparisons between the most advanced computers of the day and the human brain, but drew them not on the basis of relative problem-solving capabilities or memories or any other aspect of performance but rather on the basis of structure as complexes of divisible parts. He looked at how these parts were assembled, how large they were, what their circuitry was, how fast they operated. Despite having worked at maximum capacity right up until his death in 1956, Von Neumann was unable to finish his study, and mankind was the loser. It may be surmised from what he did complete, though, that he might in the end have reached the conclusion that there were no significant qualitative differences between the computer and the brain and that scientific advances would inevitably narrow the quantitative gaps.

What and Whom Do You Know?

Backing away for a moment from what computers will some day be able to do, let's concern ourselves with their well-known current capabilities for storing and indexing information.

One day recently, some months after a certain operation involving a piece of real estate in a remote area, a case officer unconnected with the operation commented to a colleague, "I probably know that area better than anyone in the government; I've been duck-hunting there many times." Could this officer's knowledge of the area have been of use to those planning the operation? Very probably. Would they have had any rapid way of finding out except by sheer accident whether anyone in the organization had such knowledge? No, they would not. Until the past few years, there has been no practical way to index all of the experience and talents of all of our personnel.

We have made a start, it is true, using IBM cards. It is possible to learn through machine runs how many married, German-speaking men between 33 and 35 years old with civil engineering degrees and naval service there are in the Central Intelligence Agency. But to record even this basic data taxes the capacities of the card systems in current use. Should we decide to do so, we could, over a span of a few years, index personnel knowledge and skills to a degree never before dreamed of, using more advanced forms of electronic data processing.

In a television drama a few months back, a private organization was supposed to have compiled just such data on millions of U.S. citizens. The story concerned the search by a federal agency for a man who (1) was a barber, (2) knew a lot about stamp-collecting, and (3) could pick locks. The company found the man, the agency put his talents to use, and by the end of the program Yankee ingenuity had triumphed over a slick international narcotics ring. The real hero of the story was the computer—they must have used one—that pinpointed the right man for the job. It may be less than reckless to suggest that a comparable capability to match backgrounds to job requirements might be helpful in intelligence operations.

Or take the matter of acquaintances. It is our suspicion that in many cases where someone in an intelligence organization has an interest in someone outside of it, American or foreign, there may well be sitting down the hall and two floors up from him someone who knows the object of his interest personally. If he doesn't know him directly, he knows someone who *is* directly acquainted with him. Let's just consider American citizens. Suppose that each employee of an organization knows 1000 Americans outside of the organization. Then for every 1000 employees there are 1,000,000 Americans who are known directly. Allowing for a 50% duplication rate, there remain 500,000 Americans who are known to at least one employee of the organization. These half million in turn know 1000 each, or a total of 500,000,000 people. Cutting again for duplications we are left with 250,000,000 people.

Thoughts on Computers

Maybe these figures are high, but they at least suggest that very few of our 180,000,000 American citizens are more than one step removed from direct acquaintance with someone in an organization of several thousand people.

Some interesting conclusions could be drawn from a similar approach to the question of what foreign citizens have ties of acquaintance, direct or indirect, to the staff of an intelligence organization. Would it be worth the expense to collect such information and keep it current? That is not for us to decide, but we can say that without the vast and infallible memory of a computer such an undertaking would be unthinkable.

Political Weather Forecasts

Among the many publications issued in the intelligence community is the rather recent "Weekly Survey of Cold War Crisis Situations." Among other kinds of crisis, it calls the attention of its readers to those countries of the world where things seem to be going not too well for the governments in power. The judgments on which countries belong where on the weekly list are made by competent, seasoned political analysts. Without for a moment questioning their qualifications for the job, we wonder if their work could not be effectively improved, say by around 1975, with electronic data processing.

More specifically, there might first be established a numerical scale called the "stability index" or something similar. Each country around the globe would initially be given a rating along this scale. A number near the maximum would describe a highly stable government, e.g., Switzerland's, while one near zero would denote a tottering regime. Once this rating had been assigned, every intelligence report affecting that country thereafter would be assigned a number, plus or minus or zero, reflecting the impact of the events reported upon the country's stability. These figures would be fed into a computer as fast as they were received. As often as necessary, the net result of the input could be recovered, perhaps printed out in the form of a "daily world political weather map."

Would this form of automation sell short the political wisdom of the analyst? No, it would not. In the first place, the index could not replace the written analysis but only supplement it. In the second place, any such system would acknowledgedly have plenty of bugs in it which the experts would take months or years to work out. And in the third place, the assignment of numerical values to the reports would be an exacting job, involving several levels of rechecking by highly knowledgeable people.

The system would have advantages beyond the instant production of concentrated political judgment: It would provide a basis for quantitative comparison of a given situation with other regions and other times that would be more revealing than verbal description. By drawing more people into the appraisal process, it would also reduce the effect that any single analyst's biases, permanent or temporary, conscious or subconscious, might otherwise have on the final product. Finally, it would automatically insure that all of the available intelligence is taken into consideration and would guard against the inadvertent omission of pertinent data by a harassed senior analyst under pressure.

The Electronica Britannica

IBM has developed for public use a computer-based system called the "Selective Disseminator of Information." Intended for large organizations dealing with heterogeneous masses of information, it scans all incoming material and delivers those items that are of interest to specific officers in accordance with "profiles" of their needs which are continuously updated by a feed-back device. Any comment here on the potential of the SDI for an intelligence agency would be superfluous; Air Intelligence has in fact been experimenting with such a mechanized dissemination system for some years.

As a final thought, how about a machine that would send via closed-circuit television visual and oral information needed immediately at high-level conferences or briefings? Let's say that a group of senior officers are contemplating a covert action program for Afghanistan. Things go well until someone asks, "Well, just how many schools are there in the country, and what is the literacy rate?" No one in the room knows.

Thoughts on Computers

(Remember, this is an imaginary situation.) So the junior member present dials a code number into a device at one end of the table. Thirty seconds later, on the screen overhead, a teletype printer begins to hammer out the required data. Before the meeting is over, the group has been given through the same method the names of countries that have airlines into Afghanistan, a biographical profile of the Soviet ambassador there, and the Pakistani order of battle along the Afghanistan frontier. Neat, no?

If and when computers begin to perform these and other functions, the effects will be felt fairly rapidly by every one of us, or, more likely, by the next generation of intelligence officers. Since all intelligence information will be processed by the computers, we (or they) will need to know the fundamentals of their construction and operation. Formats will change. So will collection requirements. Nearly everyone will have to go through new training. Many operational decisions formerly based on some research and a lot of educated guesswork will be reached only after consultation with the computer. A new language will be spoken; words like "digital," "analog," "programming," "game theory," "Boolean algebra," "Monte Carlo method," "stochastic process" will be commonplace. And "the monster" (as it is sure to be known) will provide a convenient target for almost all grievances, including many that no one has thought up yet.

Why do we need the computer? Partly, because of the staggering tasks and the shrinking time limits imposed on us by the space-age cold war, we need to delegate to it routine, repetitive arithmetical and logical calculations, thereby permitting fuller application of human skills to problems of judgment. But we also need it because it is available to us, because with it we can do jobs that we could never have done without it, "because," as the inveterate Alpinist explained, "it's there."

BIBLIOGRAPHY OF SOURCE MATERIALS

Books

Buchanan, James M., *The Calculus of Consent*. Ann Arbor: The University of Michigan Press, 1962

De Latil, Pierre, *Thinking by Machine*. Boston: Houghton Mifflin Co., 1957

Eckert, Wallace J. and Jones, T., *Faster, Faster*. New York: McGraw-Hill, 1956

Gardner, Martin, *Logic Machines and Diagrams*. New York: McGraw-Hill, 1958

Lazarsfeld, Paul F. (editor), *Mathematical Thinking in the Social Sciences*. Glencoe, Illinois: The Free Press, 1954

Rothstein, Jerome, *Communication, Organization and Science*. Indian Hills, Colo.: Falcon's Wing Press, 1958

Schelling, Thomas C., *The Strategy of Conflict*. Cambridge, Mass.: Harvard University Press, 1960

Stibitz, George R. and Larrivee, Jules A., *Mathematics and Computers*. New York: McGraw-Hill, 1957

Von Neumann, John, *The Computer and the Brain*. New Haven: Yale University Press, 1958

Wiener, Norbert, *Cybernetics* (second edition). MIT Press and John Wiley & Sons, Inc., New York & London, 1961

Williams, J. D., *The Compleat Strategyst*. McGraw-Hill, New York, London, Toronto, 1954

Periodicals

Adams, Robert H., "Developments in Air Targeting: The Air Battle Model." *Studies in Intelligence*, Spring 1958

Becker, Joseph, "The Computer—Capabilities, Prospects and Implications." *Studies in Intelligence*, Fall 1960

Bell, D., "Ten Theories in Search of Reality: The Prediction of Soviet Behavior in the Social Sciences." *World Politics*, Apr. 1958

Bloomfield, L. P. and N. J., "Three Experiments in Political Gaming." *American Political Science Review*, Dec. 1959

Borgatta, E. F., "Cumulative Scaling as a Routine Procedure with the IBM 101." *Sociometry*, Dec. 1957

Borgatta, E. F., and Robbin, J., "Some Implications of High Speed Computers for the Methodology of Social Research." *Sociological and Social Research*, Mar.-Apr. 1959

Dyer, Charlotte and George, "Estimating National Power and Intentions." *Annals of the American Academy of Political and Social Sciences*, July 1960

Jessel, Walter, "A National Name Index Network." *Studies in Intelligence*, Spring 1962

Newspaper Articles

"Games Used in Study of Diplomatic Affairs," by Julius Duscha. *Washington Post*, 13 Sept. 1959

"Government's Lightning-Fast Gray Boxes 'Think,'" by Julius Duscha. *Washington Post*, 9 July 1959

"Next a Predictor for the President," by Roscoe Drummond. *Miami Herald*, 4 Jan. 1960

"Super Mechanical 'Brain' in Making," by Thomas R. Henry. *Washington Star*, 19 May 1962

THE INTELLIGENCE COMMUNITY POST-MORTEM PROGRAM 1973-1975

THE INTELLIGENCE COMMUNITY POST-MORTEM PROGRAM, 1973-1975

Richard W. Shryock [1]

For roughly two years, from late 1973 to late 1975, the US intelligence community produced—fearlessly or fecklessly, depending on one's point of view—a series of critical post-mortem assessments of its own performance in one or another (usually trying) circumstance. There was, of course, some precedence for this unusual activity, but not much:

- Intelligence production offices in the community had for years prepared various kinds of post-mortems. But they did so only irregularly, and then almost always in response to the complaints of high-level policymakers and military officers who wanted to know what-had-gone-wrong within the very same production offices. Rightly or wrongly, but understandably, post-mortems produced in this fashion were frequently dismissed by their requesters and others as unresponsive and self-serving.

- A special subcommittee of the National Security Council Intelligence Committee tried a new, hybrid approach to the post-mortem problem in the early 1970s, producing, with the community's indispensable help, two or three assessments presumably untainted by the special interests of the community. (The best known of these seems to have been a paper on the community's performance concerning the Indo-Pakistani war of 1971.) But for eminently understandable reasons, including their unofficial status and bureaucratically peculiar origins, these post-mortems were largely ignored by both the policymakers who had indirectly commissioned them and the community officials who were the supposed beneficiaries.

The principal architects of the 1973-1975 post-mortem program of the Intelligence Community (IC) Staff sought to avoid problems of this character. They wanted to create a system that would, somehow, serve the community's real interests and, simultaneously, the "legitimate" (as opposed to the political and the purely policy) needs of its critics.[2]

---

[1] Author's note: This article was prepared at the request of two members of the Board of Editors of this journal. I have discussed its contents with one of them, and have conducted interviews with several past and present officers of the intelligence community, but the views expressed herein are my own.

I have not had recent access to the post-mortem documents discussed here, so I have had to use my memory and the resourceful press as major sources of information. Under the circumstances, some errors may have crept unbidden into the manuscript. If so, I extend my apologies.

I should also explain that I have deliberately omitted almost all names from this account, partly because they seem unnecessary in a non-scholarly, non-historical assay, and partly because it would be unfortunate if readers were distracted by controversial references to individual luminaries.

Finally, on a more personal note, let me record the fact that the post-mortem program, for which I bore a large responsibility, died quietly in 1975 without memorialization and without obituary. This, then—belatedly—is that memorialization and that obituary. R.W.S.

[2] Mutual suspicions between policymakers and intelligence officers have always existed but, not so surprisingly, seemed to reach a high point in the early 1970s. More than a few intelligence officers, for example, saw in the NSC-sponsored post-mortem on the 1971 Indo-Pak war (cited above), an effort to justify or shift blame for US policy before and during that conflict.

A total order. Perhaps too tall, especially inasmuch as the post-mortem program did not always enjoy the unalloyed support of the top IC Staff management. Still, the principal distinguishing characteristics of the program, as it was in fact instituted in November 1973, were: (1) official status, obtained via DCI and USIB (i.e., community) sponsorship; (2) preparation by an organization (the Product Review Division—PRD—of the IC Staff) that was separated, if not divorced, from any and all "line" production and collection offices and that was charged with, among other things, the preparation of post-mortems on a continual basis; (3) a serious, if not always successful, effort by this organization to strike a balance between objectivity (normally the privilege of the non-involved) and expertise (often the province of the involved); and (4) the great amount of favorable and unfavorable attention paid several of the papers by readers (and non-readers too) within and without the community.

Seven post-mortems were produced by PRD between December 1973 and September 1975. Five of these were specifically requested by the DCI; one was asked for by his Deputy for the Community; and one grew out of an IC Staff commitment to the DCI. Geographically, four concerned one or another problem in the Middle East, one dealt with Chile, one with India, and one with Southeast Asia. All are discussed in some detail below.[3]

It is the contention here that on the whole this series of post-mortems was a success, or at least not a failure. In any case, members of the community, together with observers and critics in Congress and the Executive Branch, should be aware that the program existed and for a time—until the unwelcome intercession of the House Select Committee on Intelligence (on which more later)—even prospered. For the community might one day decide to revive a candid post-mortem process with similar characteristics and objectives. It is likely, after all, to gain or accept only so much nourishment from granting a monopoly on post-mortems to "outsiders" in Congress or elsewhere. These, too, can be useful, but they should not be exclusive.

More important, the community could in the long run benefit from objective, mostly self-initiated post-mortems because, however embarrassing they might prove to be temporarily, they could help in a variety of ways to improve the quality of intelligence—in production, in collection, and yea, even in management. This, at any rate, is the hope of more than a few who not only understand the need for such improvement but who also comprehend the essentiality of the community's services to the nation.

The Seven Reports

1. *The Arab-Israeli War, 1973:* The cumbersomely titled "The Performance of the Intelligence Community Before the Arab-Israeli War of October 1973: A Preliminary Post-Mortem Report," was published in December 1973. Soon thereafter it became the IC Staff equivalent of a best seller; it received good reviews from prominent critics (Kissinger wrote the DCI to say that it was "outstanding"), and it was as widely read as its rather restrictive classification permitted. In a sober mood, well aware that their best estimates about the likelihood of war had turned out to be (as later headlined in the press) "starkly wrong," even members of the United States Intelligence Board (USIB) praised the document for its thoroughness, objectivity, and candor.

---

[3]Not discussed are several PRD papers issued during the same period which bore some resemblance to port-mortem studies but which did not, for one reason or another, bear post-mortem designations. One of these, interestingly enough, dealt specifically with an intelligence success; it was the only such paper ever prepared in PRD and the only one ever asked for (by policymakers, the DCI, USIB, or, indeed, any high-level community official). A post-mortem program, by its very nature, is likely to deal primarily with shortcomings—real or presumed—although there is no theoretical reason why this need be so.

Post-Mortems

The report itself reflected a prodigious amount of work and as much analytical effort as could be brought to bear on a difficult problem, the dimensions of which were clear but the causes of which were not. All pertinent intelligence published by the community from May to early October 1973—daily items, memoranda, weekly articles, Watch Reports, estimates, and research papers—was carefully read. Thousands of individual collection reports from the Department of State, CIA, DIA, NSA, and other agencies were also reviewed. Scores of intelligence officers and consumers were interviewed. All the data thus assembled were sifted and analyzed, chronologically arranged to serve as reference aids, and then interpreted in preliminary reports prepared by individual investigators. A paper (together with six annexes which were later dropped) was then produced and finally, after review by the DCI and his Deputy for the Intelligence Community, disseminated in early December.

In brief, after quoting from appropriate intelligence papers and examining the pre-war information available to the community from a variety of sources, the report concluded that: (a) a great deal of information indicating the imminence of an Arab attack on Israel had been collected and distributed to analysts in the months (especially September) prior to the outbreak of war;[4] (b) analysts, perceiving growing Arab reliance on political and economic rather than military tactics to achieve their aims vis-a-vis Israel, rejected the evidence suggesting the contrary and in almost unequivocal terms predicted no war;[5] and (c) they did so essentially because they were firmly committed to the (mistaken) proposition that an Arab attack could only result in a disastrous Arab defeat, or even "national suicide;"[6] that any rational man could foresee this; and that, inasmuch as the Arab leaders (e.g., Sadat and Assad) were indeed rational men, they would obviously not make a decision to attack.

These conclusions of the post-mortem were relatively easy to reach, given the clear record of misestimates. Not so easy to isolate, however, were the reasons why the analysts clung so tenaciously to the faulty syllogism outlined above. But surely their awareness of recent history had something to do with it; although they believed that, sooner or later, war was probably inevitable, the analysts had been hardened by previous false alarms. Further, the long string of Arab defeats helped reinforce the analysts' faith in overwhelming Israeli military superiority. And the failure of the Israelis themselves to anticipate the attack—despite all their sensitivity, experience, and efficient intelligence machinery—reinforced the analysts' no-war consensus.

But, more specifically, what caused the analysts to hold so rigidly to this belief in the face of good signs of Arab preparations for war? What led them to believe that the Arab forces were no better than they had been in 1967, despite the years of additional training and the receipt of vast quantities of new and better Soviet equipment? (A joint CIA-DIA study published in July 1973, for example, asserted flatly that the Egyptian Army could not cross the canal in force.) And—the biggest mystery of all—

---

[4] In the words of the report, as quoted in US newspaper accounts, US experts had been provided with a "plenitude of information which should have suggested, at a minimum, that they take very seriously the threat of war in the near term."

[5] As subsequently reported by the press and as stated in the report: "[A thorough search] failed to turn up any official statement from any office responsible for producing finished analytical intelligence which contributed anything resembling a warning.... Instead of warnings, the community produced reassurances ... that the Arabs would not resort to war.... The principal conclusions concerning the imminence of hostilities reached and reiterated by those responsible for intelligence analysis were—quite simply, obviously, and starkly—wrong." It should be noted, however, that an analyst from one agency (which was not responsible for finished analytical intelligence) did provide a briefing a few days before the Arab attack that suggested that war might be imminent. But this warning was strictly unofficial, was addressed to only a handful of officials, and was not put in writing.

[6] They were also beholden to the conviction that the Arabs, *in lieu of war*, had decided to resort to the use of an oil embargo, or threat of embargo, as a means to pressure the West into forcing Israeli concessions.

what made these same analysts totally forget the wisdom of the previous spring, when State/INR produced an almost prescient memorandum which concluded that, in certain circumstances (which in fact came to pass over the summer), the Arabs would probably attack Israel in the fall, principally in hopes of achieving essentially political, not military, objectives?[7]

The post-mortem study concluded with several pages of recommendations for improvements in the way the community conducted its business. Better communications between and among the collectors and producers of intelligence—a problem as old as intelligence itself—were urged, and some new machinery for accomplishing this was suggested. The publication of a single community situation report during crises—in lieu of the four discrete reports usually issued (on a several-times-a-day basis)—was suggested. Ways of relieving the analysts of the burden of reading countless "raw" information reports, including a controversial scheme calling for more active screening and highlighting procedures on the part of collectors, were explored.[8] A more effective system of community crisis "alerts" was proposed. And there were other notions advanced, some suggesting in general terms the need for budgetary reallocations (a bigger share of the pie for production offices). But, other than a proposal to find a systematic way to present the views of "devil's advocates," there were no recommendations that directly tackled the problem of analytical prejudices and preconceptions.

2. *Chile*: Soon after the anti-Allende coup in Chile in September 1973, the officer in PRD specializing in Latin American affairs was asked by the head of IC Staff to conduct an informal post-mortem examination of intelligence coverage before and during that event. His findings, issued in typescript in December 1973 (somewhat delayed by the intervention of the higher-priority Arab-Israeli post-mortem), included the judgment that although the analysts had done a respectable job of covering the increasingly turbulent domestic Chilean scene, they had been somewhat remiss in not really warning their leaders of the likelihood of a coup in the near term. It appeared to him that sufficient good information was available in time for them to do so. All in all, the PRD reviewer gave somewhat higher marks to DIA than CIA coverage.

The paper was never presented to or discussed by USIB or followed up by the DCI or any other senior community figure.

3. *The Indian Nuclear Explosion*: Though of modest size, the nuclear explosion set off by New Delhi in May 1974 set off political shock waves around the world and around Washington. The DCI wanted to know why he and his constituents had not been forewarned and called for another post-mortem.

---

[7] A full discussion of this intriguing question, under the caption "A Case of Wisdom Lost," is one of the most interesting sections in the post-mortem. The power of preconceptions, together with the analysts' understandable feeling that those who might fear war were only crying wolf, is thoroughly explored, but the paper fails to provide an altogether satisfactory answer.

[8] One way of handling the "information explosion"—in this instance the number of discrete information reports reaching analysts in the production agencies—is to computerize the data. This greatly reduces the amount of paper reaching the analyst and permits him to summon information as he needs it. Trouble is, this route is enormously expensive, is resisted by many mechanophobic analysts, and may not lead to a solution of the problem in any event.

There is at least an interim alternative, and it was proposed in the report: cut down the flow of words and paper to analysts by requiring the issuing agency to summarize, interpret, highlight, and condense (but not analyze). Many items (but of course not all) normally sent on an "as received" basis could be held, combined with other, similar documents, and disseminated in summary form, say on a weekly basis. Trouble here is that analysts—who on the one hand complain about "too much mail" and on the other want to read "everything"—do not trust anyone other than themselves to digest the material, i.e., all the material. And the collection agencies, which may lack adequate resources for the job, are in any case reluctant to take it on for a potentially ungrateful audience.

Post-Mortems

The report, published in July 1974, pointed to a curious sequence of events and raised a question about the way in which the community goes about its business. A year and a half or so before the event, a National Intelligence Estimate discussing the problem of nuclear proliferation concluded that India could (and indeed might) explode a nuclear device at almost any time. After the publication of this estimate, the flow of reports concerning Indian nuclear capabilities and intentions, hitherto reasonably heavy, almost ceased. So too, partly as a consequence, did the coverage of relevant material in intelligence periodicals and memoranda. Thus, in the months preceding the actual detonation, the possibility was simply ignored in intelligence publications.

The question, as more or less posed in the post-mortem: after the appearance of the NIE, did the community somehow feel that, having fully discharged its duties concerning this significant topic, it now could sit back and relax?

The answer was a frustrating "perhaps." At any rate, for whatever reason, the collectors and producers alike seemed to lose interest in India's nuclear effort after the NIE had pronounced on the problem. The post-mortem, in a mood of diffident daring, suggested that maybe, just maybe, this disinterest reflected a similar lack of regard in the *policy-making* community as well.

The post-mortem also concerned itself rather extensively with the problem of collection in countries with serious nuclear potential. It pointed out that, once a certain state of readiness had been achieved (as in India), the decision of whether to explode a device and to develop weapons was a political one and, in the event (again as in India), might be made on political grounds. The paper then urged (as it subsequently developed, with some success) that collection programs be revamped, requirements and priorities be revised, and the character and interests of the human collectors concerned be substantially altered.

4. *The West Bank:* A sequel to the Arab-Israeli post-mortem of December 1973 had been promised the DCI, and it appeared about a year later. Called "Military Intelligence During an International Crisis: Israel's West Bank Campaign in October 1973," it provided a brief examination of intelligence coverage of that campaign and suggested some significant possible consequences of that coverage. Although the report was in this way a valuable addition to the body of intelligence literature, it did not purport to be a post-mortem report of conventional breed.

5. *Cyprus 1974:* It was clear in late 1973 that the new Greek strongman, Ionides, was likely to cast a covetous eye on Cyprus. Intelligence memoranda of the time emphasized Ionides' aggressive interest in *enosis*, the reunion of Cyprus with the Greek motherland, and, because of this, foresaw trouble ahead between Greece and Turkey.

Six months or so later, however, in early July 1974, intelligence analysts—although by no means claiming that the issue was dead—suggested in effect that American policymakers need not be concerned with a crisis in the immediate future. *Inter alia*, they highlighted and implicitly endorsed a report from an "untested source" that Ionides would not move against Cyprus in the near term. On 14/15 July, however, Athens sponsored a coup in Nicosia that threw out the reigning Cypriot, Archbishop Makarios, installed a Greek puppet regime, and in general set the stage for *enosis*. Turkey invaded within the week, and war between the two NATO allies in the eastern Mediterranean appeared imminent.

The DCI, knowing that *he* had been surprised by the coup, was concerned that the community might have missed another one; if so, he wanted to know why; and so he called for post-mortem number five. The result was "An Examination of the

Intelligence Community's Performance Before and During the Cyprus Crisis of 1974," published in January 1975. This report, in the course of examining the published record, concluded that the analysts had misperceived Ionides' intentions in July. Perhaps they had been distracted by the Aegean seabed issue, which had flared in late June and which had then received much greater emphasis in an estimative memorandum than the Cyprus problem. Or perhaps they had made too much of the misleading report that Ionides would not soon move against Cyprus because they themselves did not wish to believe earlier signs (and their own fears) to the contrary. Indeed, perhaps the analysts had been persuaded that it would be irrational of the Greek leader to risk war with Turkey, the wrath of the United States, and the possible intervention of the Soviets, all for the sake of Cyprus; that although he was hardly less than eccentric, Ionides was not irrational; and that—in the now familiar syllogism—Ionides would thus not move precipitately (at least so long as the risks seemed so large).

The Cyprus post-mortem report also pointed out, in a positive vein, that the pre-July intelligence record on Cyprus was quite good. And concerning other topics of major interest—the possibility of Soviet intervention, the probable reaction of the Turks to the coup in Nicosia, and the outcome of the fighting on the island—it was judged that coverage ranged from right-on-target (*in re* the Soviets) to pretty good (the invasion) to adequate (the course of the fighting).

Concerning collection, the post-mortem noted some weaknesses, especially in Athens, and some strengths, as in Nicosia and Ankara.

The Cyprus report created something of a stir immediately upon publication. There were, for example, laments to the effect that the authors of the report had enjoyed the advantages of hindsight, a curious but commonly voiced complaint. (Of course they had. The process is by definition *post*, and a condition of such studies is precisely that they can be made in the light of hindsight.)

One official charged (and was partly right) that the paper contained several "factual errors," and an NIO asserted that the post-mortem fundamentally misapprehended the nature of estimative intelligence when it criticized analysts for their failure to predict the coup. Further, some of these analysts felt themselves unjustly accused of mistakes they hadn't made. This is surely not the time or place to rehearse old argument about specifics, but some general observations are in order:

- It is true, of course, as the NIO suggested, that intelligence analysts, lacking supernatural means of peering into the future, should not be expected to predict with precision. (It is also true, and too bad, that many consumers of intelligence do expect such predictions.) And certainly there is merit in the often-heard proposition that highlighting the serious possibility that an event will take place within the foreseeable future should be sufficient to alert policymakers, who are then, in the great scheme of things, supposed to devise appropriate responses.

- In the case of the Cyprus post-mortem, however, analysts were not faulted for failing to make a precise estimate about, for example, the date of the coup sponsored by Ionides. They were criticized, rather, for making what the authors of the post-mortem perceived to be a *negative* estimate, *viz.*, the clear implicit estimate made during the first half of July in daily publications that there probably would *not* be a coup in the near term. This estimate was strongly reinforced during the same period by what the analysts did *not* provide, i.e., anything akin to the kind of warning sounded earlier to the effect that a crisis or a coup or some other major move by Ionides was likely, and

Post-Mortems

fairly soon. At best, the backtracking in July muffled the alarm; at worst, it would have told the policymakers that they could afford to relax for a spell. (In fact, the policymakers did not relax, partly because in some instances they simply weren't *aware* of what intelligence analysts were saying, partly because in other cases they just didn't *care* what the analysts were saying.) Finally, in sum, as the post-mortem suggested, if the analysts were right to sound warnings in June—and they were—then they were wrong not to do so in July.

6. *Egyptian Military Capabilities:* In February 1975, the members of USIB, meeting to consider a new NIE on the Arab-Israeli situation, made a last-minute change in the paper, radically altering a key judgment concerning the likelihood of war by estimating that the Arabs might attack Israel within a few days. They did so at the urging of one member who cited a number of very recent items of information which to him seemed to portend war. This member also cited a just-published memorandum written by analysts in his agency; this offered a similarly alarmist view and also presented a singular and (as it subsequently developed) distorted view of the state of Soviet-Egyptian relations at the time.

The memorandum had been published only a day or so after the appearance of a community paper that was relatively reassuring *in re* the prospects for war; this community effort, sponsored by an NIO, had been concurred in by all major intelligence components, including the agency now offering alarmist views at USIB. Consumers (in, for example, the Office of the Secretary of Defense, on the NSC Staff, and in the State Department) were understandably indignant or confused by the alarmist position of the second paper, especially since it made no reference to the milder conclusions of the community analysis. Indeed, one consumer cabled his principal in the field to say that the alarmist position was ill-founded—based on erroneous evidence—and should be ignored.

The National Intellignce Officer responsible for the community memorandum and the NIE thought that USIB should not have been so quick to amend a critical judgment in an important estimate. The NIO asked the DCI to call for a post-mortem look at the entire affair, and the DCI thereupon did so.

It was clear that this problem could not be handled in an orthodox way. It not only involved some delicate information, several sensitive interviews, and a number of private communications at high levels of the US Government, but it also focussed on only one agency of the intelligence community. All concerned agreed that, although the paper might in most respects resemble a conventional post-mortem report, it would be (and in fact was) given only to the head of the agency involved.

The specific conclusions of this "private" post-mortem cannot be reproduced here. But two of its recommendations, which regrettably came to naught, should be mentioned.

One—rapping USIB on its collective knuckles—suggested that USIB members should not on their own alter NIEs on the basis of information presented for the first time at the meeting called to consider that NIE. USIB should return a challenged paper to the appropriate NIOs and analysts for immediate checking and possible amendment. The other suggestion proposed, in the interest of potentially confused consumers, that intelligence memoranda issued by one agency which contradict the conclusions of recent community papers dealing with the same or similar topics should acknowledge the fact, i.e., bear a specific notice acknowledging the differences.

7. *Mayaguez:* The *Mayaguez* and its crew of 39 were seized by the Cambodian Communists on 14 May 1976. Within days the administration—taken completely by

surprise—wanted to know what the intelligence community had known and reported both before and after the seizure.

There was no time for a formal post-mortem, so a hastily assembled community-wide chronology of events was prepared by the NIOs and a more ambitious narrative account was rushed into print within three days by the IC Staff. This study revealed, among many other things, that the government—intelligence and operational-policy communities alike—lacked effective machinery for warning US merchant ships of possible hostile actions.

In August of 1975, the DCI asked PRD to produce a more thorough and careful post-mortem examination of the *Mayaguez* incident. Although he did not explicitly say so, the DCI indicated that he was moved in part by his desire to show both Congress and the White House that the community could examine its own performance during an international crisis with care and publish its findings with candor. And perhaps he hoped to head off any sensational and unjustified criticisms of that performance by the staff and members of the then highly active Pike Committee.

The PRD inquiry confirmed the earlier judgment that the warning system for US merchant ships was seriously deficient. In fact, there was no real contact between the community and those elements in the departments of State and Defense involved in the issuance of such warnings; intelligence officers had not even been aware that offices in these departments were so involved.

The report also confirmed that no intelligence agency had foreseen Cambodian seizure of a US ship. Prior to the event, there was some reporting by collectors of actions against coastal shipping in the Gulf of Siam (where the *Mayaguez* was intercepted), but most of these incidents seemed to involve only small coastal craft. There were also a few reports of episodes involving larger ocean-going ships—Panamanian and South Korean—but there had been no Cambodian seizures of these ships. Analysts receiving these ambiguous reports did not see in them a harbinger of hostile moves against US ships and thus (with one minor exception) did not mention them in their publications. There were various other reasons why they failed to do so, not the least of which were: (1) the almost complete dearth of information about the organization, composition, policies, and intentions of the new Cambodian Communist regime; and (2) the weariness of the community's analysts who covered Southeast Asia, analysts who had just witnessed the sudden fall of both Cambodia and South Vietnam and who were still trying to sort out the aftermath.

If, as the DCI wondered, the community could handle two simultaneous crises in two parts of the world adequately, could it also cope with two crises in *one* part of the world? For despite all the extenuating circumstances, it was simply a fact that had to be faced that, in the week before the seizure of the *Mayaguez*, the analysts had known from unclassified radio broadcasts reproduced by FBIS that the South Korean government had issued a public warning to *its* merchant ships to avoid the Gulf of Siam.

The post-mortem also looked closely into a question initially raised by the White House: was there an excessive delay between the community's first knowledge of the seizure of the *Mayaguez* and its notification of its principals in the White House and elsewhere? The essence of the answer provided by the post-mortem was "yes." The original CRITIC (Critical Intelligence) message received concerning the *Mayaguez* arrived in the community's operations centers at about 5:30 a.m. (Washington time), roughly two and a half hours before the President and the Secretary of State got the word, much, as it turned out, to their consternation.

Post-Mortems

The senior intelligence officers on duty when that first CRITIC message came in were uncertain about both the fact and the significance of the seizure. (So too, apparently, were a number of officials not in the intelligence community who were notified well before the President and the Secretary.) Subsequent clarifying CRITIC messages should have helped to resolve this uncertainty, but did not. To be sure, there was some confusion about what had actually happened and a concomitant disinclination to grapple with the question of what the event might portend. There were also some problems associated with the incorrect handling, timing, and numbering of the CRITIC messages. And then, too, there was an understandable reluctance among operations officers and others to rouse the top figures of the government from their sleep; the CIA Operations Center, for example, was the first to notify its principal, but did not do so until 6:35 a.m., the time of the DCI's normal awakening. But, as was clear in hindsight, none of these circumstances constituted a legitimate reason for the delay. Uncertainty is likely to attend the beginnings of any crisis. And clearing up the unknowns prior to notifying those who will be responsible for managing the crisis not only risks their wrath but also may jeopardize their ability to cope.

The post-mortem highlighted some of the problems associated with the CRITIC system, and it recommended in unequivocal terms that in the future the appropriate operations centers get in touch with each other immediately following the receipt of an initial CRITIC message. Had such a procedure been in effect vis-a-vis the *Mayaguez*, senior principals would almost certainly have been notified promptly.

Some Community Post-Mortems Not Produced

A number of formal community post-mortem reports that probably should have been written during this period (1973-1975) were not. Performance concerning at least three major developments—the leftist coup in Portugal in the spring of 1974, the rapid collapse of Cambodia and South Vietnam a year later, and the Cuban intervention in Angola in the fall of 1975—merited more careful and judicious examination than it in fact received.

- The community's face was not visibly red in the aftermath of the surprise coup in Portugal, nor did the community seem to blush because it had not foreseen Lisbon's subsequent (temporary) drift toward Moscow. In any event, no one called for a post-mortem investigation at the time. That came later, in effect—during the hearings of the Pike Committee in the summer of 1975.

- In the case of Vietnam, PRD did, at the request of the DCI, hastily prepare a paper—some called it a "mini-post-mortem"—that was given very limited but high-level dissemination. This, however, was completed even before the fall of Saigon and made no pretense of examining circumstances in a thorough way and in the light of true hindsight. Several months later, again at the request of the DCI, a second paper on the subject was prepared, but this time under the aegis of an NIO. It, too, could not lay claim to any real post-mortem status, in part because in this instance its principal drafters were examining their own performance.

- Concerning the community's (and their own) performance regarding Angola, the NIOs produced another post-mortemlike paper in early 1976, again at the specific request of the DCI. This, however, was not a full-scale effort, nor could it meet a test of objectivity.

- One 1976 development, unrelated to any specific event or crisis, may have warranted post-mortem investigation, and that was the CIA's and the community's unprecedented (and highly publicized) revision—from six percent to 11 to 13 percent—of their estimate of the percentage of the Soviet Gross National Product devoted to the military budget in recent years. Long carried at the lower figure, the proportion was increased—some charged very tardily so—after the receipt of new information and a prolonged study by teams of community experts. The significance of the change seemed to lie not so much in what it revealed about the size and strength of the Soviet military establishment, but rather in what it told about the determination of the Soviet leadership to allow the economy to bear such a burden. The change also raised serious questions about the community's and especially CIA's methodology for making cost estimates.

Post-Mortem Purposes...

In a sense—because they reviewed and recounted the past—the community post-mortem studies constituted a form of history. But they were history with a special purpose: to provide present and future members of the community—analysts, collectors, and processors, and managers alike—with a new means to measure and improve their performance. These reports, in fact, sought objectively to identify the strengths and weaknesses of the community's processes, systems, and attitudes, as manifested during a particular period or vis-a-vis a particular problem, and they tried, however imperfectly, to record the truth as best as could be ascertained.

To be sure, as already indicated, not all readers of these reports looked upon them in a kindly light. Some analysts and collectors, for example, although not named in the reports, felt themselves the targets of unfair criticism. But others recognized that there was merit in a program that could, by design, avoid many of the problems afflicting previous critical reviews of intelligence performance.

It was as if the Director, in establishing an independent post-mortem capability in the IC Staff, was seeking a perspective not available either to the producers of the play (the policymakers, who often believe themselves to be the only *responsible* critics) or to the actors on stage (the performing intelligence professionals who frequently feel themselves to be the only *qualified* critics).

- Intelligence post-mortems conducted or ultimately controlled by the policymakers can suffer from two conspicuous faults. They may reflect the relative ignorance of their authors concerning intelligence matters and thus may even neglect to ask the right questions, much less provide helpful answers. More important, they may seek in a self-serving way to pin blame for one or another policy problem on alleged intelligence deficiencies.

- Post-mortems conducted by the "actors" (in community production offices and collection entities) may try to do the same sort of thing, i.e., shift blame away from themselves. Or they may simply try to deny—sometimes correctly, but only rarely convincingly—that any real problem existed in the first place.

This is not to say that community post-mortems can be immaculately conceived or ever achieve the degree of objectivity they should strive for. Still, if post-mortems are commissioned by a DCI who insists on dispassionate analysis, and are prepared by qualified officers who have little or no stake in the outcome of the review, then they hold the *promise* of a unique efficacy. Put another way, it is simply a truism that the chances are better that the system will permit a constructive concentration on the nature and causes of intelligence problems and intelligence successes if the post-mortem task is undertaken by knowledgeable parties whose interests are not directly affected by the post-mortem "verdict."

Post-Mortems

...and Principles

Little formal methodology guided (or could have guided) the preparation of the community post-mortem reports. An effort was made, however, to meet certain minimum standards in all the formally published papers. These can be stated as general "post-mortem principles:"

- All published intelligence items relevant to a post-mortem investigation should be obtained and read. These include individual current intelligence reports, or portions thereof, as well as more ambitious intelligence studies such as National Intelligence Estimates. The vast bulk of reporting from intelligence and other sources should also be reviewed.

- As many as possible of the parties involved in the reporting and preparation of relevant intelligence should be interviewed; a representative selection of appropriate supervisors and office heads should be, too; and a fair number of high-level consumers should be asked to comment as well. (The names of individuals, however, should as a general rule be omitted from the published post-mortem report.)

- The post-mortem team should doublecheck the opinions and facts it gathers in the course of the investigation. The word of one intelligence officer or group of officers cannot be taken as final, not because such officers are necessarily suspect, but because they are as capable of shading meaning, or committing inadvertent errors, or speaking from ignorance, as any other comparable group of human beings. And sometimes what appear unquestionably to be facts turn out not to be.[*]

- Many, perhaps a majority, of the members of a post-mortem team should have served successful terms as intelligence analysts; some should be familiar with the specific area or topic under scrutiny; and some should also be thoroughly conversant with the various means of collection. At the same time, none of the members of the team should have been personally involved in the work being investigated; and none should function as representatives of any of the community's components—each member should try to speak for the community as a whole.

- The product of the post-mortem exercise should reflect judgments as independent and objective as those presumably reflected in finished intelligence itself. Post-mortem investigators, however, must ask themselves if the analysis they are studying is itself in fact objective. Are there signs of institutional or personal prejudice; riding of hobby horses; covering up or defense of past errors of judgment; excessive fascination with or fondness of particular countries or particular national leaders; or capitulation to the presumed policy interests of the consumers?

- To be effective, post-mortem reports should be well presented. The way in which even an eager readership receives a given report depends in part on how

---

[*] To cite one example, during preparation of the post-mortem on the *Mayaguez* incident, investigators fixed the times of the (simultaneous) receipt in Washington of the first three CRITIC cables on the basis of machine-imprinted time stamps on the copies of those cables received by one particular operations center. Subsequently (but not too late to make the necessary corrections in the draft) it was more or less fortuitously discovered that those particular time stamps had been off by roughly half an hour, the result of a power shutdown over the previous weekend. The resultant errors exaggerated the length of the delay—bad enough as it was—between the initial receipt of the information by operations centers and the passage of that information to senior principals.

skillfully it is put together. Is it physically attractive, handy, easy to read? And are its contents pertinent, reasonably concise, well written, and above all, lucid? It is easier to extol clarity—and pertinence and concision and all the rest—than it is to achieve it, so writers should be given some help; competent editors can sometimes perform miracles.

Some Accomplishments

In the area of specific accomplishments, there is no theoretical limit to what a good post-mortem can do. As a practical matter, however, and as demonstrated by the fate of many of the recommendations of the community post-mortems issued in the past, there are a variety of hard constraints. It is a lot easier to isolate problems than to propose workable remedies. And it is, in turn, easier to propose such remedies than to implement them.

The post-mortems and the Product Review Division were responsible, however, for some specific and tangible improvements in the way the community conducted its business and, perhaps, the way in which the rest of the government responded to the community as well. For example:

- PRD's extensive work with watch and operations centers and in the general area of warning intelligence was in large part an outgrowth of post-mortem findings. Its various enterprises helped to lower the surprisingly high barricades surrounding all the intelligence operations centers and to establish mutually profitable contacts between these centers and similar centers in the White House, State Department, and Pentagon. The old, almost exclusively vertical lines of communication leading upward from each of these centers to its own prinicipals were (loosely) tied—through telephone conferencing systems, personal contacts, a series of mutually profitable "business conventions," and the adoption of a number of important common procedures—into a horizontal network serving the government as a whole.

- In work that followed the revelations of the *Mayaguez* inquiry, PRD tackled and solved a number of problems associated with the CRITIC system. It was discovered that the CRITIC procedures and "rules"—designed to move vital all-source information from the field to the President and other top officials in Washington via the operations centers—badly needed overhauling. They were in certain respects out-of-date, unrealistic, and incomplete, and they varied from agency to agency. Indeed, there was no single system, only sets of systems, and not all these were compatible with one another. As was the case in the *Mayaguez* incident, this disarray had led to some problems and delays but, fortunately, no intelligence disasters. A failure to bring community-wide order into CRITIC, however, would have surely risked such a disaster in the future.

- Partly as the consequence of the revelations of the 1973 Arab-Israeli postmortem, the DCI and the community (working through the IC Staff and PRD) in 1974 established a new form of estimative warning paper, the Alert Memorandum. The inspiration of a senior officer in one of the community's current intelligence offices, this kind of paper could when necessary be produced very quickly with light coordination by secure telephone, and could be delivered to top-level consumers in such a way as to virtually guarantee that they would read it.[10] A survey of Alert Memoranda was made by PRD in the

---

[10] These consumers had long complained that even when intelligence had "called it right," they sometimes hadn't gotten the word. Kissinger, for example, is said to have told one of the rare meetings of the National Security Council Intelligence Committee that a warning was not a warning unless it reached *him*. And, of course, he had a point.

summer of 1975 at the request of the DCI. It revealed that the system was working well—more than a score had been produced under the aegis of the National Intelligence Officers, and top consumers were in fact receiving and reading the memoranda.

- The same Arab-Israeli post-mortem pointed in 1973 to the excessive number of situation summaries published by components of the community during crises and to the complaints of consumers about this unnecessary and confusing duplication of effort. It then took three years of sporadic effort by PRD and others to work out procedures for the production of a single national crisis "sitsum" for high-level consumers.[11] But a "charter" was finally drafted by PRD and agreed upon by the community in 1976, and a national sitsum was actually issued during a crisis some two months later.

The Decline and Fall of the Post-Mortem

There were many reasons why the once-promising community post-mortem program died in the fall of 1975. Not least among them were shortcomings of the program itself, the departure from the community of its principal sponsors, the effects of bureaucratic politics and reorganizations, and a growing conviction among many intelligence officers that candid critical reviews of past performances represented, at best, an unbalanced look at the condition of the profession and, at worst, an unnecessary exercise in self-flagellation. It seems unlikely, however, that any of these circumstances, individually or in the aggregate, would have been controlling had it not been for: (1) the public reaction against the Constitutional and ethical abuses, both real and imagined, committed by CIA and the community over the course of two decades; and (2) the effort to exploit that reaction by the House Select Committee on Intelligence and its staff.

Although the House Committee initially professed a serious interest in evaluating the activities of the community and especially of CIA—how much did they cost, what were their risks, how successful were they?—its staff soon demonstrated that it was more anxious to condemn the community than to examine it.[12] It also demonstrated that for this purpose it was eager to concentrate on the substantive end of the intelligence business. Some of the post-mortems—forwarded to the Committee staff under threat of subpoena—may have helped to inspire this strategy and were in any event extremely useful to it.

In the end, the use and misuse of the post-mortems by the House Committee, together with the reactions of those in the community who had to contend with the Committee, were simply too much for the program. Still, the post-mortems then died with more than a mere whimper. They died, in fact, to the rousing accompaniment of a Constitutional confrontation between Congress and the President of the United States, occasioned by the President's refusal to grant Congress permission to release classified information drawn from the Mid-East post-mortem of 1973, and the Pike Committee's determination to assert its right to do so, no matter what the position of the Executive Branch.[13]

---

[11] It had also taken an order from the President to get the effort moving again. Truth is, both the practical and bureaucratic problems associated with this sort of enterprise were and are enormously complex.

[12] It did not really explore the reasons for the community's problems or show much interest in so doing—although the post-mortems and other available sources provided a clear opportunity for sober inquiry. Nor did it reflect on the Community's successes, of which, of course, there were many.

[13] Neither side seemed at all anxious to bring this matter to a head. The Chairman of the Committee was apparently not sure he enjoyed the support of the House as a whole. The Executive was far from confident that it would win a test in the Supreme Court, which is presumably where the matter would have been decided had the stalemate persisted. Ultimately, of course, the Committee in effect caved in, although the issue as such was not resolved.

The Future

A post-mortem assessment of the 1973-1975 post-mortem program would no doubt reveal many ways in which it could have been improved. It might, in addition, uncover means to persuade in-house skeptics that future programs of comparable intent need not resemble an exercise in masochism.

If, in fact, the decision is ever made to resurrect candid post-mortem procedures, those responsible could do worse than to ponder some of the lessons of the recent past:

- Large, formal post-mortem reports should only concern the community's performance vis-a-vis especially important circumstances—such as major international crises and key analytical or collection problems—and should be produced only with the approval and bearing the imprimatur of the DCI. They should receive a broad readership within the community, subject of course to restrictions imposed by classification, and should be presented to the National Foreign Intelligence Board (or its equivalent) for rumination, discussion, and—if appropriate—action.

- The community's performance in less dramatic circumstances, involving particular incidents, might best be treated in shorter, more informal papers, disseminated on a more selective basis. These papers should be quite flexible in content and form and could appear as often as events seemed to warrant. Such papers might be issued as "Special Studies" or "Special Reviews," rather than as post-mortem reports *per se*.

- The successes of the community should receive greater attention than was customary in the 1973-1975 post-mortem series; not because the public relations aspects of such emphasis are tempting, but because it is as easy—perhaps easier—to learn from honest successes as it is from honest mistakes.

- Post-mortem reports and similar papers should be disseminated outside the community only with the approval of the DCI. There should be no blanket proscription of such dissemination; some papers could usefully inform, say, the NSC, or even respond to its requests for post-mortem reviews. But it should be generally understood that the primary audience for most community post-mortems should be the community itself.

- The subjects of post-mortems should not be confined to assessments of analytical and collection performance vis-a-vis a particular international incident or development. Some papers should address such broad (and sensitive) topics as: the quantity and quality of reporting and analysis on a given country (e.g., China) over a period of years; the controversial procedures followed last year during the preparation of the annual NIE on Soviet strategic forces; and the benefits and costs of the community's maintenance of competitive and duplicative analytical centers and collection programs.

Clearly, any future post-mortem staff would have more than enough to do. Even so, to allay apprehensions, it should be made obvious to all that there would be no trespass on the functions of the inspectors-general or the prerogatives of managers, that it would not be the role of "post-mortemists" to seek out mis-or-malfeasance or to supervise personnel. "Post-mortemists" are, however, historians of community error and accomplishment and as such—if it is true that those who do not know history are condemned to repeat it—are better read than ignored.

BASIC NATIONAL SECURITY STRATEGY
NSDD 238

~~TOP SECRET~~ TOP SECRET

THE WHITE HOUSE
WASHINGTON

SYSTEM II
90475

September 2, 1986

NATIONAL SECURITY DECISION
DIRECTIVE NUMBER 238

DECLASSIFIED IN PART
NLS M02-028 #1
By CJJ, NARA, Date 10/27/05

BASIC NATIONAL SECURITY STRATEGY (C)

Significant progress has been made during the past six years in strengthening the position of the United States in world affairs. The constancy of purpose we have demonstrated in defending U.S. global interests and pursuing our policy objectives has strengthened global security. Yet, important changes have evolved in international affairs that must be considered as we further develop our strategy of peace for the future. (U)

This directive supersedes NSDD-32 and its supporting documents as the primary source of U.S. national security strategy. It shall serve as the starting point for further development of policy and strategy where appropriate. Policy guidance now in effect is being reviewed to ensure its consistency with this document. Supplemental directives will be structured to ensure conformance with this guidance. (TS)

Broad Purposes of U.S. National Security Policy

The primary objective of U.S. foreign and security policy is to protect the integrity of our democratic institutions and promote a peaceful global environment in which they can thrive. The national security policy of the United States shall serve the following broad purposes:

-- To preserve the political identity, framework and institutions of the United States as embodied in the Declaration of Independence and the Constitution.

-- To protect the United States -- its national territory, citizenry, military forces, and assets abroad -- from military, paramilitary, or terrorist attack.

-- To foster the economic well-being of the United States, in particular, by maintaining and strengthening the nation's industrial, agricultural and technological base and by ensuring access to foreign markets and resources.

-- To foster an international order supportive of the vital interests of the United States by maintaining and strengthening constructive, cooperative relationships and alliances, and by encouraging and reinforcing wherever possible and practicable, freedom, the rule of law, economic development and national independence throughout the world.

Grand Strategy

The grand strategy of the United States is to avoid nuclear war while preventing a single hostile power or coalition of powers from dominating the Eurasian land-mass or other strategic regions from which threats to U.S. interests might arise. The success of this strategy is dependent on the maintenance of a strong nuclear deterrent, dynamic alliances, and a Western-oriented world economy. It is also dependent on the U.S. ability to wage successfully a competition for influence among less developed countries, the ability to influence events beyond our direct control, and ultimately, the ability to project military power abroad in defense of U.S. interests. The strength of this grand strategy is founded upon the convergence of interests between the U.S. and the community of nations as a whole. The national independence and individual freedoms we seek to uphold are in harmony with the general desires and ideals common to all mankind. The U.S. must therefore remain the natural enemy of any country threatening the independence of others, and the proponent of free trade, commerce, and economic stability.

This grand strategy requires the development and integration of a set of strategies to achieve our national objectives, including political, diplomatic, military, informational, economic, intelligence, and arms control components. These strategies are necessarily shaped by our values and our vision of the future; the national and international policy objectives we have set for ourselves; by dynamic trends in the global economy and the military balance; and by the demands of our geographical position. Such strategies must also take into account the capabilities and intentions of those hostile countries or coalitions which threaten to undermine the achievement of U.S. policy objectives.

Threats to U.S. National Security

The primary threats to U.S. national security in the years ahead will continue to be posed by the armed forces of the Soviet Union and Soviet exploitation of regional instabilities.

The geopolitical objectives of the Soviet Union include the dissolution of Western alliances in Europe and Asia, the erosion of China's ties to the West, and the attainment of strategic position in all key regions of the world. The U.S. faces potential military threats to its interests across the entire spectrum of potential conflict from multiple sources in widely separated parts of the world. It also faces a concerted effort by the Soviet Union and its surrogates to diminish U.S. influence through diplomacy, propaganda, selective commercial activity and subversion.

The most severe threat to the United States is the offensive and defensive nuclear capability of the Soviet Union. While the probability of a nuclear war appears low, and can be influenced by the overall conduct of our relations, the ongoing Soviet attempt to achieve nuclear superiority over the U.S. threatens to undermine the credibility of our nuclear deterrent which provides the basis for Western security policy. The Soviet Union seeks nuclear superiority for the broad political purpose of deterring the U.S. from threatening the use of nuclear weapons in defense of Western interests; to increase the effectiveness of its conventional military advantages; and to increase the probability of a successful outcome, in relative terms, if nuclear war should occur. The continued Soviet modernization of their larger conventional forces, and the growth of Soviet power projection capabilities, also challenge the ability of the U.S. and its allies to maintain an adequate and stable military balance.

The Soviet Union remains aware of the potential consequences of initiating military action directly against the United States or its allies. For this reason, a war with a Soviet client arising from regional tensions or attacks against U.S. personnel and facilities is more likely than a war involving U.S. and Soviet forces in direct combat. In a conflict with a Soviet client, however, the risk of direct confrontation with the Soviet Union remains.

The Gorbachev leadership is more vigorous and dynamic than its predecessors since the late Brezhnev period. The potential now exists for more creative and energized Soviet foreign policies inimical to U.S. interests. Moscow will continue to try politically to isolate and undermine the efforts of Western governments to resist Soviet blandishments in those areas of arms control and economic cooperation that are detrimental to Western security interests. The USSR will seek to capitalize on any changes in Western governments that portend lesser resistance to Soviet interests and increased friction with the United States.

The intelligence services of the Soviet Union and its surrogates will continue to present a strategic threat to U.S. national security. This threat includes espionage, hostile

SIGINT against U.S. telecommunications and automated information systems, and the illegal diversion and acquisition of sensitive U.S. technology. The Soviets will continue to attempt to penetrate our most sensitive secrets in order to undermine our political integrity and reduce the costs of their military buildup.

The Soviet leadership also will persist in its efforts to consolidate previous Third World gains and will try to take advantage of new opportunities which may arise. Unstable governments, weak political institutions, inefficient economies, and local conflicts will continue to create opportunities for Soviet expansion in many parts of the developing world. Economic uncertainty, terrorism, the trafficking of illicit drugs, the dangers of nuclear proliferation, reticence on the part of a number of Western countries, and the assertiveness of Soviet foreign policy, all threaten Western interests.

One of the most challenging issues confronting the United States and its allies is the dedicated effort of the Soviet Union and others to subvert democratic processes and interests by whatever means. Western interests on all continents are threatened by direct and indirect actions on the part of the Soviet Union and its allies to undermine and take over other governments. They undertake this through destabilization and subversion, support of insurgencies, coups, infiltration and domination of local security and military services, use of propaganda and agents of influence, and other methods.

Instability is not always the product of Soviet design nor always harmful to U.S. interests. Historical and other forces also shape the evolution of regional affairs. Nevertheless, the Soviets share mutual interests with several radical and ambitious Third World states, and use arms transfers and both direct and indirect military support as catalysts through which such states can upset regional military balances and threaten U.S. and other allied interests. While the possibility of nuclear confrontation or a major conventional conflict between the U.S. and the Soviet Union cannot be ruled out, the continuing and prolonged challenge at this lower end of the spectrum of potential conflict (including regional instability and organized terrorism sponsored by radical states and hostile coalitions), exploited by the Soviet Union, constitutes the most likely threat we face in the years ahead.

The underlying competition between the United States and the Soviet Union is in the realm of ideas and values, and in our contrasting visions of the future and the conditions for peace. Our way of life, founded upon the dignity and worth of the individual, depends on a stable and pluralistic world order within which freedom and democratic institutions can thrive. Yet, the greatest threat to the Soviet system, in which the

State controls the destiny of the individual, is the concept of freedom itself. The survival of the Soviet system depends to a significant extent upon the persistent and exaggerated representation of foreign threats, through which it seeks to justify both the subjugation of its own people and the expansion of Soviet military capabilities well beyond those required for self-defense.

The Soviet system challenges not just our values, but the stable political environment in which they flourish. Few value systems are as irreconcilable with our own, and no other has the support of a great and growing center of military power capable of threatening our national survival. While we will seek and experience periods of cooperation with Soviet leadership, there will be no change in the fundamentally competitive nature of our relationship unless and until a change occurs in the nature of the Soviet system.

Global Objectives

In support of our grand strategy, and in response to the threats we face, the national security policy of the United States shall be guided by the following global objectives:

- To deter military attack by the USSR and its allies against the U.S., its allies, and other important countries across the spectrum of conflict; and to defeat such attack should deterrence fail.

- To strengthen the influence of the U.S. throughout the world by strengthening existing alliances, by improving relations with other nations, by forming and supporting coalitions of states friendly to U.S. interests, by promoting democracy, and by a full range of diplomatic, political, economic, and information efforts.

- To contain and reverse the expansion of Soviet control and military presence throughout the world, and to increase the costs to the Soviet Union and other countries that support proxy, terrorist, and subversive forces.

- To neutralize the efforts of the USSR to increase its influence through its use of diplomacy, arms transfers, economic pressure, political action, propaganda, and disinformation; weaken the links between the Soviet Union and its client states in the Third World; and isolate the radical regimes with whom the Soviets share mutual interests.

- To foster, if possible in concert with our allies, restraint in Soviet military spending, discourage Soviet adventurism, and weaken the Soviet alliance system by forcing the USSR to bear the brunt of its economic shortcomings, and to encourage long-term liberalizing and nationalist tendencies within the Soviet Union and allied countries.

- To reduce over the long term our reliance on nuclear weapons and nuclear retaliation, by strengthening our conventional forces, by pursuing equitable and verifiable arms control agreements and insisting on compliance with such agreements, and in particular, by pursuing technologies for strategic defense.

- To limit Soviet military capabilities by strengthening the U.S. military, by using both strategy and technology to force the Soviets to redirect assets for defensive rather than offensive purposes, and by preventing the flow of militarily significant technologies and resources to the Soviet Union, and others where appropriate.

- To prevent the reinstitution of a Moscow-Beijing axis of strategic cooperation in international security affairs.

- To improve our intelligence collection capabilities so as to provide maximum information in peacetime and continuing information in times of crisis and war.

- To identify, counter, and reduce the hostile intelligence threat to U.S. national interests.

- To discourage the further proliferation of nuclear, biological and chemical weapons.

- To ensure U.S. access to foreign markets, and to ensure the U.S. and its allies and friends access to foreign energy and mineral resources.

- To ensure U.S. access to space and the oceans.

- To encourage and strongly support aid, trade, and investment programs that promote economic development and the growth of humane social and political orders in the Third World.

- To promote a well functioning international economic system with minimal distortions to trade and investment, stable currencies, and broadly agreed and respected rules for managing and resolving differences.

- To combat threats to the stability of friendly governments and institutions from the international trafficking of illicit drugs.

Requirements for Military Forces

The United States requires military forces that are organized, manned, trained, and equipped to deter aggression across the entire spectrum of potential conflict. Our grand strategy, global objectives, and the nature of the threat require that we defend our interests as far from North America as possible. In coalition with our allies we will continue to maintain in peacetime major forward deployments for land, naval, and air forces in both Europe and the Pacific, and other deployments in the Western Hemisphere and the Indian Ocean. The overall size and composition of the armed forces must be planned accordingly. (C)

The challenge we face is dynamic and complex. Overall, there remains a significant imbalance of forces which would favor the Soviet Union in several important contingencies. In addition, Third World states are increasingly armed with modern and sophisticated military equipment. (S)

Comprehensive and imaginative integration of U.S. and allied military capabilities is required to reduce future risks to our national security. Since our political and social heritage militates against our raising and supporting large forces in peacetime, this impels us to seek security in America's national genius for technological innovation, industrial efficiency, and alliance cooperation. The U.S. must pursue strategies for competition which emphasize our comparative advantages in these areas. (C)

The full range of U.S. military capabilities must be appropriately balanced among combat and support elements, and mixed within active duty and reserve components. The U.S. must have specialized forces for nuclear deterrence and anti-terrorism; and must also have general purpose forces both capable of sustaining high intensity conflict, and trained and equipped for lesser contingencies and special operations. (C)

U.S. military forces must also be supported by plans and doctrine which provide for their effective integration and employment. While the possible use of nuclear weapons must remain an element in our overall military strategy, nuclear forces will not be viewed as a lower-cost alternative to conventional forces. U.S. forces must be capable of rapid deployment to deter wider crises or conflicts, and capable of expanding the scope and intensity of conflict as appropriate should deterrence fail. We must also have the capability to exploit U.S. technological advantages across the entire spectrum of conflict. The U.S. must maintain effective and robust reserve forces, trained and equipped at levels commensurate with their wartime missions, as well as Coast Guard and other capabilities which support the national security establishment. The U.S. must also continue to enhance its capabilities to surge or mobilize manpower and key industrial resources, planning for the effective use of available warning in the event of crisis or war. (C)

Strategic Forces

Deterrence of nuclear attack constitutes the cornerstone of U.S. national security and that of its allies. Maintaining that deterrence requires that Soviet war planners be assured that any direct conventional attack, or an attack involving the use of nuclear weapons, would result in an outcome unfavorable to the Soviet Union. In strengthening deterrence, U.S. strategic forces must be effective, survivable, and enduring. Such forces must be able to respond flexibly against an array of targets under a variety of possible contingencies. (S)

The U.S. will retain a capable, credible, and diversified strategic Triad of land-based ballistic missiles, manned bombers, and submarine launched ballistic missiles. While each leg of this Triad should be as survivable as possible, the existence of all three precludes the destruction of more than one by surprise attack and guards against technological surprise which could similarly undermine the effectiveness of a single leg. (C)

In addition to maintaining and strengthening deterrence in the near term, the U.S. must now also take steps to provide future options for ensuring deterrence and reducing the risk of nuclear attack over the long term. We must do so in a way that allows us both to negate the destabilizing growth of Soviet offensive forces, and to channel longstanding Soviet propensities for defenses toward more stabilizing and mutually beneficial ends. The Strategic Defense Initiative is specifically aimed toward these goals. Research through the Strategic Defense Initiative will investigate the possibility of making deterrence stronger and more stable by reducing the role of ballistic missiles and placing greater reliance on defenses which threaten no one. (C)

The United States will enhance its strategic nuclear deterrent by completing its five-part Strategic Modernization Program, which includes the Strategic Defense Initiative, in accordance with guidance provided in NSDD-178, except as may be modified by new decisions concerning the basing mode for the second 50 Peacekeeper missiles. This Program will be complemented by related programs to provide for the continuity of government and civil defense. Strategic objectives and concepts will be developed for future strategic offensive and defensive forces to meet U.S. security needs early in the next century. (TS)

General Purpose Forces

General purpose forces support U.S. national security policy in peacetime by deterring aggression, by demonstrating U.S. interests, concern, and commitment, by assisting the forces of other friendly nations, and by providing a basis to move rapidly from peace to war. In wartime, these forces would be employed to achieve our political objectives and to secure early war termination on terms favorable to the U.S. and allies, preferably without the use of nuclear weapons. U.S. general purpose forces must, however, be prepared for both prolonged conflict and the use of nuclear weapons if required.

The U.S. shall maintain a global posture and shall strive to increase its influence worldwide through the maintenance and improvement of forward deployed forces and rapidly deployable U.S.-based forces, together with periodic exercises, security assistance, and special operations. U.S. general purpose forces must provide the flexibility to deal quickly, decisively and discriminately with low-level conflict contingencies requiring U.S. military involvement. The U.S. will further enhance its capabilities for global mobility, including appropriate protection and support for points of embarkation and debarkation. The United States will continue to improve its conventional warfare capabilities and to improve its ability to deter chemical attack through the production of binary chemical munitions.

Resource Priorities

In order to reduce the risk that we may not be able to execute wartime strategy, the U.S. must undertake a sustained and balanced force development program. This program must complement our diplomatic, economic, and security assistance strategies, and should be guided by periodic net assessments of U.S. and Soviet nuclear and conventional capabilities. We must consider the capabilities for which there would be immediate, high-level, and sustained demand in the event of general war; capabilities which cannot be provided by allies, and which cannot be mobilized or produced within a short period of time. We must consider our own capability for technological innovation, which represents one of our most significant military advantages vis-a-vis the Soviets, and consider how most effectively to exploit it to affect the military balance in ways that are favorable to the U.S. At the same time, we must balance expenditures among the vital needs of readiness, sustainability, modernization and force expansion. The relative priority of these four pillars is not the same in all mission areas.

The following general guidance applies:

-- In the overall context of Western security, it is the responsibility of the United States to maintain a nuclear balance with the Soviet Union. Thus, the strategic modernization program (including SDI), and particularly strategic command, control, communications and intelligence, has the highest overall priority.

-- To preserve a credible conventional deterrent, we will establish and maintain an appropriate level of combat readiness and sustainability, and ensure the maintenance of a robust logistics infrastructure.

   - We must ensure that compensation, unit integrity, and quality leadership are all maintained at a level sufficiently high to recruit and retain our most capable service men and women. In this regard, we must emphasize individual and unit training in the active forces and early deploying reserves through specific training programs and major exercises.

   - In achieving an appropriate level of sustainability, preferential attention shall be given to meeting inventory objectives for precision munitions and other advanced guidance weapons systems which can multiply force effectiveness, particularly in the critical early days of conflict, and help alleviate the effects of numerical imbalances between U.S. and Soviet forces.

-- To support the U.S. strategy of forward deployment and rapid reinforcement, we must build and maintain adequate strategic airlift, sealift, and tanker support to transport and sustain our forces abroad.

-- Force structure expansion of U.S. maritime, air, and ground forces shall be prioritized in accordance with the national military strategy. This strategy recognizes that we must continue to build and modernize national forces sufficient to retain maritime superiority.

-- U.S. military systems which particularly stress Soviet defenses, or require a disproportionate expenditure of Soviet resources to counter, represent an especially attractive investment relative to competing systems, provided their cost and military effectiveness otherwise warrant the systems' procurement.

-- In keeping with this approach, for general purpose forces, modernization shall seek to exploit opportunities created by the application of high-leverage advanced technology. Particular attention should be paid to those areas with

the potential for near-to-mid-term payoff in significantly
enhanced combat capabilities. These include low observable
technologies; improved surveillance, reconnaissance and
targeting capabilities; new generations of "smart" and
"brilliant" weapons; and systems which extend the effective
strike range and survivability of conventional forces.
Tactical ground and air forces will have sufficient priority
for modernization to regain and maintain U.S. qualitative
advantages to offset the Soviets' quantitative superiority.

-- Special attention should be given to the continued
   development and acquisition of capabilities which enhance
   the effectiveness of joint or combined operations.

-- Special operations forces shall be expanded and forces
   specifically designed for counter-terrorism shall
   give priority to near-term readiness, deployability
   and command, control, communications and intelligence
   improvements. (S)

Priorities and Objectives in Peacetime

U.S. grand strategy is fundamentally a coalition strategy.
Its success depends upon robust and dynamic alliances based on
shared interests. The development of these shared interests
is built upon political and economic strengths of the industrial
democracies, a common perception of the potential threats, and
the continued importance of Third World resources. We not only
seek to strengthen our traditional bilateral and multilateral
alliance relationships, but to fundamentally broaden our base of
support abroad, influencing to the extent possible the pace and
direction of political change. The U.S. will assist democratic
and nationalist movements where possible in the struggle against
totalitarian regimes and will seek the cooperation of allies and
others in providing material support to such movements. We will
also pursue broader cooperation among all governments in the
fight against terrorism and the international trafficking of
illicit drugs. (C)

In peacetime, the achievement of our regional
objectives will be based on political, diplomatic and economic
strategies which promote the peaceful resolution of disputes,
regional stability, unrestricted trade and economic growth,
financial stability, and the further development of democratic
institutions. Such strategies will complement U.S. regional
military objectives. (C)

The international economic policy of the United States
is built upon the principle that economic growth is one of the
free world's greatest strengths. It is vital not only for our
standard of living but also for our political cooperation and

mutual defense. The source of economic growth is individual creativity expressed through the marketplace. The U.S. seeks to foster an environment in which growth can occur through domestic economic policies that minimize government interference in markets, by ensuring stable exchange rates through international cooperation, and by negotiating the elimination of barriers to trade and investment flows. The U.S. also must encourage cooperation among its Allies in preventing the transfer to Soviet bloc and other countries of goods and technologies that are critical to the military balance.

In peacetime, we will seek to deter military attack against the U.S. and its forces, allies and friends; to contain and reverse the expansion of Soviet influence worldwide; to isolate radical regimes hostile to U.S. interests; and promote regional stability and the capabilities of allies and friends for self-defense. In drawing upon the cooperation of allies and others to support and protect our mutual interests, the growth of Soviet power projection capabilities and indigenous regional threats require stronger and more effective collective defense arrangements between the U.S. and its allies. We will continue to consider the status of these arrangements in military planning concerning the size, composition, and disposition of U.S. forces.

Western Hemisphere

The defense of North America is our primary security concern. In this context the U.S. must continue to build on interests shared with Canada. We must modernize the strategic air defense system for North America, to include development of true strategic defenses against both ballistic missiles, through the SDI, and against air-breathing threats. In Central America we must reverse the success of the Soviet bloc in developing Nicaragua into a hostile base on the American mainland. In El Salvador we will support the government's effort to defeat an insurgency which poses the threat of another Soviet client state. The U.S. must also continue to promote the Caribbean Basin Initiative and the trend towards democracy throughout the Caribbean and Latin America. We must achieve greater cooperation from Mexico and other governments in the region to establish effective control over our southern borders, and to reduce the threat to friendly governments and to our own well-being from the trafficking of illicit drugs. The U.S. must strengthen military-to-military contacts and further develop the capabilities of Caribbean and Central American countries, and their mutual cooperation, for territorial defense. And we will seek to maintain and acquire as necessary base and facilities access, logistical support, and operating, transit, and overflight rights which would support U.S. military objectives in crisis or war.

Western Europe and NATO

The security of Europe remains vital to the defense of the United States, and a strong and unified NATO indispensable to protecting Western interests. The U.S. will maintain its commitment to forward deployment and early reinforcement. While encouraging all NATO allies to maintain and increase their contributions in Europe, the U.S. should specifically encourage those Allies who can contribute outside Europe to allocate their marginal defense resources preferentially to capabilities which could support both out-of-area and European missions. We will work within the alliance framework to achieve improvements in the modernization of NATO's nuclear, chemical, and conventional deterrent, including the further development of innovative operational concepts. The U.S. will also seek additional bilateral arrangements for host nation support and facilities access which enhance the effectiveness of both U.S. and allied forces. In addition to supporting the achievement of approved force goals within NATO, we will promote as priorities the resolution of the Aegean dispute, the modernization of the armed forces of Turkey, and the full integration of Spain into the alliance. (S)

East Asia

In the Far East and the Pacific basin, the foremost U.S. peacetime objective, in conjunction with allies and other friends in the region, is to prevent the Soviet Union and its allies from expanding their influence in the region. Most important to this strategy is a close alliance relationship with Japan, encouraging its development of military capabilities more commensurate with its economic status. We will seek a Japan more capable of sharing U.S. military and naval burdens in the region as well as contributing on its own to regional defense and deterrence. We will continue to develop our relationship with China in ways which ▓▓▓▓▓▓▓ enhance the durability of Sino-U.S. ties, and further lay the foundation for closer cooperation in the future as appropriate. The U.S. will also seek the withdrawal of Vietnamese forces from neighboring states in Indochina. Within the United Nations context, we will maintain sufficient U.S. and allied strength on the Korean Peninsula to deter aggression. While continuing to strengthen longstanding relationships in this region, the U.S. will continue to promote economic and political development, and to assist regional states in a manner that will reduce our vulnerability to Soviet exploitation of potential instabilities. We must continue to maintain and further develop access to forward bases, and other logistical infrastructure, essential to the efficient forward deployment of U.S. forces in the Pacific Basin. (S)

1.4 (c)
3.3 (b)
(5)(6)

Near East/Southwest Asia

The primary U.S. objective in this pivotal region is to prevent the Soviet Union or its client states from extending their influence in the region in a manner that would threaten the security of our allies and U.S. interests in Europe and Asia. To accomplish this objective in peacetime, the U.S. must rely on regional states to contribute to the extent possible to their own defense. To deter direct Soviet involvement we will continue to improve U.S. global capabilities to deploy and sustain military forces in the region. The U.S. must enhance its support for the development of balanced and self-contained friendly regional forces, especially in Saudi Arabia and Pakistan, and will increase peacetime planning with friendly states for wartime contingencies, including host nation support, prepositioning, and combat roles for indigenous forces. The U.S. will continue to actively oppose radical and terrorist elements in the region, support moderate states against external aggression and subversion, and maintain Israel's qualitative military advantage ████████████████████████████████
The United States also remains committed to securing Western access to oil resources and maintaining freedom of commerce in the Persian Gulf. We will maintain a strong naval presence in the region, and seek to develop a land presence to the extent regional sensitivities and local political constraints will permit.

Africa

U.S. peacetime objectives in Africa, in concert with our allies, are to preempt and defeat foreign aggression, subversion, and terrorism sponsored by Libya or other forces hostile to U.S. interests; to secure the withdrawal of Soviet and proxy forces from the continent; to ensure U.S. and allied access to oil and mineral resources; to prevent the Soviets from attaining strategic advantage; to support accelerated reform in African economic policies so as to promote stability, pluralism and the role of market forces and reduce possibilities for hostile destabilization; and to promote peaceful reform in South Africa while maintaining U.S. influence. We will assist friendly countries that are the targets of subversion, and we will seek to create, and respond to, opportunities to weaken the ties between the Soviet Union and regional governments.

Foreign and Security Assistance Programs

Resources for the conduct of U.S. foreign policy, including security assistance, economic aid, and public information programs are vital parts of our peacetime national security strategy.

In meeting U.S. security objectives abroad, security assistance is a cost-effective and essential complement to our own force structure. Security assistance will develop indigenous forces for local and regional defense, enhance interoperability between U.S. and other forces, and promote the broader objectives of our coalition strategy. Where local forces play a key role in the success of our regional or coalition strategy, or can significantly reduce our own military requirements, resources for security assistance may share the same importance as those resources devoted to U.S. forces. U.S. security assistance objectives should be structured to give priority to the requirements of countries with whom we are joined in formal mutual security agreements, so-called frontline states which confront direct threats from the Soviet Union or its clients, and access states which enhance the global mobility of U.S. forces. We must also help meet the needs of other states where a prudent investment of resources can prevent subversion or other broader regional problems.

Economic assistance programs should support economic growth in Third World countries through market-oriented policies that will increase political stability. Public diplomacy programs will also enhance U.S. objectives by promoting the development of democratic institutions abroad.

The U.S. foreign and security assistance program should undergo periodic review to identify emerging requirements and priorities. In addition, we will work with non-governmental and commercial enterprises, and with other friends and allies, to develop creative and flexible alternatives to direct U.S. funding.

Priorities and Objectives in War

Deterrence can best be achieved if our defense posture makes the assessment of war outcomes by the Soviets or any other adversary so dangerous and uncertain, under any contingency, as to remove any incentive for initiating conflict. Deterrence depends both on nuclear and conventional capabilities and on evidence of a collective will to defend our interests. If deterrence fails, we must have the capability to counter aggression, to control escalation, and to prevail.

In a conflict not involving the Soviet Union, the United States will rely primarily on indigenous forces to protect their own interests. Commitment of U.S. combat forces will be made only when other means are not considered viable. Such commitment is appropriate only if political objectives are established, our political will is clear, and appropriate military capabilities are available. If U.S. combat forces are committed, the United States will seek to limit the scope of the conflict, avoid involvement of the Soviet Union, and ensure that U.S. objectives are met as quickly as possible.

REDACTED

1.4(a),
1.4(d)
1.4(g)

[REDACTED]

In global war ████████████████ our overall objectives are to limit damage to the United States and its allies, control the scope and intensity of the conflict, and terminate hostilities on terms favorable to the United States and its allies. This requires defeating the geopolitical objectives of our enemies, preserving the territorial integrity and political independence of our allies, and emerging from the conflict with a global political orientation favorable to the United States and in which the long term threat from the Soviet Union is reduced and the prospects for lasting peace enhanced. In implementing these objectives, we will seek to prosecute the war as far forward and as close as possible to the sources of greatest threat. The following regional objectives apply: (TS)

3.3 (b)
(5)(6)

1.4(a)
1.4(c)
1.4(g)

[REDACTED]

1.4(a)
1.4(d)
1.4(g)
3.3(b)
(5)(6)

Supplemental Guidance

Warfighting strategy and contingency planning concerning the potential employment of U.S. forces will continue to be developed through operational plans which are prepared by Combatant Commanders and the Joint Chiefs of Staff, and reviewed and approved by the Secretary of Defense and the President. (TS)

Further development of policy and strategy, in both regional and functional areas, should continue to emphasize the need for coordination to ensure consistency with overall policy objectives and maintain the interlocking character of supporting strategies. (C)

Ronald Reagan

CIA PUBLIC AFFAIRS AND THE DRUG CONSPRIACY

Without editorializing, I highly recommend that after reading the following CIA report on the drug conspiracy that you also review the *Drugs, Law enforcement and Foreign Policy* report by the subcommittee on Terrorism, Narcotics and International Operations prepared by the United States Senate Committee on Foreign Relations. The investigation and report was prepared during the 100th Congress, 2nd Session in 1989. The subcommittee was chaired by Senator & Secretary of State John F. Kerry and included senators Brock Adams, Daniel P. Moynihan, Mitch McConnell and Frank H. Murkowski.

Additionally, review the Boland Amendments which were passed in 1982, 1983 and 1984.

After reviewing the items mentioned above, you'll possess a wealth of knowledge that will assist in placing the following report in proper context.

Managing a Nightmare

CIA Public Affairs and the Drug Conspiracy Story

> "In the world of public relations, as in war, avoiding a rout in the face of hostile multitudes can be considered a success."

The charges could hardly be worse. A widely read newspaper series leads many Americans to believe CIA is guilty of at least complicity, if not conspiracy, in the outbreak of crack cocaine in America's inner cities. In more extreme versions of the story circulating on talk radio and the Internet, the Agency was the instrument of a consistent strategy by the US Government to destroy the black community and to keep black Americans from advancing. Denunciations of CIA—reminiscent of the 1970s—abound. Investigations are demanded and initiated. The Congress gets involved.

But, after this surge of publicity that questions the Agency's integrity, the media itself soon begins to question the veracity of the original story. A completely one-sided media campaign is averted, and reporting on the issue becomes polarized rather than wholly anti-CIA. By one count, press stories skeptical of the charges against CIA actually begin to outnumber those giving the story credence. A review of the CIA drug conspiracy story—from its inception in August 1996 with the *San Jose Mercury-News* stories—shows that a ground base of already productive relations with journalists and an effective response by the Director of Central Intelligence's (DCI) Public Affairs Staff (PAS) helped prevent this story from becoming an unmitigated disaster.

This success has to be viewed in relative terms. In the world of public relations, as in war, avoiding a rout in the face of hostile multitudes can be considered a success. Obviously, it is not an ideal situation. We would rather promote CIA and its missions and people all the time, stopping occasionally only to correct errors in a reporter's story—but that is not realistic. As an important public relations resource book advises:[1]

> Crisis and controversy can strike any organization, regardless of its size or line of business...the rule is: Anything can happen. No organization with the remotest chance that its regimen could be upset by surprise happenings should fail to keep at least one eye open for the unexpected.... No organization can expect to be immune to events that engage **public attention**, affect **key constituencies**, and arouse **emotions**.

With the drug conspiracy allegations, public attention was certainly engaged, as the story was carried nationwide by major and local press, TV, and radio. Emotions were aroused. The more virulent of the public attacks against CIA charged the Agency with engaging in "chemical warfare," "systematic genocide," and "attempted mass murder" against black Americans.[2] Were "key constituencies" affected negatively by the story? Inasmuch as the American public is the ultimate "constituency" for any element of our democratic form of government, the answer has to be yes. The Congress—a constituency for CIA due to its budget and oversight responsibilities—also became involved. Finally, the men and women who work for CIA themselves are a constituency; we all are affected to some degree by such allegations, and many of us have been confronted with questions about it from friends, neighbors, and others. By anyone's definition, the emergence of this story posed a genuine public relations crisis for the Agency.[3]

Alarming Allegations

The firestorm began when the *San Jose Mercury-News* ran its three-part series, "Dark Alliance," by staff writer Gary Webb. In the series, Webb alleged that the US-backed Contra rebels in Nicaragua forged a "union" with gangs in Los Angeles to sell tons of cocaine in black neighborhoods and to use "millions" of dollars in profits to fund the Contras' war against the Sandinista regime. "Dark Alliance" did not state outright that CIA ran the drug trade or even knew about it, but CIA complicity was heavily implied by the graphics accompanying the story and by the frequent use of the phrase "the CIA's army" to describe the Contras and anyone working with them.

The series appeared with no warning. Generally speaking, reporters working stories on CIA will call the PAS for comment, background, specific information, or requests to speak with retired Agency employees. Part of Public Affairs' planning for crisis involves an ongoing, active engagement with media representatives. The telephone and fax numbers for CIA Public Affairs are well known among US and foreign journalists, as evidenced by the quantity and variety of calls fielded every day by the Agency's media relations spokesmen. Webb, who reportedly investigated this story for a year, would later claim—during the media

> **Because of the ongoing IG review, CIA was limited in its response, and requests for CIA spokesmen to appear on talk radio or TV programs had to be turned down.**

criticism that emerged in the coming weeks—that he tried to call the Agency but was unsuccessful: "Essentially, our trail stopped at the door of the CIA. *They wouldn't return my phone calls.*"[4]

CIA was caught unawares by the *Mercury-News* series because Gary Webb had never called or spoken with anyone on the PAS. Touted as an investigative journalist—Webb was named Northern California's Journalist of the Year for this series—he apparently could not come up with a widely available and well-known telephone number for CIA Public Affairs. It is difficult to escape the conclusion that he spoke to no one at CIA because he was uninterested in anything the Agency might have to say that would diminish the impact of his series.[5]

The story quickly spread through wire services and the *Mercury-News* website. CIA complicity in drug smuggling into US cities was more strongly implied or explicitly stated with every "bounce" of this story. Public Affairs received its first call on the story from a journalist on 21 August, the day after the series ended. In the first few days, CIA media spokesmen would remind reporters seeking comment that this series represented no real news, in that similar charges were made in the 1980s and were investigated by the Congress and were found to be without substance. Reporters were encouraged to read the "Dark Alliance" series closely and with a critical eye to what allegations could actually be backed with evidence. Early in the life of this story, one major news affiliate, after speaking with a CIA media spokesman, decided not to run the story.

Gaining Momentum

The story languished with little attention for a week or so, during which DCI John Deutch received a letter from Representative Maxine Waters of California, who had asked for an investigation into the charges. In his response, the DCI reiterated his belief that the allegations were groundless; at the same time, he said, he was requesting a review by CIA's Inspector General (IG), in light of the serious nature of the charges. The Director sent a similar letter to Senator Barbara Boxer of California and to the chairmen of the House and Senate intelligence committees. At this point, the story began to pick up steam.

Because of the ongoing IG review, CIA was limited in its response, and requests for CIA spokesmen to appear on talk radio or TV programs had to be turned down. Nevertheless, Public Affairs emphasized to callers the independence of CIA's IG (although press commentary often distorted the IG review as an "in-house" or "internal" investigation) and that the Agency would willingly cooperate with any external investigation. Public Affairs also began to distribute to media contacts copies of the Director's letter to Waters, and, beginning in early September, many stories made use of the DCI's words.[6]

On 11 September, activist Dick Gregory and local Washington talk radio host Joe Madison were arrested at CIA's front gate when they insisted on personally delivering a letter to Director Deutch. This incident added momentum to the story. Overall coverage peaked over the next two weeks. Of particular concern to the CIA community was the fact that the majority of stories or commentaries in the press seemed to give credence—implicitly or explicitly—to the allegations of CIA complicity in drug smuggling.[7]

This heightened media interest was accomplished by a surge in the number of calls by journalists to CIA Public Affairs. This reflects the fact that most journalists are professionals genuinely interested in getting the story right. By the middle of September, Public Affairs was fielding calls from a variety of reporters who were skeptical of the allegations and who were planning to write articles casting doubt on the *Mercury-News* series. But the more balanced media treatment was still days or weeks away.

Meanwhile, CIA continued to get hammered. Joe Madison made CIA's "leading role" in the inner-city crack epidemic a daily subject in his local talk show. One nationally syndicated columnist pointed to Director Deutch's "typical vague denial" and called for "an investigation that can wring the truth out of the CIA, where coverups and 'plausible denials' are standard operating procedures." *Newsweek* quoted Maxine Waters saying "I think it is unconscionable that…the CIA could think so little of people of color that they would be willing to destroy generations in order to win the war in Nicaragua."[8]

The DCI addressed the charges on 19 September, when he testified before the Senate Select Committee on Intelligence (SSCI). That same day, he met for an hour with the Congressional Black Caucus (CBC), members of which were denouncing CIA and seemed to be accepting the wider allegations—that CIA was part of an antiblack conspiracy—at face value.[9] Wire services and others began to claim that the CIA's IG review came about because of pressure from the CBC. This connection was false; as noted earlier, the Director had ordered the IG review in early September.

> " … most journalists are professionals genuinely interested in getting the story right. "

Spreading Skepticism

That third week in September was a turning point in media coverage of this story. Respected columnists, including prominent blacks, began to question the motives of those who uncritically accepted the idea that CIA was responsible for destroying black communities. Others took a hard look at the evidence provided by the *Mercury-News*—something Public Affairs encouraged from the beginning—and found it unconvincing. A *New York Daily News* reporter concluded the *Mercury-News* series "just doesn't say what everybody seems to think it says." *The Baltimore Sun*, after running articles giving credence to the allegations, reported that the series was "weak" in documentation; the *Sun* also quoted a CIA spokesman to the effect that the *San Jose Mercury-News* never called CIA for comment and should have called "in the interest of fair and balanced reporting." *The Weekly Standard* published a piece that discredited the *Mercury-News* series. *The Washington Post* ran two articles by leading journalists that criticized the assumptions and connections made by the original series. Public Affairs made sure that reporters and news directors calling for information—as well as former Agency officials, who were themselves representing the Agency in interviews with the media—received copies of these more balanced stories. Because of the *Post's* national reputation, its articles especially were picked up by other papers, helping to create what the Associated Press called a "firestorm of reaction" against the *San Jose Mercury-News*.[10]

The *Mercury-News* soon found itself the target of so much media-generated criticism that it resorted to the unusual measure of scrutinizing its own series, addressing the criticism, and conceding the paper might have done some things differently, including calling the CIA, not using the CIA logo, clarifying its use of the term "CIA's army," and including a statement that the paper found no evidence that CIA ordered or sanctioned the drug trade.[11] One reporter of a major regional newspaper told Public Affairs that, because it had reprinted the *Mercury-News* stories in their entirety, his paper now had "egg on its face," in light of what other newspapers were saying.

By the end of September, the number of observed stories[12] in the print media that indicated skepticism of the *Mercury-News* series surpassed that of the negative coverage, which had already peaked. In fact, for three weeks the number of skeptical or positive pieces observed in the media constantly exceeded the number of negative treatments of CIA. After a brief surge in negative reporting in mid-October, the observed number of skeptical treatments of the alleged

CIA connection grew until it more than tripled the coverage that gave credibility to that connection. The growth in balanced reporting was largely due to the criticisms of the *San Jose Mercury-News* by *The Washington Post*, *The New York Times*,[13] and especially *The Los Angeles Times*.

In its own three-part series, *The Los Angeles Times* debunked Gary Webb's claims and insinuations regarding the alleged role of CIA in drug smuggling, the amount of money that went to the Contras, and even such basic elements of the story as the chronology of events. Published almost exactly two months after the *San Jose Mercury-News* stories, *The Los Angeles Times* series[14] itself became a newsworthy story and was picked up by many media outlets across the country.

By the time the SSCI ended its first round of hearings on the matter in late October, the tone of the entire CIA-drug story had changed. Most press coverage included, as a routine matter, the now-widespread criticism of the *Mercury-News* allegations. DCI Deutch's much publicized "town meeting" in Watts in mid-November, other than sparking a small surge of stories, ironically seemed not to have made much difference on the generally factual character of news reporting—other than possibly generating some public sympathy for the way he was treated.

The Role of Public Affairs

Of the journalists and columnists who wrote pieces skeptical or critical of the CIA-cocaine connection, about one-third called Public Affairs before going to print. Some called to

> **"Because of CIA's secret history and public interest in its work, whatever CIA spokesmen say—even denials—can make news."**

check facts; many called for an official CIA comment; most called for further information.

It is in providing information that Public Affairs can best do its job. I have spoken with some CIA employees who are angry that Public Affairs "does not do more" when adverse publicity hits the papers; a few even seem to think CIA can and should write the media's stories for them. It is important to reiterate that the PAS aims above all to inform rather than to pressure or to persuade. When dealing with the media, the rule practiced by Public Affairs is to provide as much information as possible, consistent with the need to protect sensitive information, sources, and methods. Often, CIA spokesmen cannot comment. Frequently, they can say something to the media, but it can take days to figure out within the Agency what it is that can be said. For example, in order to help a journalist working on a story that would undermine the *Mercury-News* allegations, Public Affairs was able to deny any affiliation of a particular individual—which is a rare exception to the general policy that CIA does not comment on any individual's alleged CIA ties. But coordinating that response took time.

Because of CIA's secret history and public interest in its work, whatever CIA spokesmen say—even denials—can make news. So Public Affairs fields a lot of calls from journalists—up to 300 a month, if CIA is having a particularly bad time—and these journalists tend to pay attention to the information CIA provides. CIA benefits from the good track record the PAS has with journalists for returning phone calls promptly, providing background briefings on occasion, and helping journalists as much as possible. This record gives CIA a certain level of credibility when a public relations crisis occurs.

Public Affairs cannot dictate stories to the media—nor would we want to live in a society where that was possible. CIA's relationship with the media can be an extremely sensitive matter, as demonstrated by the public flap in 1996 over the possible intelligence use of information from journalists. What CIA media spokesmen can do, as this case demonstrates, is to work with journalists who are already disposed toward writing a balanced story. Even when dealing with a breaking story that puts the Agency in a bad light, CIA Public Affairs can help the journalist with information he might not have or a perspective that might not have crossed his mind. The result is a more balanced story: better for the reporter, because the facts are right; better for CIA, because the Agency gets a fairer hearing; and better for the public, which is better informed than it otherwise might be. In a few cases, it may be possible, through simply providing information, to change the mind of a reporter whose initial inclinations toward CIA were negative but who is willing to listen to the other side of the story. The influence Public Affairs wields has its limits, but at least it exists.

Some Self-Policing

What gives this limited influence a "multiplier effect" is something that surprised me about the media: that the journalistic profession has the will and the ability to hold its own members to certain standards. This self-policing phenomenon reached its apogee early in 1997, when the *American Journalism Review* (AJR) published a skeptical piece on "The Web That Gary Spun." This piece also revealed that some of Gary Webb's harshest critics were his own colleagues on the *Mercury-News* staff. The editor of the *AJR* later wrote that the *Mercury-News* deserved all the heat leveled at it for "Dark Alliance." The criticism from within the journalistic community had its effect; in May 1997, the executive editor of the *Mercury-News* made nationwide news by apologizing in print for the flaws and shortcomings of "Dark Alliance." This mea culpa was reported by every major newspaper in the country.[15]

The CIA-drug story has largely run its course. It is by no means a dead issue, however. The *Mercury-News* disclaimer "didn't change things at all" for Representative Waters, and she continued to conduct her own investigation.[16] She and other critics publicly disparaged CIA again in late 1997, when the IG announced its investigation came up with no evidence to support the charges. About the same time, Gary Webb resigned from the *Mercury-News*. He evidently is considering writing a book in which he would expand his theories to include the notion that the war in Nicaragua—far from being a battle in the Cold War—was not a real conflict at all but rather a charade to cover up drug smuggling by rogue CIA agents. As Howard Kurtz of *The Washington Post* remarked, "Oliver Stone, check your voice mail."[17]

A Question of Trust

There will be other public relations crises with which CIA will have to contend. As John Ranelagh suggested 10 years ago in his history of CIA,[18] the attitude of the American people toward the Agency parallels its view of government generally; when the public's trust in politicians and government institutions sinks, CIA can expect to be a target, with the media the obvious delivery vehicle. If historians such as Samuel Huntington and Arthur Schlesinger, Jr., are correct, we can expect periodic displays of public distrust in government roughly every 20 to 30 years—and we are just beginning such a phase.[19] In such times, even fantastic allegations about CIA—JFK's assassination, UFO coverups, or importing drugs into America's cities—will resonate with, and even appeal to, much of American society. At those times, it is especially important to have a professional public affairs staff help limit the damage and facilitate more balanced coverage of CIA.

Societal Shortcomings

As a personal postscript, I would submit that ultimately the CIA-drug story says a lot more about American society on the eve of the millennium that it does about either CIA or the media. We live in somewhat coarse and emotional times—when large numbers of Americans do not adhere to the same standards of logic, evidence, or even civil discourse as those practiced by members of the CIA community.[20] Venom against "CIA thuggery" can still be found in place of reasoned discourse in the public square. "Freeway Ricky" Ross, whom all agree actually brought the drugs into Los Angeles, was treated with deference and even respect on talk shows, while CIA—which is helping fight the drug scourge—was dragged through the mud. Public hearings on the allegations—even Congressional hearings—were marked by jeering or cheers from audiences less interested in truth than in having personal beliefs vindicated. Journalists who wrote articles skeptical of the charges against CIA were pilloried in print—one was accused of serving as a CIA lackey—and even threatened with physical harm over their articles.

Because of episodes like the drug story, some Agency employees might conclude that there is scant public appreciation of their dedication and hard work and of the fact, that as citizens themselves, they are just as outraged as any other responsible group in American society about the damage done by drug trafficking. But most CIA employees probably will see the drug story as yet another bum rap—one that, in this case, was belatedly acknowledged as such by reputable journalists.

NOTES

1. See the chapter on "Crisis Communications: Dealing With the Unforeseen," in Robert Dilenschneider and Dan Forrestal, *The Dartnell Public Relations Handbook* (Chicago: Dartnell, 1990), pp. 330-347; emphasis by the author.

2. For example, "State NAACP Vows To Act on CIA-drug Reports," *The Sunday Record* (New Jersey),

29 September 1996. See also Paul Shepard, "CIA Drug Allegations Revive Black Fears of Anti-Black Conspiracy," Associated Press, 5 October 1996.

3. In October 1996, I went on a speaking tour to Brigham Young University, Washington and Jefferson College, and the US Coast Guard Academy. While I encountered no hostility at any of these institutions, one of the first questions raised in Q&A was the drug conspiracy issue.

4. Quoted in Howard Kurtz, "Running With the CIA Story," *The Washington Post*, 2 October 1996, p. B1. Emphasis by the author.

5. According to journalism's primary trade journal, Webb's former employer, the *Cleveland Plain Dealer*, lost a libel suit and was assessed over $13 million in damages because of stories Webb wrote that alleged improprieties surrounding the Cleveland Grand Prix. See Susan Revah, "A Furor Over the CIA and Drugs," *American Journalism Review*, November 1996, p. 11. Those who followed General Westmoreland's unsuccessful suit against CBS several years ago can appreciate how difficult it is to win a libel suit against the press.

6. For example, "Deutch Orders CIA Probe of Drug Reports," *The Washington Post*, 7 September 1996, p. A1.

7. Typical pieces included: Andrea Lewis, "A CIA Plot Against Black America? Crack Sales May Not Be Just a Case of Paranoia," *The Baltimore Sun*, 15 September 1996, p. E1; Annette Leslie Williams, "Probe CIA Drug Ties to Bloody L.A. Gangs," *USA Today*, 13 September 1996, p. 15A; and Jesse Jackson, "Did the CIA Trade Lives for Contra Funds?," *The Los Angeles Times*, 15 September 1996, p. M5.

8. Jeffrey York, "Joe Madison, Leading the Charge," *The Washington Post*, 17 September 1996, p. B7. Carl T. Rowan, "Some Answers, Please!," *The Baltimore Sun*, 18 September 1996, p. 19A. Gregory Vistica and Vern Smith, "Was the CIA Involved in the Crack Epidemic?" *Newsweek*, 30 September 1996, p. 72.

9. Congressman Waters was only the most vocal of the Congressional critics. For example, Congressman Cynthia McKinney on the House floor called CIA the "Central Intoxication Agency." See Jim Wolf, "CIA on Defensive Over Drug-Peddling Charges," Associated Press, 18 September 1996.

10. William Raspberry, "The Crack Story: Who's Buying It?," *The Washington Post*, 23 September 1996, p. A19. Claude Lewis, "Even if the CIA Flooded Inner Cities with Crack, Blacks Didn't Say 'No'," *Philadelphia Inquirer*, 25 September 1996, p. A23. Lars Erik Larsen, "Contra-Coke Tale Is Not What It's Cracked Up To Be," *New York Daily News*, 25 September 1996. Mark Matthews, "CIA's Dubious role in Crack Deals," *The Baltimore Sun*, 27 September 1996, p. 2A. Tucker Carlson, "A Disgraceful Newspaper Exposé and Its Fans," *The Weekly Standard*, 30 September 1996, pp. 27-30. Howard Kurtz, "Running with the CIA Story," *The Washington Post*, 2 October 1996, p. B1. Robert Suro and Walter Pincus, "The CIA and Crack: Evidence is Lacking of Alleged Plot," *The Washington Post*, 4 October 1996, p. A1. The Associated Press reported on *The Washington Post's* critical treatment of the story, which in turn received some "bounce" among newspapers: see, for example, "CIA Drug Link Report Challenged," *Miami Herald*, 5 October 1996. See also Associated Press, "Mercury News Has Reporter Evaluate CIA-Contra-Crack Series," 21 October 1996.

11. Pete Carey, "'Dark Alliance' Series Takes on a Life of its Own," *San Jose Mercury-News*, 13 October 1996.

12. PAS Research and Services staff regularly clips articles relevant to intelligence and national security issues.

13. Tim Golden, "Tale of C.I.A. and Drugs Has Life of Its Own," *The New York Times*, 21 October 1996, p. A1.

14. Doyle McManus, "The Cocaine Trail," three-part series, *The Los Angeles Times*, 20-22 October 1996.

15. Alicia Shepard, "The Web That Gary Spun," *American Journalism Review*, January/February 1997. Rem Rieder, "The Lessons of Dark Alliance," *American Journalism Review*, June 1997. Jerry Ceppos, "To Readers of Our 'Dark Alliance' Series," *San Jose Mercury-News*, 11 May 1997.

16. Robyn Gearey, "Troubled Waters," *The New Republic*, 30 June 1997.

17. Eleanor Randolph and John Broder, "Cyberspace Contributes to Volatility of Allegations," *The Los Angeles Times*, 22 October 1996, p. 14. Howard Kurtz, "A Webb of Conspiracy," *The Washington Post*, 28 October 1996, p. A12.

18. John Ranelagh, *The Agency: The Rise and Decline of the CIA* (New York: Simon and Schuster, 1986), pp. 532-533.

19. Samuel Huntington, *American Politics: The Promise of Disharmony* (Cambridge: Harvard University Press, 1981); Arthur Schlesinger, Jr., *The Cycles of American History* (Boston: Houghton Mifflin, 1986).

20. (b)(3)(n)

"If you do not know others and do not know yourself, you will be in danger in every single battle."

Sun Tzu

Printed in Great Britain
by Amazon